First World War
and Army of Occupation
War Diary
France, Belgium and Germany

50 DIVISION
150 Infantry Brigade,
Brigade Machine Gun Company
1 February 1916 - 31 March 1918

WO95/2837/3

The Naval & Military Press Ltd
www.nmarchive.com
Published in association with The National Archives

Published by

The Naval & Military Press Ltd

Unit 10 Ridgewood Industrial Park,
Uckfield, East Sussex,
TN22 5QE England
Tel: +44 (0) 1825 749494

www.naval-military-press.com

www.nmarchive.com

This diary has been reprinted in facsimile from the original. Any imperfections are inevitably reproduced and the quality may fall short of modern type and cartographic standards.

© **Crown Copyright**
Images reproduced by permission of The National Archives, London, England, 2015.

Contents

Document type	Place/Title	Date From	Date To
Heading	WO95/2837 50 Div. 150 Inf Bde Bde M.G.C. Feb 16-March 18		
Heading	50th Division 150th Infy Bde 150th Machine Gun Coy. Feb 1916-Mar 1918.		
War Diary	In The Field Billet Near Dickebusch Map Ref. H.27c 4.7 Sheet 28.	01/02/1916	05/02/1916
War Diary	Field	06/02/1916	17/02/1916
War Diary	Billet Farm At H.27c4.7 Sheet 27. (Near Dickebusch)	18/02/1916	23/02/1916
War Diary	In The Field	24/02/1916	29/02/1916
Heading	150 Bde M.G. Coy Vol II March 16		
War Diary	In Trenches Ypres "Sanctuary Wood" District	01/03/1916	02/03/1916
War Diary	In Trenches	02/03/1916	10/03/1916
War Diary	In Billets Farm H.27.C.H.7 Sheet 28 Near Dickebusch	11/03/1916	22/03/1916
War Diary	In Trenches	23/03/1916	24/03/1916
War Diary	In Billet	25/03/1916	29/03/1916
War Diary	Billet X.1d.3.3 Sheet 27	29/03/1916	31/03/1916
Operation(al) Order(s)	50th Division Operation Order No. 27	09/03/1916	09/03/1916
Operation(al) Order(s)	50th Division Operation Order No. 28.	10/03/1916	10/03/1916
Miscellaneous	150th Infantry Brigade.	10/03/1916	10/03/1916
Operation(al) Order(s)	151 Bde M.G. Company Operation Order No. 5	12/03/1916	12/03/1916
Miscellaneous	Operation Order No. 5		
Operation(al) Order(s)	151st Infantry Brigade Operation Order No. 16	12/03/1916	12/03/1916
Miscellaneous	Orders For Local Releif Of M.G. Team	16/03/1916	16/03/1916
Operation(al) Order(s)	Operation Order No. 6	16/03/1916	16/03/1916
Operation(al) Order(s)	150th Infantry Brigade Operation Order No. 20	16/03/1916	16/03/1916
Operation(al) Order(s)	150th Infantry Brigade Operation Order No. 2.	15/02/1916	15/02/1916
Operation(al) Order(s)	151st Brigade Machine Gun Company. Operation Order No. 6.	17/03/1916	17/03/1916
Operation(al) Order(s)	149th Brigade Machine Gun Coy. Operation Order No. 8	17/03/1916	17/03/1916
Miscellaneous	O.C., Brigade Machine Gun Coy.	19/03/1916	19/03/1916
Miscellaneous	149th Brigade Machine Gun Coy Operation Order No. 9	21/03/1916	21/03/1916
Operation(al) Order(s)	151 Brigade Machine Gun Coy Operation Order No. 7	21/03/1916	21/03/1916
Operation(al) Order(s)	50th Division Operation Order No. 30	17/03/1916	17/03/1916
Operation(al) Order(s)	Operation Order No. 10	23/03/1916	23/03/1916
Miscellaneous	O.C., Brigade Machine Gun Coy.	27/03/1916	27/03/1916
Miscellaneous	O.C., Brigade Machine Gun Coy.	26/03/1916	26/03/1916
Miscellaneous	Lorry Programme For Move Of 150th Infantry Brigade	28/03/1916	28/03/1916
Miscellaneous	O.C., Brigade Machine Gun Coy.	27/03/1916	27/03/1916
Miscellaneous	150th Infantry Brigade-March Table	28/03/1916	28/03/1916
Operation(al) Order(s)	150th Infantry Brigade Operation Order No. 22	27/03/1916	27/03/1916
War Diary	Sheet 28. In Trenches About N.29.	01/04/1916	07/04/1916
War Diary	Sheet 28. In Trenches A Billet M24d4.8	09/04/1916	22/04/1916
War Diary	Sheet 28. Trenches & Billet	24/04/1916	28/04/1916
War Diary	Sheet 27 Rest Billet Q.35.d.7.4	29/04/1916	30/04/1916
Miscellaneous	O.C., Brigade Machine Gun Coy.	01/04/1916	01/04/1916
Miscellaneous	Distribution Of Machine Guns		
Operation(al) Order(s)	150th Infantry Brigade. Operation Order No. 23	05/04/1916	05/04/1916
Operation(al) Order(s)	150th Infantry Brigade. Operation Order No. 24	13/04/1916	13/04/1916

Type	Description	Date 1	Date 2
Operation(al) Order(s)	150th Infantry Brigade. Operation Order No. 25	17/04/1916	17/04/1916
Miscellaneous	O.C., Brigade Machine Gun Coy.	19/04/1916	19/04/1916
Operation(al) Order(s)	150th Infantry Brigade Operation Order No. 26	22/04/1916	22/04/1916
Miscellaneous	O.C. Brigade Machine Gun Coy.	30/04/1916	30/04/1916
War Diary	In The Field "Resting" Near Thieushoek 27.Q35d7.5	01/05/1916	23/05/1916
War Diary	Resting Farm At Q35d7.5	24/05/1916	25/05/1916
War Diary	In Trenches In Front Of Kemmel Village	26/05/1916	31/05/1916
Miscellaneous	O.C. Brigade Machine Gun Coy.	22/05/1916	22/05/1916
Diagram etc	Rough Sketch Of Divisional Parade		
Operation(al) Order(s)	150th Infantry Brigade Operation Order No. 28	31/05/1916	31/05/1916
Operation(al) Order(s)	Operation Order No. 2 c/6th Coy Machine Gun Corps 76th Inf Brigade	25/05/1916	25/05/1916
Miscellaneous	150th Bde. M.G. Coy. Operation Order.	25/05/1916	25/05/1916
Miscellaneous	Trenches	26/05/1916	26/05/1916
Miscellaneous	Operation Orders. 150th Inf. Bde M.G. Coy.	24/05/1916	24/05/1916
Miscellaneous	Appendix 5	30/05/1916	30/05/1916
Miscellaneous	150th Infantry Brigade	02/05/1916	02/05/1916
Operation(al) Order(s)	150th Infantry Brigade Operation Order No. 27	09/05/1916	09/05/1916
Miscellaneous	150 Bde M.G. Coy		
Operation(al) Order(s)	76th Brigade Machine Gun Company Operation Order No. 1	26/04/1916	26/04/1916
War Diary	In Trenches In Front Of Kemmel Village	01/06/1916	26/06/1916
War Diary	Kemmel Trenches	26/06/1916	26/06/1916
War Diary	Billet 28.m.26.c.5.4	27/06/1916	30/06/1916
Miscellaneous	Appendix 1.	04/06/1916	04/06/1916
Miscellaneous	Appendix 2.	08/06/1916	08/06/1916
Miscellaneous	Appendix 3	13/06/1916	13/06/1916
Miscellaneous	150th Brigade Machine Gun Coy.		
Operation(al) Order(s)	Operation Order No. 32 150th Bde. M. Gun Coy	19/06/1916	19/06/1916
Miscellaneous	Table Referred To In Clause (2)	19/06/1916	19/06/1916
Operation(al) Order(s)	150th Infantry Brigade Operation Order No. 32	16/05/1916	16/05/1916
Operation(al) Order(s)	50th Division Operation Order No. 36	14/06/1916	14/06/1916
Miscellaneous	Amendment To Operation Order No. 32	17/06/1916	17/06/1916
Operation(al) Order(s)	Operation Order No. 33 150th Bde. M. Gun Coy	19/06/1916	19/06/1916
Miscellaneous	Table Referred To In Of Order No. 3		
Operation(al) Order(s)	Operation Order No. 34	25/06/1916	25/06/1916
Miscellaneous	Table Referred To Teams		
Heading	War Diary Of 150th Brigade Machine Gun Coy July 1916 Vol 6		
War Diary	Sheet 27. Billet R. 23b 6.7.	01/07/1916	03/07/1916
War Diary	Sheet 28 M.18.c.4.8 Trenches F3-L5.	06/07/1916	19/07/1916
War Diary	In Trenches	21/07/1916	31/07/1916
Operation(al) Order(s)	150th Infantry Brigade Operation Order No. 33.	01/07/1916	01/07/1916
Miscellaneous	Operation Order No. 33	03/07/1916	03/07/1916
Operation(al) Order(s)	Operation Orders No. 35		
Miscellaneous	Table Referred To In O.O. 35	04/07/1916	04/07/1916
Miscellaneous	Amendment To O/Order No. 35	04/07/1916	04/07/1916
Operation(al) Order(s)	Op. Order No. 36	08/07/1916	08/07/1916
Miscellaneous	150th Infantry Brigade.	09/07/1916	09/07/1916
Operation(al) Order(s)	Operation Order No. 34	08/07/1916	08/07/1916
Miscellaneous	150th Bde. M.G. Coy.	09/07/1916	09/07/1916
Operation(al) Order(s)	Op. Order No. 38	12/07/1916	12/07/1916
Miscellaneous	150th Bde M.G. Coy	13/07/1916	13/07/1916
Miscellaneous	The following alterations in dispositions will be made on the night of the 15/16 July. Appendix 10.	15/07/1916	15/07/1916
Miscellaneous	150th Bde. M.G. Coy.	17/07/1916	17/07/1916

Miscellaneous	150th Bde. M.G. Coy.	21/07/1916	21/07/1916
Operation(al) Order(s)	150th. Bde. Machine Gun Coy.-Op. O. No. 42	23/07/1916	23/07/1916
Miscellaneous	150th Bde M.G. Coy.	25/07/1916	25/07/1916
Miscellaneous	150th Bde M.G. Coy.	29/07/1916	29/07/1916
Operation(al) Order(s)	150th Machine Gun Coy. O.O. 46	30/07/1916	30/07/1916
War Diary	In The Trenches Infront of Vierstraat.	01/08/1916	07/08/1916
War Diary	In Billet St. Jean Fm Thieushoek	08/08/1916	10/08/1916
War Diary	In Train Travelling Doullens	11/08/1916	11/08/1916
War Diary	In Billet At Autheux	12/08/1916	15/08/1916
War Diary	Flesselles	15/08/1916	15/08/1916
War Diary	Molliens Au Bois	16/08/1916	16/08/1916
War Diary	Millencourt	17/08/1916	31/08/1916
Miscellaneous	150th M. Gun Coy. O. O. 46.	02/08/1916	02/08/1916
Miscellaneous	War Diary. 150 M.G. Coy	03/08/1916	03/08/1916
Operation(al) Order(s)	Operation Order 47	07/08/1916	07/08/1916
Miscellaneous	War Diary 150 M.G. Coy.	06/08/1916	06/08/1916
Operation(al) Order(s)	150th Infantry Brigade Operation Order No. 38	13/08/1916	13/08/1916
Miscellaneous	50th Division.	15/08/1916	15/08/1916
Miscellaneous	150th Machine Gun Coy.	13/08/1916	13/08/1916
Operation(al) Order(s)	Operation Order No 48 150th Machine Gun Coy Appendix VI	14/08/1916	14/08/1916
Operation(al) Order(s)	150th Infantry Brigade Operation Order No. 39	15/08/1916	15/08/1916
Miscellaneous	Brigade Headquarters Signal Section.		
Miscellaneous	To L/Cpl Barret Please AcKnowledge to Brigade receipt of this		
Operation(al) Order(s)	150th Infantry Brigade Operation Order No. 40	16/08/1916	16/08/1916
Miscellaneous	Brigade Headquarters Signal Section.		
Miscellaneous	150th M. Gun Coy. Brigade Scheme	31/08/1916	31/08/1916
Miscellaneous	150th Inf. Bde. Scheme Orders For 150th M. Gun Coy.	24/08/1916	24/08/1916
Heading	150th. Infantry Brigade 50th. Division 150th. Machine Gun Company September 1916.		
War Diary	In Billets At Millencourt	01/09/1916	11/09/1916
War Diary	Mametz Wood	11/09/1916	14/09/1916
War Diary	In Trenches S. Of Martin Puich.	15/09/1916	18/09/1916
War Diary	In Captured Trenches S.W Of Martin Puich	18/09/1916	19/09/1916
War Diary	In Dugouts At Edge Of Mametz Wood	20/09/1916	21/09/1916
War Diary	In Trenches Infront Of Eaucourt L'Abbaye	23/09/1916	28/09/1916
War Diary	In Dugouts In Edge Of Mametz Wood	28/09/1916	30/09/1916
Operation(al) Order(s)	150th Infantry Brigade Operation Order No. 41	08/09/1916	08/09/1916
Miscellaneous	Relief Complete By 11p.m SHA Store		
Operation(al) Order(s)	150th Infantry Brigade (Preliminary) Operation Order No. 42	14/09/1916	14/09/1916
Miscellaneous	Table Of Moves.	14/09/1916	14/09/1916
Operation(al) Order(s)	150th Infantry Brigade Operation Order No. 43	14/09/1916	14/09/1916
Miscellaneous	Addendum No. 1 To 150th Infantry Brigade Operation Order No. 42	14/09/1916	14/09/1916
Operation(al) Order(s)	Preliminary Operation Order No. 50		
Miscellaneous	Provisional Order For Relief Of The 150th M.G. Coy.		
Miscellaneous	Relief Orders. Appendix 7		
Operation(al) Order(s)	Operation Order No. 48		
Operation(al) Order(s)	150th Infantry Brigade Operation Order No. 43	23/09/1916	23/09/1916
Operation(al) Order(s)	150th Infantry Brigade Operation Order No. 45	26/09/1916	26/09/1916
Miscellaneous	Time Table		
Miscellaneous	Notes		
Miscellaneous	Tactical Considerations Reference Operation Order 45 Para. 6.		

Operation(al) Order(s)	150th Infantry Brigade Operation Order No. 46	27/09/1916	27/09/1916
Operation(al) Order(s)	150th Infantry Brigade Operation Order No. 47	28/09/1916	28/09/1916
War Diary	In Reserve In Mametz Wood	01/10/1916	01/10/1916
War Diary	In German Deep Dugouts	02/10/1916	02/10/1916
War Diary	Billets In Albert.	03/10/1916	03/10/1916
War Diary	Baizieux Camped Near The Wood	04/10/1916	19/10/1916
War Diary	In Camp At Bazieux Wood	20/10/1916	22/10/1916
War Diary	Billets In Millencourt	23/10/1916	24/10/1916
War Diary	Bazentin Le Grand	24/10/1916	24/10/1916
War Diary	In Trenches Near Labutte de Warlencourt	25/10/1916	31/10/1916
Operation(al) Order(s)	150th Infantry Brigade Operation Order No. 48.	30/09/1916	30/09/1916
Miscellaneous	Artillery Programme		
Miscellaneous	150th Machine Gun Coy.	30/09/1916	30/09/1916
Miscellaneous	A Form Messages And Signals.		
Operation(al) Order(s)	Operation Order No. 51	30/09/1916	30/09/1916
War Diary	In Trenches In Front Of The Butte De Warlencourt	01/11/1916	02/11/1916
War Diary	In Comp Near Mametz Wood	04/11/1916	05/11/1916
War Diary	In Trenches As Before	06/11/1916	11/11/1916
War Diary	In Camp Near Bazentin Le Grand	12/11/1916	17/11/1916
War Diary	Becourt Camp	18/11/1916	30/11/1916
Operation(al) Order(s)	150th Infantry Brigade Operation Order No. 55	01/11/1916	01/11/1916
Miscellaneous	Addendum To Operation Order No. 55	01/11/1916	01/11/1916
Miscellaneous	Relief Orders For 3/4 Nov. 1916	02/11/1916	02/11/1916
Miscellaneous	War Diary Appendix 3		
Miscellaneous	Relief Order	10/11/1916	10/11/1916
Miscellaneous	2/Lt DADD	10/11/1916	10/11/1916
Miscellaneous	Sgt Brown Mill	10/11/1916	10/11/1916
Miscellaneous	2/ Lt Commins Relief Order	10/11/1916	10/11/1916
Miscellaneous	2/Lt Carpenter		
Operation(al) Order(s)	150th Infantry Brigade Operation Order No. 60		
Miscellaneous	Table Of Moves.		
War Diary	Vadencourt	01/12/1916	14/12/1916
War Diary	Map Ref. Sheet 57 1/40000 U.21.c.4.3.	15/12/1916	20/12/1916
War Diary	Vadencourt	21/12/1916	31/12/1916
War Diary	Mametz Wood	01/01/1917	10/01/1917
War Diary	High Wood	11/01/1917	26/01/1917
War Diary	Fricourt	27/01/1917	29/01/1917
War Diary	Buire	30/01/1917	31/01/1917
War Diary	Buire Sur L'Ancre	01/01/1917	08/01/1917
War Diary	Macourt to Foucourcourt	09/01/1917	28/01/1917
War Diary	Estre's Trenches	01/03/1917	09/03/1917
War Diary	Bayonvillers	10/03/1917	30/03/1917
War Diary	Bussy	31/03/1917	31/03/1917
War Diary	Raineville	01/04/1917	01/04/1917
War Diary	Vicogne	02/04/1917	02/04/1917
War Diary	Bagneux	03/04/1917	03/04/1917
War Diary	Ligny-Sur-Canche	04/04/1917	06/04/1917
War Diary	Houvigneul	07/04/1917	07/04/1917
War Diary	Sars-Lez-Bois	08/04/1917	09/04/1917
War Diary	Latre St. Quentin	10/04/1917	10/04/1917
War Diary	Arras	11/04/1917	11/04/1917
War Diary	Ronville	12/04/1917	24/04/1917
War Diary	Arras	25/04/1917	25/04/1917
War Diary	Grenas	26/04/1917	30/04/1917
War Diary	Grenas	01/05/1917	01/05/1917
War Diary	Rosignal	02/05/1917	02/05/1917

War Diary	Blairville	03/05/1917	03/05/1917
War Diary	Rosignal	04/05/1917	05/05/1917
War Diary	Grenas	06/05/1917	17/05/1917
War Diary	Rosignal	18/05/1917	18/05/1917
War Diary	Douchy	19/05/1917	23/05/1917
War Diary	Rosignal	24/05/1917	31/05/1917
War Diary	Rosignal Farm Bayencourt	01/06/1917	14/06/1917
War Diary	Bovelles In The Line West Of Fontaine Croiselles	15/06/1917	26/06/1917
War Diary	In The Field Fontaine Croiselles	27/06/1917	30/06/1917
War Diary	Boyelles	01/07/1917	31/07/1917
War Diary	Camp At. M. 24 Central Sheet 51B S.W.	01/08/1917	03/08/1917
War Diary	Camp At. M. 24 Central Sheet 51B S.W. and Coy HQ. N 16a 2.9 51b S.W: 1/20,000	04/08/1917	09/08/1917
War Diary	Coy H.Q. N 16a 2.9 Sheet 51B S.W	09/08/1917	15/08/1917
War Diary	Coy H.Q. N. 16a 2.9 (51B S.W. 1/20000)	16/08/1917	20/08/1917
War Diary	Coy HQ M. 24 Central	21/08/1917	24/08/1917
War Diary	Coy HQ. M. 24 Cent (51b.S.W)	24/08/1917	27/08/1917
War Diary	Coy H.Q. N.30.b.6.2 (51b. S.W.)	28/08/1917	31/08/1917
War Diary	Coy H.Q. N.30.b.8.2 (Quarry)	01/09/1917	13/09/1917
War Diary	N36. C. 5.8 Concrete Tr:	14/09/1917	15/09/1917
War Diary	Coy H.Q. Carlisle Lines M.14.a.8.6.	16/09/1917	21/09/1917
War Diary	N.16a 2.9	22/09/1917	22/09/1917
War Diary	Coy. HQ. N.16.a.2.9.	23/09/1917	30/09/1917
War Diary	Coy, H.Q. N.16a 2.9. (51b S.W)	01/10/1917	05/10/1917
War Diary	Achiet-Le-Petit G.8.c.0.2 (57c N.W.)	06/10/1917	14/10/1917
War Diary	Achiet-Le-Petit	15/10/1917	16/10/1917
War Diary	Cassel Later Rubrouck	17/10/1917	20/10/1917
War Diary	Rubrouck and Ledringhem	21/10/1917	21/10/1917
War Diary	Ledringhem and Proven	22/10/1917	22/10/1917
War Diary	Proven	23/10/1917	23/10/1917
War Diary	Proven and Elverdinghe	24/10/1917	25/10/1917
War Diary	Coy HQ.-Line U.18.a.9.4. Sheet 20. S.W. 4.	26/10/1917	31/10/1917
Operation(al) Order(s)	150th Machine Gun Coy Operation Order No. 96	02/10/1917	02/10/1917
War Diary	Coy H.Q. U.18a.9.4. Sheet 20 S.W. 4.	01/11/1917	01/11/1917
War Diary	Dublin Camp A.11.c.1.7.	02/11/1917	11/11/1917
War Diary	Mentque P.16.a.2.1 (Sheet 27a S.E.)	12/11/1917	24/11/1917
War Diary	Tournehem J.31.a.5.9. 27A. S.E.	25/11/1917	30/11/1917
Heading	War Diary Of 150th Machine Gun Coy From Decr 1st-1917 To Decr 31st-1917		
War Diary	Tournehem J.31.a.5.9. (Sheet 27a N.E.)	01/12/1917	01/12/1917
War Diary	Ouestmont K.27.a.1.3. (Sheet 27a NE.)	02/12/1917	09/12/1917
War Diary	Ridge Camp G.11.A.8.2. (Sheet 28 N.W.)	10/12/1917	11/12/1917
War Diary	Sheet 28 N.E 1	12/12/1917	16/12/1917
War Diary	Potijze Camp (I.9.a.8.2) Sheet 28. N.W.	17/12/1917	19/12/1917
War Diary	Sheet 28. N.E. (Passchendaele)	20/12/1917	22/12/1917
War Diary	Passchendaele Sheet 28 N.W.	22/12/1917	24/12/1917
War Diary	Potizje Camp (I.9.a.8.2) Sheet 28 N.W.	25/12/1917	27/12/1917
War Diary	Passchendaele Sheet. 28 N.E.	28/12/1917	31/12/1917
Heading	150 M.G Coy Vol 24		
War Diary	Potijze 1.3.c.0.3 Sheet 28 N.W.	01/01/1918	02/01/1918
War Diary	Winnizeele J.35.d.7.9 Sheet 27.	03/01/1918	15/01/1918
War Diary	Setques E.8.a.95.00	16/01/1918	26/01/1918
War Diary	No 2 Camp Potijze	27/01/1918	28/01/1918
War Diary	Dan House D.21.b.3.8	29/01/1918	31/01/1918
War Diary	Potijze No.2 Camp I.4.d.0.8. (Sheet 28 N.W.)	01/02/1918	04/02/1918
War Diary	Adv. HQ. Heine House D.11.c.7.3	05/02/1918	07/02/1918

War Diary	No2 Camp Potijze 1.4.d.2.8 (Sheet 28 N.W.)	08/02/1918	11/02/1918
War Diary	Coy. HQ. D.26.6.9.4 (Zonnebeke)	12/02/1918	16/02/1918
War Diary	No2 Camp Potijze 1.4.d.2.8 (Sheet 28 N.E)	17/02/1918	19/02/1918
War Diary	Westbecourt V.14.a.5.8 (27a S.E)	20/02/1918	28/02/1918
Heading	War Diary Of 150th Machine Gun Coy From Feby 1st 1918 To Feby 28th 1918		
Operation(al) Order(s)	2nd Bn Northumberland Fusiliers Operation Order No48	17/12/1918	17/12/1918
Heading	50th Division Became "B" Company 50th Machine Gun Battalion 150th Machine Gun Company March 1918		
Miscellaneous	B. Coy		
War Diary	Westbecourt (Pas-De-Calais)	01/03/1918	08/03/1918
War Diary	Glisy Sur Somme	09/03/1918	10/03/1918
War Diary	Harbonniers	11/03/1918	20/03/1918
War Diary	Harbonniers Sur.Somme	21/03/1918	21/03/1918
War Diary	Hancourt and Bouvincourt	22/03/1918	22/03/1918
War Diary	St. Cren and Belloy-En-Santerre	23/03/1918	23/03/1918
War Diary	Belloy-En-Santerre	24/03/1918	24/03/1918
War Diary	Foucaucourt and Proyart	25/03/1918	25/03/1918
War Diary	Proyart and Hangard	26/03/1918	26/03/1918
War Diary	Hangard	27/03/1918	28/03/1918
War Diary	Rouvel and Boves	29/03/1918	29/03/1918
War Diary	Sains En Amienois	30/03/1918	30/03/1918
War Diary	Saleux and Argoules	31/03/1918	31/03/1918

WO 95/2837 ③
50 Div. 150 Inf Bde
Bde M.G.C.
Feb '16 - March '18

50TH DIVISION
150TH INFY BDE

150TH MACHINE GUN COY.

FEB 1916. - MAR 1918.

WAR DIARY
or
INTELLIGENCE SUMMARY

Army Form C. 2118.

150 Brigade Machine Gun Company
att: 150 Infantry Brigade.

Place	Date	Hour	Summary of Events and Information	Remarks and references to Appendices
In the Field Billet near DICKEBUSCH Map Ref. H.2.C.4.7 Sheet 28.	Feb 1st 1916.		Previous to this date Lt. G. B. PURVIS. 5th YORK. REGT. had been sent down to Billet to prepare it for the Transport and 4 machine gun sections of the 150 Infantry Brigade which were to form the Brigade Machine Gun Company. On night March 31st/Feb 1st the M.G. sections belonging to 4 Bn East Yorkshire Regt. 4th Yorkshire Regt. came out of trenches. 4th Yorkshire they billeted ruede X trench, Glasgow Goro. H.9. 50. A1 - A.2. 5th E. York Regt. A.3. A.4. A.5. in A 12. by 4th York Regt. The teams arrived at Billet between 1 - 2 A.M. Feb 1st. 2nd Lt. J. R. BARR in charge of 4th E.York Section. LT. G. W. DAWSON & 2nd Lt. R. C. MOON in charge of 4th YORK Section. 5th Bn DURHAM. L.I. Machine Gun Section came out of trenches on	E.R.P.
	Feb 2nd		night of Feb 1st/2nd. TRANSPORT FARM. spent day cleaning up & ammunition etc. Reserve from TRANSPORT FARM. Road very much blocked by traffic. A.M.T. lorry in the ditch in one case, and an A.A Gun on lorry in the middle of the road in another, caused a great deal of congestion. Day spent in cleaning up. 5th YORK. Sect. came from trenches.	E R.P.
	3rd		4th sections out of trenches go to baths at DICKEBUSCH afternoon as gun half morning spent doing parades. Selecting ... range near DICKEBUSCH HUTS afternoon spent with football match. 2nd Lt N. B. STEPHENS arrived from 4th E. York Regt.	E.R.P.
	4th		Morning spent preparing for trenches. All sections marched off for trenches at 4.30 p.m. marched via KRUISSTRAAT R.E. Dump. SHRAPNEL CORNER. TRANSPORT FARM. Line went through YPRES. All sections relieved sections of 4th, 5th, 6th & 7th Northumberland FUSILIERS. Headquarters at BEDFORD HOUSE. Guns in various positions	E.R.P.
	5th		extending from BLAUPORT FARM. to A 5 trench. Quiet relief no casualties	E.R.P.

Army Form C. 2118.

WAR DIARY
or
INTELLIGENCE SUMMARY
(Erase heading not required.)

150 Brigade M.G. Coy.
150 Inf. Brigade.

Place	Date	Hour	Summary of Events and Information	Remarks and references to Appendices
Field	Feb 6th		Section in trenches. No Casualties. BEDFORD HOUSE & R4 & R8 heavily shelled.	G.B.P.
	7th		No Casualties. Clear fine day. A lot of shelling.	G.B.P.
	8th		In trenches	G.B.P.
	9th		In trenches. Two maxims sent to DICKEBUSCH RANGE to be tested by officer from A.O.C. Both condemned as unserviceable.	G.B.P.
	10th		In trenches no casualties.	G.B.P.
	11th		Heavy rain all day. A good deal of shelling. Transport shelled going through YPRES.	G.B.P.
	12th		3 MAXIM guns tested on DICKEBUSCH RANGE. One condemned. A great deal of shelling. A gas barrage with lachrymatory - smoke shells made at KRUISTRAAT. No Casualties.	G.B.P.
	13th		Quiet day. Not much shelling. In trenches.	G.B.P.
	14th		2 MAXIM GUNS tested on DICKEBUSCH RANGE. One condemned. BLUFF attacked and captured from 17th DIVISION. Two abortive attacks were made on our Divisional front without success. R4, R7, R8 & REDFORD HOUSE also B7 8 & 41 8 heavily shelled. Barrage of fire chiefly shrapnel - woolly bear - between BEDFORD HOUSE & BLAUPORT FARM. MACHINE GUNS in rear positions fired directly on to line of communication behind German front line. Everybody standing to day & night. Fairly quiet day. Certain amount of shelling.	G.B.P.
	15th		Bombing attack by bombers on to Bluff commenced at 8 p.m. Did not succeed. Roads very heavily shelled at night. No Casualties.	G.B.P.
	16th		Fine clear day. Still in trenches. Shrapnel brought back a G.S. wagon which had been found derelict on the road. Not so much shelling as last night.	G.B.P.
	17th		Windy day. Company relieved from trenches tonight by 151 Brigade M.G. Coy. Quiet relief with no casualties. Wind dying down. Last section returned to billet about 2 A.M. morning of 18th.	G.B.P.

WAR DIARY or INTELLIGENCE SUMMARY

Army Form C. 2118.

150 Brigade Machine Gun Company
attached 150 Infy Brigade.

Place	Date	Hour	Summary of Events and Information	Remarks and references to Appendices
Billet Farm at H.29.c.4.9. Sheet 27.	18th		Very wet stormy day. Men cleaning themselves & guns & ammunition all day.	G.R.P.
	19th		LT. PURVIS went to lecture at BAILLEUL by BRIG. GEN. HOTHAM on HORSE MANAGEMENT. Company during gun drill & ordinary inspections.	G.R.P.
	20th		Guns on DICKEBUSCH RANGE. Clear day with a lot of aeroplanes about. All high the engaged with M.G. fire.	G.R.P.
(near DICKEBUSCH)	21st		Change in the weather. Frosty with some snow. Company Inspected by BRIG. GEN. PRICE (150 Bde) Rest of day spent cleaning ammunition etc. M13/6 LENA ASHWELL'S CONCERT PARTY gave Concert at Y.M.C.A. Hut at DICKEBUSCH HUTS.	G.R.P.
	22.		CAPT. SHARP proceeded on 9 days leave to-day. LTS. PURVIS, HESSLER ROSE and STEPHENS went to reconnoitre new line which was being taken over from 14th Infy Brigade. Enemy put up heavy fire Barrage between SWAN CHATEAU & KRUISTRAAT VILLAGE. during clear a smoke shells. Also the Boat House on ZILLEBEKE LAKE was heavily bombed. 24th Division had some casualties. Snowed hard at Night.	G.R.P.
	23rd		Company packing limbers ready for trenches. Snowy day. Company moved off 3.45.p.m. Some shelling on the way up. LT. WOOD and 3 guns at PROMENADE DUGOUTS. LT. DAWSON & 3 guns at MAPLE COPSE. LT. HESSLER and 4 guns in WARRINGTON AVENUE trenches B2 & B4. LT. ROSE 4 guns at A.5. A.12.R + A.12.L. + R.2. 2nd LT BARR with guns in VIGO ST.	G.R.P.
In the field.	24th		Still very cold. LT. BALDWIN R.E. interviewed with reference to making gun emplacements in reserve positions. Snowing hard at night, not much work could be done.	G.R.P.
	25th		Finished No 2 Divisional emplacement tonight. Quiet day. Flew at us at night. No casualties.	G.R.P.
	26th		Quiet day. A lot of snow still lying about. Some shelling of the Dump at night.	G.R.P.
	27th		LT FOSTER R.E. interviewed about emplacement near VALLEY COTTAGES. Working party started here at night. Snowed again.	G.R.P.
	28th		LTS PURVIS & STEPHENS went round near position and eighty aiming sticks for indirect firing onto roads approached behind the enemy lines.	G.R.P.

WAR DIARY or INTELLIGENCE SUMMARY

Army Form C. 2118.

150 Brigade Machine Gun Company att. 150 Inf: Brigade

Place	Date	Hour	Summary of Events and Information	Remarks and references to Appendices
In the Field	Feb 29th		2nd LT A.R. BARR returned from leave. Thirs men returned from months leave. CAPT WILKINSON O/C 149 Bde M.G. Coy came round to arrange about opening fire in case of German attack. Heavy bombardment tonight in its severity. Report that Germans were massing opposite the "A" trenches so would up reserve guns from PROMENADE DUGOUTS to positions in front of ZILLEBEKE VILLAGE.	G.B.P.

C.B. Purvis Lt.
for O/C 150 Brigade Machine Gun Company

50

150 Bde M.G. Coy

Vol II

March 16

WAR DIARY or INTELLIGENCE SUMMARY

Army Form C. 2118.

150 Brigade Machine Gun Company

Place	Date	Hour	Summary of Events and Information	Remarks and references to Appendices
In trenches YPRES. "SANCTUARY WOOD" DISTRICT	1916 March 1st		Lt. G.B. PURVIS attended Conference at Right-Battalion Headquarters, MAPLE COPSE, 150 Inf: Brigade held by BRIG. GEN. PRICE, to discuss arrangements for Co-operation with 3rd Division in the Counter attack at the BLUFF. It was decided to blow up several mines and generally try to draw fire on to our Divisional front and so make it easier for the 3rd Division on our Right. The Machine Guns of the Brigade were to form a barrage behind the German line and search Communications trenches and Reverse slopes near CLONMEL COPSE, STIRLING CASTLE, CHARING CROSS etc. 10 (ten) Machine Guns were used for this purpose and fire at ranges varying from 1500 x to 3000. There was to be a mine demonstration commencing at 5.30 p.m. in which the infantry got "the wind up" and did rapid fire, which was to stop at this point. The Germans was anticipated. This drew a fair amount of shell fire as was intended. The main demonstration was to begin at 4.30 A.M. March 2nd.	G.B.P. The chatter this induced finally was Killed to Relieving Coy.
	March 2nd	4.30 A.M. 4.32	Two salvos by an 18 pdr Battery were fired, at about 30 sec interval. Pandemonium let loose. In the interval the 1st Gordons rushed the BLUFF and took the Germans by surprise catching them while a relief was in progress. A barrage was formed behind the BLUFF area by shell fire and the machine guns of 150 Bde formed a barrage behind the SANCTUARY WOOD trenches. There was a very heavy trench mortar Bombardment of our trenches in retaliation for our Mine explosions & trench mortars. The object of the mines was to blow up the BIRD CAGE, an advanced German trench. This did that & but arrived as tip of the crater was just short of the parapet. Two other mines were blown up the first mine the German Parapet two minutes afterwards. On blowing up the first mine the Germans apparently evacuated their front line, sent up green flares and	G.B.P.

WAR DIARY or INTELLIGENCE SUMMARY

Army Form C. 2118.

Place	Date	Hour	Summary of Events and Information	Remarks and references to Appendices
In trenches	Mar 2nd 1916	4:32 A.M.	almost immediately their own artillery began shelling the German front line trench with whizbangs & shrapnel "Crumps", finding that no infantry came over they sent up Red flares. The artillery lengthened the range & shelled our support line and SANCTUARY WOOD and the Germans re-opened 15" Bombards & trench mortar rapid fire, and machine gun fire. Infantry casualties from trench mortar fire. No machine gunner casualties except 1 slightly wounded.	G.B.P.
		9:30pm	Heavy bombardments on night during the day. Two machine guns sent up from Brigade reserve to R1 & R2 at night. Very dark stormy night.	
	3rd		Heavy showers during the day. Enemy fairly quiet. CAPT SHARP returned from leave. 2nd Lt MOIR & Cottrell went to M.G. School at WISQUES.	G.B.P.
	4th		Moved gun in B2 back to MAPLE COPSE. This evacuated emplacement was blown in about 4 hours after leaving it, by a 5-9 Howitzer Shell. Bored dugout in night.	G.B.P.
	5th		Fine quiet day, very clear. Commenced emplacement near VALLEY COTTAGES at night. Snowing hard all night.	G.B.P.
	6th		Fine day. Position near Valley Cottage continued work on	G.B.P.
	7th		fine day, morning straight. Commenced emplacement in front of ZILLEBEKE VILLAGE. Germans shelled ZILLEBEKE DUMP with whizbangs shrapnel, about 50 yards from working party.	G.B.P.
	8th		Working parties at night, clear cold night. Quiet fine day.	G.B.P.
	9th		Bright day FOKKER brought down one of our spotting aeroplanes near Railway DUGOUTS in morning. Pct. Men killed to R + R escaped unharmed. Handed over 6th 17th Brigade Machine Gun Company who relieved the company at night. CAPT BIRCH took over 2 guns slewed shortly 11pm.	Q.B.P.
	10th		Lt. J.K.M. Keasler went to hospital, I & then A.Q.R. ARR sick. 149 Bde took over emplacement by first issuing new clothing spare parts of time from 3rd Division.	G.B.P. Appendix No 1.

2449 Wt. W14957/Mgo 750,000 1/16 J.B.C. & A. Forms/C.2118/12.

WAR DIARY or INTELLIGENCE SUMMARY

Army Form C. 2118.

150 Bde M.G. Coy

Place	Date	Hour	Summary of Events and Information	Remarks and references to Appendices
In Billets at Toun.	Mar 11th		Spent day washing clothes & cleaning up generally. BRIG. GEN. PRICE inspected the Company in the afternoon. Heavy day's drizzling work of the time.	6/150.
H.27.C.H.7 Sheet 28. near DICKEBUSCH	12th		Resting. Company Bath in afternoon.	9m @ 9.P.
	13th		2nd Lt ROSE with No. 4 Section 2nd Lt STEPHENS with No.1 Section went up to positions in support of 151 Inf Brigade. Relief carried out all right. No casualties.	Appendix No. 3 4. No. 5, 6.
	14th		Fine Day. Usual routine work. Lt HESSLER went to Hospital.	
	15th		Two men from cohort E.P.M. Sgt replaced by M.G. Corps. No casualties	6/150
	16th		Obtained a new Vickers gun for a moment Maxim gun from ordnance. Fine. Intermediate	6/150
	17th		Officers & men continue to fired's support line to relieve 151 Bde M.G. Coy. Fairly quiet relief. No casualties. Silent Susie Shelled BLAUPORT FARM just before team arrived. 149 Bde M.G. Coy came into our billet at Toun was occupied by 151 Bde M.G. Coy.	Appx 7 & 9/150 No. 8 A. 7.
	18th		Infantry of 150th Bde relieved 149th Bde. Heavy quiet day, and shelling	7-9A E/150
	19th		Usual trench routine. W'ship enemy at 147 & 393	
	20th		Lt HESSLER returned from hospital. DICKEBUSCH heavily shelled with 5.9" & 4.7" & much enemy	6/150
	21st		Lt MOON & Lt H.V.R. landed in Railway line of Billet. Some heavy shelling of trenches. carried out in company relief. 2nd Lt STEPHENS hit by squares of Bde HQS. This day. No casualties. 2nd Lt DAWSON. 3rd Lt STEPHENS hit by team relieved by team of 151 Bde MG Coy	Appendix No. 10 11,
	22nd		Lt MOON relieved Lt DAWSON. 3rd Lt STEPHENS hit by team relieved by team of 151 Bde MG Coy from positions in 35, 36, B93 & feet great relieved about 3 A.M.	15, 12A 266.

WAR DIARY or INTELLIGENCE SUMMARY

Army Form C. 2118.

150 Bde M.G. Coy.

Place	Date	Hour	Summary of Events and Information	Remarks and references to Appendices
In trenches	Mar 23rd		Quiet stormy day.	
	24th		Snowing last night. CAPT SHARP & 2nd LT ROSE with 4 teams were relieved in trenches tonight by June 4 & 149 Bde M.G. Coy. The other 8 guns are left in trenches in Dugouts. Jds 1 & 4 Bde M.G. Coy	
In billet	25th		CAPT SHARP, LTS PURVIS & DAWSON rode to C/K Bde (Canadian) Machine Gun Coy Billet at M2 & 2.8 near Kemmel Hill to reconnoitre route & see trenches. Received Signal time. Carried out a local relief of the 8 teams who were in reserve positions with 8 teams who were in rest.	
	26th		CAPT SHARP, LTS PURVIS, WOOD, ROSE & STEPHEN rode to 6th Canadian Bde M.G. Coy Billet K.90 round trenches in new area about midday. CAPT SHARP now taken over. Billet K.90 round. Returned to billet at 4 afternoon.	
	27th 5		Heavy bombardment. Mine explosion felt at billet from mine blown up at ST. ELOI. Heavy bombardment all round. Trenches captured at ST. ELOI present arms fast billet. LT PURVIS in charge of Coy went to Brigade H Qrs to arrange about move to new area.	
	28th		LT DAWSON went to new area to take over Machine Gun School. LT PURVIS 2nd LT STEPHEN with 8 teams & baggage left billet at 10 P.M. marched across road area road. OUDERDOM - WESTOUTRE - VIA BAIGNE - METEREN. Majors Billet. Staff 29. x.1.a.3.3. arrived about 4.30 a.m. & commenced turn in by 15th Bn M.G. half Company left in Salient relieved last night marched this morning to 6th Bde Canadian M.G. Coy other half Coy resting. LT PURVIS attended conference at 150 Bde H.Q. and afterwards rode over to see O/C 6th Canadian Bde M.G. Coy	

WAR DIARY
or
INTELLIGENCE SUMMARY

150 Brigade Machine Gun Company.

Army Form C. 2118.

Place	Date	Hour	Summary of Events and Information	Remarks and references to Appendices
Billet X.1d 3.3 Sheet 27	29th		4 teams & 2nd Lt STEPHENS go to take up position at S.P.8. S.P.9. S.P.10 & S.P.11.	G.H.Q.
	30th		6th Canadian Bde M.G. Coy. Limbers left at 12.30 p.m. for Coy H Quarters. 2nd Lt Ross Morningshed parking limbers & took up reserve position at S.P.1. FARM. HOLLEBEKE and H. Adam went up to take up reserve position at ROLFA FARM, FRENCHMAN'S FARM and ROLFA FARM.	G.H.Q.
	31st		Sent up 4 more VICKERS guns and reduced number of men with each gun. Lt STEPHENS relieved by Lt G.W. DAWSON. Parties arrived from 5th YORK Regt & 5th Durham L.I. to undergo course of instruction. LT. HESSLER went up to relieve 2nd Lt. to-day	appendix No 15 W.D.P.

E.A. Purvis Lieut
for O/C 150 Brigade Machine Gun Company

No. 1

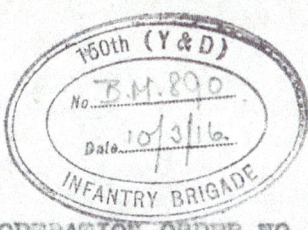

SECRET.

50TH DIVISION OPERATION ORDER NO. 27.

Trench Map 1/40000
HOOGE & HOLLEBEKE.

9th March 1916.

1. The 149th Infantry Brigade will take over on the 10th March from the 9th Infantry Brigade, 3rd Division, the front from junction of THORN STREET with trench 34 at I.34.b.4.3½. to Trench 37 R inclusive (trenches 34 (part) 35, 36, and 37R) and the supporting point R 9, with Battalion H.Q. at I.34.b.2.8.

   All details to be arranged between Brigades concerned.

2. One Battalion 151st Infantry Brigade will be placed at the disposal of G.O.C., 149th Infantry Brigade from 10th March, under arrangements made between these Brigades.

3. 3rd Division is responsible for Artillery Support of the front taken over.

4. The 149th Infantry Brigade will have use of the 3rd Division trench tramway for the Battalion holding the front taken over, under arrangements between 149th and 9th Infantry Brigades.

5. Dividing line between 3rd and 50th Divisions will be I.34.b.4.3½ - to road junction at I.27.d.9.6. and thence as at present.

6. Command of the front taken over will pass from G.O.C., 9th Infantry Brigade and 3rd Division to G.O.C. 149th Infantry Brigade and 50th Division on completion of relief, which will be reported by wire to D.H.Q.

7. Acknowledge.

(signed) A.G.Stuart, Lt.Colonel,
General Staff,
50th Division.

Issued at 6.30 a.m. 10th March.

- 2 -

O.C.,
Brigade Machine Gun Coy.
————————————————

For information.

Major,
Staff Captain,
150th Infantry Brigade.

Headquarters,
150th Infantry Brigade.
10th March 1916.

SECRET.

50TH DIVISION OPERATION ORDER No. 28.

Ref. Map
1/40,000
Sheet 28.

No 2.   10.3.16.

1. On Tuesday 14th March, the 151st Infantry Brigade will relieve the 149th Infantry Brigade, which will go into Corps Reserve at POPERINGHE (3 battalions) and at Camp D. near OUDERDOM (1 Battalion), with Brigade H.Q. at 53 Rue d'YPRES.

   The personnel of the three battalions 149th Infantry Brigade for POPERINGHE will be railed to that place from GOLDFISH CHATEAU under arrangements to be notified separately; transport by road.

2. The 150th Infantry Brigade will place two battalions and two sections 150th Bde. Machine Gun Company at disposal of G.O.C., 151st Infantry Brigade on same date.

   The 150th Infantry Brigade (less two battalions and two sections Bde. Machine Gun Company) will relieve the 151st Infantry Brigade in Divisional Reserve at DICKEBUSCH and CANADA Huts.

3. Arrangements for above reliefs to be made direct between Brigades concerned; the usual receipts for trench stores will be taken by 151st Infantry Brigade from 149th Infantry Brigade.

4. Command of the front will be assumed by G.O.C., 151st Infantry Brigade on completion of relief, which will be reported to D.H.Q.

5. Acknowledge.

                    (signed) A.O. Stuart, Lt. Colonel,
                                    General Staff,
Issued at 3 p.m.   50th Division.

- 2 -

O.C.,
Brigade Machine Gun Coy.

For information.

                                    Major,
                                    Brigade Major,
                                    150th Infantry Brigade.

Headquarters,
150th Infantry Brigade.
10th March 1916.

SECRET.

50th Division.
G. X. 1295

150th Infantry Brigade.

No 3.

1. While the Division has only one Brigade in the line trench and rest periods will be 6 days in the line and 12 days out.

2. The Brigade coming out will be in Corps Reserve, and be accommodated for 6 days at POPERINGHE (3 battalions) and at Camp D (G.30.a) near OUDERDOM (1 Battalion). It will then proceed to DICKEBUSCH and CANADA Huts for 6 days and will be in Divisional Reserve while there before going into the line.

3. As far as can be foreseen at present reliefs will be carried out as follows during the present month :-

   14th MARCH
   151st Inf.Bde. relieves 149th Inf.Bde in front line.
   150th "   "   (less Units detached) relieves 151st Inf.Bde. in Divisional Reserve.
   149th "   "   relieves 150th Inf.Bde. in Corps Reserve.

   20th March.

   150th Inf.Bde. relieves 151st Inf.Bde. in front line.
   149th "   "   (less Units detached) relieves 150th Inf.Bde. in Divisional Reserve.
   151st "   "   relieves 149th Inf.Bde. in Corps Reserve.

   26th March
   149th Inf.Bde. relieves 150th Inf.Bde. in front line.
   151st "   "   (less Units detached) relieves 149th Inf.Bde. in Divisional Reserve.
   150th "   "   relieves 151st Inf.Bde. in Corps Reserve.

4. The Brigade in Divisional Reserve will find such extra troops as are required for special purposes with the Brigade in the line; viz (at present)
   1 Battalion, and Half Brigade M.G.Company to reinforce the Brigade in front line; 1 Battalion to hold extra front taken over from 3rd Division.

   Arrangements will be made to bring the battalions coming out of the line back to POPERINGHE by rail from GOLDFISH CHATEAU (transport by road); other movements will be by road.

                    (signed) A.G.Stuart, Lt.Colonel,
                                         General Staff,
10th March 1916.   50th Division.

- 2 -

O.C.,

Brigade Machine Gun Coy.

                    For information.

Headquarters,
150th Infantry Brigade.
10th March 1916.
                                    Major,
                                    Brigade Major,
                                    150th Infantry Brigade.

Map. Ref.
Sheet 28.
1/40,000.

151 Bde M.G. Company.

Operation Order No. 5.

SECRET.
Copy No 3

4.

1. The 151 Bde M.G. Coy will relieve 149 Bde. M.G. Company on night 13/14th March.

   8 guns of 150 Bde M/G Company will be attached to 151 Bde M.G. Coy.

2. 8 guns of 150 Bde M.G. Coy will arrive at Transport Farm (TRANSPORT FARM) at 7.30 p.m. on 13th March and will relieve 8 guns of 151 Bde M.G. Company as follows:-

   1 gun at "Dump".
   1 "   " LARCH WOOD.
   1 "   " VERBRANDEN MOLEN.
   1 "   " KNOWLE FARM.

   Guides for these 4 positions to be at TRANSPORT FARM at 7.20 p.m.

   4 guns at PROMENADE and RAILWAY dugouts.

   2 Officers to RAILWAY DUGOUTS.

3. 16 guns of 151 Bde M.G. Coy will occupy following positions:-

   'A' Section   { A 3 front line }
   (6 D.L.I.)   { M.G. Mansion   }   1 Officer to A 3.
                 { M.G. HOUSE   }

   'B' Section   { 2 at "DUMP" }
   8 D.L.I.   { 41 S   }   1 Officer to DUMP
                 { 39 S   }

   'C' Section   { R 7   }
   9 D.L.I.   { R 8   }   1 Officer to
                 { BLAUWEPOORT FM}   BLAUWEPOORT

2

D Section { GLASGOW X
(5 Border R).   X trench.   } 1 officer to
              FOSSE WAY   X trench.

3. 1 Gun of "A" Section - GUNNERS LODGE.
   1 "   " C   "   - I B.
   1 "   " D   "   - I C.
   C.S.M   to BEDFORD HOUSE.

4. GUIDES.
   A 3.
   M.G. Mansions. }
   M.G. House.   } 1 guide per gun will be
   Dump.   } at ZILLEBEKE STATION
   41 S.   } at 7.30 A.m.
   39 S.

   GUNNERS LODGE - 1 guide to be at crossing
                    tramway + road (I 20 c)
                    at 7.15 P.M.

5. 2 guns of "C" Section at RAILWAY
   dugouts will relieve BLAUWEPOORT FARM.
   and I B respectively and 2 guns of "D"
   Section at RAILWAY DUGOUTS will relieve
   FOSSE WAY and I c. in daylight under
   arrangements of O.C. 149 Bde M.G. Coy.

6. On being relieved by 150 Bde M.G. Coy
   2 guns of "C" Section at KNOWLE FM
   and LARCH WOOD will move to R 8 and
   R 7 respectively.
   2 guns of "D" Section at "DUMP" and
   VERBRANDEN MOLEN will move to GLASGOW
   X and X trench respectively. O.C. 149 Bde
   M.G. Coy will arrange for guides.

3

7. Tripod mountings and amm. belt boxes will be taken over in every case.

8. Section Officers will report completion of relief to M.G.C. at E.Z.A.

W.A. Emerson.
Capt.
Cmdg 151 Bde. M. Gun Coy.

12.3.16.

Copy No 1 - Filed.
     2 - O.C. 149 Bde M/G Coy.
     3 - O.C. 150
     4 - 151 Inf. Brigade.

Sheet 28
1/10،000

No 5.

Operation Order No 5.
by Capt B.W.R. Sharpe
Cmdg 150th Bde M.G. Coy

SECRET

1. 8 guns of 150 Bde M.G. Co will be placed at disposal of G O C 149 Inf Bde on night 13/14th March and will pass to G O C 151 Inf Bde on relief of the 149 Inf Bde by 151 Inf Bde.

2. Dispositions as follows 4 Vickers guns with 4 teams of No 2 Section to consist of 4 men & No 1 G O each under 2 Lt Rose guns of No 3 section will be taken up to occupy positions in rear of DUMP.
4 Maxim Guns (No 1 Section) and 4 teams No 1 Section of 1 No. G.O and 3 men per team under 2 Lt STEPHENS at RAILWAY and ST JAMES DUGOUTS.
Each gun will be accompanied by 2 belts (steel if use-able in gun) & no tripods.

(2)

3/ Guides will be at TRANSPORT FARM at 7.20 pm 13/14th.

4/ Limbers will arrive at Transport Farm at 7.30 pm night 13/14th.

5/ The Officers named above will be at RAILWAY DUGOUTS to reconnoitre the new portion of line at 2.30 pm & will arrange to meet their limbers as in (4). Their HQ will be at RAILWAY DUGOUTS where they will report to O C 151 Bde M G Co and to O C 150 Bde M G Co who were at DICKEBUSH, on completion of relief.

            J Nutthanp
            Capt
     O C 150 Bde M G Co

issued at 3 pm.

G

SECRET.

151ST INFANTRY BRIGADE.

OPERATION ORDER No.16.

Ref.Map.
Sheet 28
1/40,000

No 6.

12th March 1916.

1. On the night of the 14th/15th March the 151st Infantry Brigade and attached units will relieve the 149th Infantry Brigade and attached units in trenches 54 from the junction of THORN STREET to A.3 inclusive.

2. The 151st Brigade Machine Gun Company with 2 sections attached from 150th Infantry Brigade will relieve the 149th Brigade M.G. Company on the night of 13/14th March under inter-company arrangements.

3. (a) The 4th East Yorks. Regt. will relieve the 9th D.L.I. in 54 from the junction of THORN STREET, 35, 36, 37 R. and R.9.

   (b) The 8th D.L.I. will relieve the 5th N.F. in 37 L. and 37 L.S. and the 4th N.F. in 38, 39, 40, and supports.

   (c) The 5th Border Regt. will relieve the 4th N.F. in 41, 41 S., 47 S, and the 5th N.F. in GLASGOW CROSS, X.TRENCH, LARCH WOOD DUGOUTS, R.7.

   (d) The 6th D.L.I. will relieve the 6th N.F. in 49, 50, A.1, A.2., and A.3.

   (e) The 4th Yorkshire Regiment will occupy :-

   RAILWAY DUG-OUTS...   ...Half Company.
   ARMAGH WOOD ?.. ...   ...One Company.
   H. 30. a....   ...One Company & Battn. H.Q.
   BLAUWEPOORT FARM...   ...One and a half Companies.

   (f) The 9th D.L.I. on relief will occupy:-

   SUNKEN ROAD   ...   ...One Company.
   BEDFORD HOUSE   ...   ...Battalion H.Q. & 2
                             Companies.
   SWAN CHATEAU   ...   ...One Company.

4. The 5th Border Regt. will relieve the centre sub-sector as soon as possible after dark.

   Head of 5th D.L.I. will pass TRANSPORT FARM at 7.0 p.m.
   "   " 8th D.L.I.   "   "   "   "   "   " 7.30 p.m.
   "   " 4th Yorks.   "   "   "   "   "   " 7.40 p.m.
   "   " 4th East Yorks. will pass
                    WOODCOTE HOUSE   at 7.0 p.m.

5. Guides from 9th D. L. I. -

   1 Officer per Company.
   1 N. C. O. per platoon.
   1 N. C. O. for Battn. H.Q.
   1 guide per Lewis Gun.
   will be at WOODCOTE HOUSE at 7.0 p.m.

   Guides for Lewis Guns from each gun in the line (less 9th D. L. I.) will be at BLAUWEPOORT FARM at 9.0 p.m.

6. Advance parties from relieving Battalions will arrive at Battalion H.Q. at 2 p.m. on 14th as under :-

   1 Officer and 2 other ranks per Company.
   Battalion Lewis Gun Officer, Signalling Officer,
   Grenade Officer and Intelligence Officer.

/Transport.

(2)

Transport. 7. All 151st Brigade and attached units transport will be clear of LILLE GATE by 8.30 p.m.

149th Brigade Transport will not pass LILLE GATE until 8.30 p.m.

8. Completion of all reliefs to be reported immediately to Brigade H.Q.

9. Please ACKNOWLEDGE.

(signed) J.Harter,
Captain,
Brigade Major,
151st Infantry Brigade.

- 2 -

O.C.,
Brigade Machine Gun Coy.,
149th Infantry Brigade (for information)
151st Infantry Brigade "   "

For necessary action.

In para 4, opposite 4th Yorks.Regt. erase "will pass TRANSPORT FARM," and insert "will leave POPERINGHE by train at 7.30 p.m. and will march direct to positions named in para 3 (e)".

Jackson
Major,
Brigade Major,
150th Infantry Brigade.

Headquarters,
150th Infantry Brigade.
13th March 1916.

Orders for local relief of M.G. Teams

Y.A.

1. The teams of No 1 Section at BLAUWEPOORT positions will be relieved on night 16/17th inst by teams at RAILWAY DUGOUTS.

2. The teams of No 2 Section will be relieved by teams of No 3 Section night 16/17. guides will be at TRANSPORT FARM to meet the party at 7.30pm. Lieut Dawson will relieve 2 Lt Stephens and will be at Bde Hq RAILWAY DUGOUTS at 4pm to take over. The teams of No 2 Section will return to billets under senior N.C.O.

Rudolph
Capt

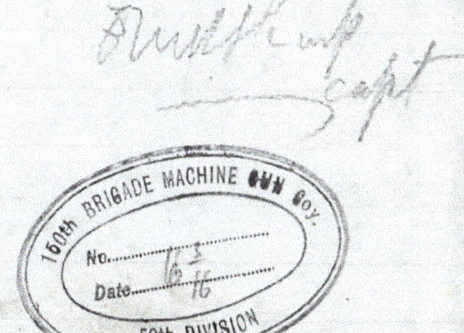

Ref th:
28
1/10,000

SECRET

Operation Order No 6
by Capt D.M.R. Sharp
cmdg 150 Bde M.G. Coy

8.A.

1. The 150 Bde M G Coy will relieve 151st Bde M G Coy in trenches on night 17/18th March.

2. 8 guns of 149 Bde M G Coy will relieve 8 guns of 150 Bde M G Coy in their present positions on night 17/18th.

3. Relief will be carried out as per table attached. Transport will not pass X. s TRANSPORT FARM before 7.30 pm

4. Tripods and belt boxes will be taken over, excepting by Nos 3 & 4 Sections of 150 Bde M G Coy who will take up 14 belt boxes per gun.

5. Spare numbers No 1 Section will be attached to No 4 Section. Spare numbers No 2 Section will be attached No 3 Section.

2

6. Completion of relief will be reported by officers i/c groups to CoHQ at RAILWAY DUGOUTS, & by wire.

7. Acknowledge as understood.

Capt
cmdg 150 D.M.G.Co

Copy No. 1 filed
✓ 2 OC 149 B.M.G.Co
  3 OC 151 —
  4 150 Inf Bde
  5
  6 } So.S. 50 Inf Bde
  7
  8

issued at 9.20 pm
pm 16 3/16

SECRET.

150TH INFANTRY BRIGADE.   Copy No. 5

OPERATION ORDER NO. 20.

Ref.Map
Sheet 28
1/40,000

No 8.   18th March 1918.

1. On the night of the 18th/19th March, the 150th Infantry Brigade and attached units will relieve the 151st Infantry Brigade and attached units in trenches 34 from the junction of THORN STREET, to A 3 inclusive.

2. The 150th Brigade Machine Gun Coy. with two sections attached from 149th Infantry Brigade will relieve the 151st Brigade Machine Gun Coy. on the night of 18th/19th March under inter-company arrangements.

3. (a) The 4th East Yorks. stand fast in right sub-sector Trench 34 from the junction of THORN STREET, 35, 36, 37 R, and R 9.

   (b) The 5th Durham L.I. will relieve the 8th D.L.I. in 37 L, 37 LS, 38, 39, 40, and Supports.

   (c) The 4th Yorks. will relieve the 5th Borders in 41, 41 S, 47 S, GLASGOW CROSS, X TRENCH, LARCH WOOD DUGOUTS, R 7.

   (d) The 5th Yorks. will relieve the 8th D.L.I in 49, 50, A 1, A 2, and A 3.

   (e) The 4th N.F. will occupy :-

       RAILWAY DUGOUTS   - Half Company.
       ARMAGH WOOD   - One Company.
       H. 30. a.   - One Coy. & Batt. H.Q.
       BLAUWEPOORT FARM - One and a half Companies.

   (f) The 7th N.F. will occupy :-

       SUNKEN ROAD   - One Company.
       BEDFORD HOUSE   - Batt. H.Q. & 2 Coys.
       SWAN CHATEAU   - One Company.

4. The 4th Yorks. will relieve the Left Centre Sub-sector as soon as possible after dark.

   Head of 8th D.L.I. will pass TRANSPORT FARM at 7.0 p.m.
   "   " 5th Yorks.   "   "   "   "   " 7.30 p.m.
   "   " 4th N.F.   "   "   "   "   " 7.40 p.m.
   "   " 7th N.F.(less"   " BRIDGE 13   " 7.0 p.m.
       Batt.H.Q. & 1 Coy.)

5. Advance parties from relieving Battalions will arrive at Battalion H.Q. at 2 p.m. on 18th inst. as under:-

       1 Officer and 2 Other Ranks per Company.
       Battn. Lewis Gun Officer, Signalling Officer,
       Grenade Officer, & Intelligence Officer.

6. TRANSPORT.
   All 150th Brigade and attached units transport will be clear of LILLE GATE by 8.30 p.m.

   151st Brigade Transport will not pass LILLE GATE until 8.30 p.m.

= 2 =

7.   Completion of all reliefs to be reported immediately to Brigade H.Q.

        Acknowledge.

                                        Major,
                                        Brigade Major,
                                        150th Infantry Brigade.

Issued at 6.0 p.m.

Copy No. 1. 4th East Yorks.
        2. 4th Yorks.Regt.
        3. 5th Yorks.Regt.
        4. 5th Durham L.I.
        5. Brigade Machine Gun Coy.
        6. 149th Inf. Bde.
        7. 151st   "   "
        8. File.
        9. War Diary.

S E C R E T.
Copy No. 7.

No 9.

151st Infantry Brigade.

Reference Map, Sheet 28.

OPERATION ORDERS NO. 2.
----

1. The 151st Infantry Brigade will relieve the 150th Infantry Brigade in trenches 57 left to A.3 (both inclusive) on the night of the 18/19th Feb.

   Machine Gun Company relief will take place on the night of 17/18th Feb. under arrangements to be made between the Companies.

2. The 8th D.L.I. will relieve the 4th Yorkshire Regiment in the Right sub-sector.

   The 6th D.L.I. will relieve the 4th East Yorkshire Regiment in the Left sub-sector.

   The 5th Border Regiment will relieve the 5th Yorkshire Regiment in Support.

   The 9th D.L.I. will relieve the 8th D.L.I. in Brigade reserve.

3. The 6th D.L.I. will pass Bridge 18 at 5.30 p.m.

   " 8th D.L.I.   "   "   " 18 " 6.0 p.m.

   " 5th Border
         Regt.   "   "   " 18 " 6.30 p.m.

   " 9th D.L.I. (less 1 Company moving to DUG-OUTS H.30.a.1.8) will pass Bridge 18 ... ... at 7.0 p.m.,

   proceeding from the present area via Cross Roads H.29.b.6.4 - Cross Roads H.30.d.2.0½ - BELLEGOED FARM.

Guides. 4.   1 for Battalion H.Q.
              1 Officer per Company.
              1 Guide per Platoon.
              1 Guide per Lewis Rifle,

   will be at Bridge 18 for 8th D.L.I. and Headquarters and 3 Companies of 9th D.L.I., and at TRANSPORT FARM for 6th D.L.I. and 5th Border Regiment.

/5.

O.O.2.   Page 2.   Copy No. 7.

Transport.   5.   150th Brigade Transport will be clear of
                  SHRAPNEL CORNER by ~~6.30 p.m.~~ 7.30pm
                  151 Bde transport will follow 150 Bde transport

6.   151st Brigade Signalling Officer and Grenade
     Officer will arrive at 150th Brigade H.Q. at 10 a.m.
     on the 18th.

         1 Officer and 4 other ranks per Company,
         Battalion Grenade Officers,
         Battalion Signalling Officers,

     will arrive at 150th Brigade H.Q. at 2 p.m. on the
     18th to proceed to trenches and take over trench
     stores.

7.   Completion of reliefs to be reported to
     Brigade H.Q.

8.   Brigade H.Q. will close at G.30.d. at 6 p.m.
     and open at RAILWAY DUG-OUTS at 6 p.m.

9.   Acknowledge.

                                            J.G. Harter
                                            Captain,
                                            Brigade Major,
                                            151st Infantry Brigade.
15.8.1916.

         Copy No. 1 filed.
         Copy No. 2 to 5th Border Regt.
         Copy No. 3 to 6th D.L.I.
         Copy No. 4 to 8th D.L.I.
         Copy No. 5 to 9th D.L.I.
         Copy No. 6 to 150th Inf. Brigade.
         Copy No. 7 to 151 Bde. M.G. Coy.
         Copy No. 8 War Diary.

SECRET.
Copy No. 2

151st Brigade Machine Gun Company.
OPERATION ORDER NO.6.

Ref. Map
Sheet 28,
1/40,000.

No 67

17th March, 1916.

1. The 150th Bde. M.G. Coy. with 2 Sections of 149th Bde. M.G. Coy. will relieve 151st Bde. M.G. Coy. on the night of the 18/19th Mch. from 37.L. to A.3 inclusive.

2. 8 Guns of 149th Bde. Coy. will relieve 8 guns of 150th Bde. Coy. in following positions:-

    KNOLL FARM   )
    LARCH WOOD   )   1 Guide from each gun to be at
    DUMP   )   ZILLEBEKE STATION at 7.30 p.m.
    VERBRANDEN MOLEN)

    2 Guns at BLAUWEPOORT FARM - 1 Guide to be at
                                  TRANSPORT FARM at 7.30p.m.
    1 Gun at RAILWAY DUGOUTS   - 1 Guide   do.   at 7.30 "
    1 Gun at PROMENADE DUGOUTS - 1 Guide   do.   at 7.30 "

3. On being relieved 8 guns of 150th Bde. M.G. Coy. will move as follows:-

    KNOLL FARM   to   FOSSEWAY   )
    LARCH WOOD   to   DUMP Tunnel) No guides.
    DUMP   ..   to   DUMP Tunnel)
    VERBRANDEN
      MOLEN .. to   R.7.   .. 1 Guide.
    2 Guns at BLAUWEPOORT to GUNNERS LODGE and
      BLAUWEPOORT FARM.
    2 Guns at Brigade H.Q. to I.B. and I.C.

4. Remaining guns of 150th Bde. Coy. will occupy:-

        A.3,   X TRENCH.
        M.G. MANSIONS,   39.S.
        M.G. HOUSE,   41.S.
        GLASGOW CROSS.,   R.8.

5. Guides. 151st Bde. M.G. Coy. will furnish the following guides:-

    A.3.   .. ..) 1 Guide per gun at RUDKIN HOUSE
    M.G. MANSIONS.   )   on OBSERVATORY RIDGE at 8 p.m.
    M.G. HOUSE   ..   )

    GLASGOW CROSS.   )   1 Guide per gun at LEICESTER SQUARE
    X TRENCH   ..   )   at 8 p.m.

    39.S.   ..   ..   )   1 Guide per gun at ZILLEBEKE
    41.S.   ..   ..   )   STATION at 8 p.m.
    R.8.   ..   ..   )

    I.B.   ..   ..   )   1 Guide per gun at TRANSPORT
    I.C.   ..   ..   )   FARM at 7.50 p.m.

    R.7.   ..   ..   1 Guide to be at VERBRANDEN MOLEN
                           position at 8 p.m.

/Para. 6.

O.O. 6. Page 2.

6. Limbers for 151st Bde. M.G. Coy. will arrive at 9.30 p.m.

        BEDFORD HOUSE   ...   Limbers 1.
        R.1.   ...   " 1½.
        ZILLEBEKE STATION   ...   " 1½.
        BLAUWEPOORT FARM   ...   " 1.
        LEICESTER SQUARE   ...   " 1½.

7. Following will be handed over:-

        Gum Boots Thigh.
        Salvus Oxygen Apparatus.
        Vermorel Sprayers.
        Tripods.

8. The following gun teams will take 14 belt boxes out to billets:-

        A.3.   X TRENCH.
        M.G. MANSIONS.   39.S.
        M.G. HOUSE.   41.S.
        GLASGOW CROSS.   R.8.

Remaining 8 gun teams will hand over belt boxes in clean condition.

9. On being relieved detachments will march back independently under their officers to billets at FARM at H.27.c.4.6 near DICKEBUSCH - late billets of 150th Bde. M.G. Coy.

10. Completion of relief to be wired to M.G.C. at Z.4.

11. Please ACKNOWLEDGE.

                                    Captain,
                    Commanding 151st Bde. M.G. Coy.

        Copy No. 1 filed.
        " " 2 to 150th Bde. M.G. Coy.
        " " 3 to 151st Bde. H.Q.
        " " 4 to Lt. Gelsthorpe.
        " " 5 to Lt. Brock.
        " " 6 to Lt. Marley.
        " " 7 to Lt. Allison.
        " " 8 to C.S.M.

No. 4

9.A.

Secret

149th Brigade Machine Gun Coy.

Ref Map
Sheet 28
1/10000

Operation Order No 8

(1) 8 Guns of the 149th Brigade M.G. Coy will relieve 8 Guns of the 150th Brigade M.G. Coy on the night of 18/19 March in their present positions on the Divisional front.

(2) On relief the 8 guns of the 149th Brigade M.G. Coy will be attached to and come under the orders of the G.O.C 150th Inf Brigade.

(3) Teams will be disposed of as follows:—

No			
13	to	Dump	} Under
15	"	Verbrandenmolen	} Lt Cowen
3	"	Larch Wood	
1	"	Knowle Farm	
5	"	Blauepoort Farm	} Under
8	"	— do —	} 2/Lt
12	"	Promenade Dug outs	} Bell.
9	"	— do —	

(4) Guides   Guides will meet the teams as follows.

Time	Place	Destination
7.30 pm	Transport Farm	Blauepoort Farm / Promenade Dug outs
7.30 pm	Zillebeke station	Dump / Verbrandenmolen / Larch Wood / Knowle Farm

(5) 1 Tripod, 4 Belt boxes and 3300 rounds of S.A.A. will be taken over at each position.

(6) Limbers will be packed and ready to move off at 5.30 pm under 2/Lt Mawson.

(7) Officers in charge of Sections will report completion of relief to O.C. 150th

Brigade M.G. Coy and also wire the same to Coy HQ at DICKEBUSCH Huts.

Lt Cowen and 2/Lt Bell will report at Railway Dug-outs to O.C. 150th Bde M.G. Coy at 5.30 p.m.

(8) Teams 3 and 15 will each take up a disappearing mounting which will be ~~made~~ sited at their respective ~~positions~~ positions

J.H. Adam (?)
Capt.
Comm-g 149th Infy Bde
Machine Gun Coy

17/3/16

SECRET.

O.C.,

Brigade Machine Gun Coy.

10.

[Stamp: 150th (Y & D) INFANTRY BRIGADE No. B.M.971 Date 19/3/16]

1. The following reliefs will probably take place on the night of the 21st/22nd March.

   (a) The 4th East Yorks. will be relieved by the 6th N.F. in trenches 34, 35, 36, 37 R, and R 9.

   The 4th East Yorks. on relief will occupy -

   Battn. Hd. Qrs. and 2 Companies — BEDFORD HOUSE.
   One Company   — SWAN CHATEAU.
   One Company   — ARMAGH WOOD DUGOUTS.

   (b) The 7th N.F. will move to CANADA HUTS on relief by 4th East Yorks.

   (c) The 4th Yorks. will be relieved by 5th N.F. in trenches 41, 41 S, 47 S., GLASGOW CROSS, SQUARE WOOD, X TRENCH, and R 7.

   The 4th Yorks. on relief will occupy -

   Battalion Hd. Qrs. and One Company — DUGOUTS R. 30. a.
   One Company   — SUNKEN ROAD.
   Two Companies   — BLAUWEPOORT FARM.

   (d) The 4th N.F. will move to DICKEBUSCH HUTS on relief by 4th Yorks.

2. On the night of 23rd/24th March.

   The 6th N.F. will be relieved in trenches 34 - 37 R. by a Battalion of 151st Infantry Brigade and will move to BEDFORD HOUSE, SWAN CHATEAU, and ARMAGH WOOD DUGOUTS.

   The 4th East Yorks. will move after relief to DICKEBUSCH HUTS "A".

3. On night of 24th/25th March.

   (a) The 5th Durham L.I. will be relieved in trenches 37, 37S, 38, 38S, 39, 39S, 40, 40S, by the 7th Bn. N.F. and after relief will move to SCOTTISH LINES.

   (b) The 5th Yorks. will be relieved in trenches ~~Square~~, 40 - A.3, by the 4th Bn. N.F. and will occupy -

   Battalion Hd.Qrs. and One Company — DUGOUTS, R.30.a.
   One Company   — SUNKEN ROAD.
   Two Companies   — BLAUWEPOORT FARM.

   (c) The 4th Yorks. will move after dark to CANADA HUTS, on relief by 5th Yorks.

4. On nights of 21st/22nd March and 23rd/24th March, working parties from 4th N.F., 7th N.F., and 4th East Yorks. will probably be required until midnight.

5. Arrangements for relief of Brigade Machine Gun Companies will be communicated later.

Acknowledge.

Headquarters,
150th Infantry Brigade.
19th March 1916.

Major,
Brigade Major,
150th Infantry Brigade.

No. 2

Secret

119th Brigade Machine Gun Coy.

11.

Map Ref
Sheet 28
1/10000

Operation Order No. 9

(1) The following reliefs will take place within the Company on the night 21/22 March in the sector of trenches now held by the Division.

(2) Teams will relieve as under:—

No. 2 will relieve	No. 1	at KNOWLE FARM	}	Under
" 4	"	" 3	LARCH WOOD	}
" 6	"	" 5	BLAUPOORT FARM	} 2/Lt Taylor
" 7	"	" 8	do	
" 10	"	" 9	PROMENADE DUGOUTS	} Under
" 11	"	" 12	do	}
" 14	"	" 13	DUMP	} 2/Lt
" 16	"	" 15	VERBRANDENMOLEN	} Challoner

(3) Guides will meet the teams as follows:—

For PROMENADE DUGOUTS and BLAUPOORT FARM at TRANSPORT FARM at 7.30 pm

For VERBRANDENMOLEN, LARCH WOOD, DUMP and KNOWLE FARM at ZILLEBEKE STN at 7.30 pm

2

The 150° Bde M/Gun Coy will furnish one guide per gun to be at BLEAUWEPOORT FARM at 8 P.M.

5. Tripods and 14 belt boxes per gun will be taken to trenches.

6. Completion of relief to be reported to Capt Grierson, HQ 76° Infantry Bde.

7. Please acknowledge.

W.A.Grierson.
Captain.
Cmdg 151 Bde M/Gun Coy.

21.3.16.

Copy no 1 — Filed.
" 2 — HQ 151 Bde.
" 3 — HQ 76 Bde. M/G. Coy.
" 4 — HQ 150° Bde M/G Coy.

(4) 2/Lts Challoner & Taylor will report to Lt Cowen at PROMENADE DUG-OUTS at 3 pm for the purpose of reconnoitering the positions to be occupied by their guns relieving.

(5) Teams will take over guns, spare parts, tripods, belt boxes, S.A.A., blankets and gum boots, etc.
The Section Officers in charge will be responsible that rations and a fresh supply of oil are taken up.

(6) Completion of relief to be reported verbally to O.C. 150th Brigade Machine Gun Coy at RAILWAY Dug-outs and to Company Headquarters by wire.

Acknowledge.

Copy No 1. H.Q. 150 Infy Bde
2. O.C. 150th B.M.G. Coy
3. 2/Lt Challoner Cowen
4. " Taylor
5. War Diary
6. File

G. Challoner
Capt
Comm'dg 150th Infy
Brigade Machine
Gun Coy.

March 20th 1916

12

COPY No 4

Secret

151 Brigade Machine Gun Coy

Operation Order No 7.

Map Ref
Sheet 28 1/40000

21.3.16.

1. The 151 Brigade M/Gun Coy will relieve the 76th Bde M/Gun Coy (8 guns) and 4 guns of the 150th Brigade M/Gun Coy, on the night of the 22/23rd March 16; from the BLUFF to 37.R inclusive.

2. The following positions will be taken over from the 76th Brigade M/G Coy —

   2 guns at North Canal Post.
   1 gun, - 30.R
   2 guns, Gordon Post.
   2 guns, - Gordon Terrace.
   1 gun, - R.10.
   2 " s. - In hedge So. of BLEAUWEPOORT FARM. (NOT OCCUPIED AT PRESENT).

3. The following positions will be taken over from the 150th Bde M/G Coy.
   35, 36 S, 37 S, and Grand Fleet Street.

4. Guides One guide per gun will be furnished by 76 Bde M/G Coy and will be at WOODCUT HOUSE I 20 c at 8 P.M.

50TH DIVISION

OPERATION ORDER No. 30

SECRET.

Copy No.4.

Ref.Map
1/10000 VOORMEZEELE.   17th March 1916.

No 12A

1. The 50th Division will take over the front from their right to the CANAL at the BLUFF on the night 23rd/24th March, from the 3rd Division.

2. The 151st Inf. Bde. with affiliated Companies R.E. and Pioneers will take over on the night 23rd/24th March.

   (a) from the 76th Brigade, 3rd Division, from the CANAL (exclusive) to the junction of THORNE STREET with Trench 34 at I.34.b.4.3½ (exclusive), and

   (b) from the 150th Inf. Bde. from lastnamed place (inclusive) to Trench 37 R. (inclusive).

   Brigade H.Q. at WOODCOTE HOUSE, Supporting Points and all accommodation in the area, together with Log Books, defence scheme, maps and orders appertaining to the front in question, and R.E.Material and stores in the area will be taken over.
   All details to be arranged between Brigades concerned.

3. Artillery Support of the front taken over will be arranged between C.R.As. 3rd and 50th Divisions and reported to D.H.Q. for approval.

4. O.C. Trench Mortars will arrange in communication with G.O.C. 151st Inf. Bde. for trench mortars required.

5. Dividing line between 3rd and 50th Divisions will be North bank of CANAL to Bridge 21 inclusive (I.26.c.2.6) and thence following present interdivisional boundary via CAFE BELGE ,H.29.b.7.5)

6. Trench Stores will be taken over on relief, the usual receipts given and a complete list furnished to D.H.Q.

7. Command of the front taken over will pass from the G.Os. C. 76th and 150th Inf. Bdes. to G.O.C. 151st Inf. Bde. and from G.O.C. 3rd Division to G.O.C. 50th Division on completion of the entire relief.
   Completion of relief to be reported by wire to D.H.Q.

8. On completion of this relief the 149th Inf. Bde. will be in 50th Divisional Reserve with Brigade Headquarters at G.30.d.4.8. near OUDERDOM.

(signed) A.G.Stuart, Lt.Col.,
General Staff,
Issued at 6.30 a.m. 18.3.16.   50th Division.

- 2 -

O.C.,

Brigade Machine Gun Coy.

For information.
Please acknowledge.

Headquarters,
150th Infantry Brigade.
18th March 1916.

Major,
Brigade Major,
150th Infantry Brigade.

Rtn.

Map Ref   Copy No 2.   Secret.
Sheet 28   Operation Order No 10
1/10000.   by
                 Capt G. E. Wilkinson
    13   Comm.g 149th Infy Brigade
                 Machine Gun Coy.

                                    23rd March 1916

1. The 149th Infy Brigade Machine Gun Coy will relieve the 150th Brigade Machine Gun Coy in trenches 37.L to A.3. both inclusive on the night of 24th March. 8 guns of the 150th Brigade Machine Gun Coy will be attached to the 149th Brigade Machine Gun Coy.

2. Dispositions will be as follows:-
(a) No 1 team (Maxim) will move to BEDFORD HOUSE
    " 2   "   "   "   "   "   DO
    " 3   "   (Vickers) "   "   "   Top of DUMP
    " 8   "   "   "   "   "   VERBRANDENMOLEN
    " 9   "   "   "   "   "   PROMENADE DUG-OUTS
    " 12   "   "   "   "   "   DO
    " 13   "   "   "   "   "   39S
    " 15   "   "   "   "   "   41S

Cont'd

(b) Eight guns of the 150th Bri Machine Gun Coy will remain in their present positions viz A3. M.G. House. M.G. Mansions. Glasgow Cross. X Trench. Fosse Way. R7. and R8.

(c) There will be the following moves of the guns of the 149th Brigade Machine Gun Coy at present in position, on relief:-

No 16 will move to   DUMP (Left emplacement)

" 14 " " "   DUMP (Right emplacement)

3/ Guides will be found by the 150th Brigade Machine Gun Coy vig. for 415 and 395. These guides to be at ZILLEBEKE Station at 9.45 pm.

4/ Teams will come under command of Officers as follows:-

BEDFORD HOUSE   2/Lt Taylor
                           H.Qrs BEDFORD HOUSE.

GLASGOW CROSS
X TRENCH
FOSSE WAY
KNOWLE FARM
} 2/Lt Moon
(150th M.G.Coy).
H.Qrs. X TRENCH.

Con⁰

R7.
BLAWEPOORT FARM.
I B
R 8
VERBRANDENMOLEN
} 2/Lt Mawson

H.Qrs
BLAWEPOORT
FARM.

A 3
M.G. HOUSE
M.G. MANSIONS
} 2/Lt Kessler
(150 M.G.Coy)

H.Qrs A.3.

39S
41S
DUMP (12.and 53)
LARCH WOOD
} 2/Lts Bell &
Turnbull

PROMENADE Dugsouts   2/Lt Challoner

5. 1 Tripod, 14 Boxes belts, S.A.A,
Salvus apparatus, Vermoral Sprayers
Bombs and Range cards will be
taken over at each position
except by the teams for PROMENADE
Dug-outs and BEDFORD HOUSE who
will take up 1 tripod and 14
belt-boxes per gun.

6. Teams N⁰s - 1.5.8.9 and 12 will
take up one blanket per man
and all teams will take up
2 pairs of Gum-boots, thigh.

Cont.

7. The Coy Sgt Major and No 2065 Pte Currins. E.W. (Range-finder) will move to PROMENADE DUG-OUTS. and two Signallers to RAILWAY DUG-OUTS.

8. The sections will parade at 5.30pm under their Section Officers. Limbers will be packed and ready to move off from Coy H.Qrs at this time.

9. Nos. 5 and 8 teams will each take up a Disappearing Mounting.

10. Officers in charge of sections will report completion of relief by wire to me at Brigade H.Qrs RAILWAY DUG-OUTS.

Acknowledge.

Copy No 1. 149th Infy Bde
2. 150 Bde M.G.Coy
3. } Section Officers
4. }
5. War Diary
6. Filed.

R. Atkin
Capt.
Commdg 149th Infy
Brigade Machine-Gun Coy

O.C., ~~5th Yorks.Regt.~~,
 "   Brigade Machine Gun Coy.
~~6th Canadian Brigade (for information)~~.

      At 11 a.m. on the 29th March the Brigade Grenade School at KEMMEL SHELTERS will be taken over from the 6th Canadian Brigade by the Grenadier Officer 5th Yorkshire Regiment. This Officer, with 4 other ranks, will live at the School until his Battalion goes into trenches.

2.   At the same date and time the O.C., Brigade Machine Gun Coy. will send an Officer to take over the Machine Gun School M. 24. d. 3. 5. from 6th Canadian Brigade.

Major,
Brigade Major,
150th Infantry Brigade.

Headquarters,
150th Infantry Brigade.
27th March 1916.

SECRET.

14

O.C.,

Brigade Machine Gun Coy.

Herewith copy of Lorry Programme for the move of this Brigade to the new area.

The distribution will be as follows:-

March 28th.

1st Journey
(2 Lorries - 4th East Yorks.
(2 " - 4th Yorks.Regt.
(2 " - 5th Yorks.Regt.
(2 " - 5th Durham L.I.
(2 " - Brigade M.G.Coy.

2nd Journey
(1 Lorry - 4th East Yorks.
(1 " - 4th Yorks.Regt.
(1 " - 5th Yorks.Regt.
(1 " - 5th Durham L.I.
(2 Lorries - Brigade M.G.Coy.
(2 " - Brigade H.Q.

Guides from Units will meet lorries as detailed in attached programme.
Units will send sufficient men to unload the lorries and send them back at once so that the second journey may be made.

March 30th:-

3 Lorries for each Unit moving.

April 1st:-

2 Lorries for each Unit moving.

Please acknowledge receipt.

Major,
Staff Captain,
150th Infantry Brigade.

Headquarters,
150th Infantry Brigade.
26th March 1916.

QX/2523/5   LORRY PROGRAMME FOR MOVE OF 150TH INFANTRY BRIGADE.   S E C R E T.

Date.	Time	UNIT	No. of Lorries	Starting Point.	Destination	Remarks.
March 28th	7 a.m.	150th Bde.	8	Road Junction H.19.b.central (Sheet 28)	II Canadian Rest Area Sheet 27.	150th Bde. will arrange for lorries to be met on arrival at H.19.b. central and conducted to Battn. billets in 2nd Canadian Rest area. Lorries to be ordered to return to their Park on completion of work. Two journeys may be made if necessary.
30th	7 a.m.	2 Battns. 150th Bde.	6	SCHAEXKEN	LOCRE	150th Brigade will arrange guides to be at SCHAEXKEN to conduct lorries to Battn. Billets and then to LOCRE. Lorries may make two journeys if necessary. After unloading at LOCRE, 3 lorries to return to their Park, the other lorry to proceed to 150th Bde. H.Q. X.17.d.6.3. Sheet 27 (guide to be provided by Brigade) N/4 for work the following day and return to its Park on completion.
31st.	7 a.m.	150th Bde. H.Q.	1*	2nd Canadian Rest area, X.17.d.6.3. Sheet 27.	Near LOCRE M.30.t.3.5. Sheet 28.	
* kept back from previous day.
April 1st.	7 a.m.	2 Battns. 150th Bdes.	4	BERTHEN	LOCRE	150th Bde. will arrange for guides to be at SCHAEXKEN to conduct lorries to battalion billets and then to LOCRE. Lorries may make two journeys if necessary. On completion of work lorries will return to their Park.

U R G E N T.   S E C R E T.

O.C.,

Brigade Machine Gun Coy.
~~50th Division. (for information)~~
~~50th Divl. Train Coy. (for information.)~~

        March Table issued with 150th Infantry Brigade Operation Order No.21 is cancelled.

2.   The Brigade will march tomorrow, to new area, as under:-

    9.55 a.m. - Brigade Headquarters.
    10.0 a.m. - 4th East Yorks.
    10.5 a.m. - 4th Yorks.Regt.
    10.10 a.m. - 5th Yorks.Regt.
    10.15 a.m. - 5th Durham L.I.
    10.20 a.m. - 2nd Field Coy.R.E.
    10.25 a.m. - Half Coy. Pioneers.
    10.30 a.m. - Brigade Machine Gun Coy.

        The Heads of Units will pass the starting point, i.e. road junction G.30.c.3.8. (OUDEZEM) at times stated opposite their names.

3.   The Transport of Units will march Brigaded under the Brigade Transport Officer in order of march stated in para 2. The Brigade Headquarters Transport will be ready to move at 11 a.m. 200 yards N.E. of road junction G.34.b. central. Transport of remaining Units will form up on the road in rear of Brigade Headquarters Transport.

        Route for Transport only:-

REININGHELST - HEKSKEN - WESTOUTRE - BURTERN - SCHAEXKEN.

4.   One Mounted N.C.O. from each Unit's Transport will report to Brigade Transport Officer at 10. a.m. tomorrow at Cross Roads G.29.b. central.

                                                  Major,
                                                  Brigade Major,
                                                  150th Infantry Brigade.

Headquarters,
150th Infantry Brigade.
27th March 1916.

SECRET.

150TH INFANTRY BRIGADE - MARCH TABLE.

Ref.Maps Sheet 27 & 28.   28th March 1918.

1.	2.	3.	4.	5.	6.	7.
UNIT.	Starting Point.	Time.	Route.	To	Thence to billets at	Remarks.
Brigade H.Q.	Road Junction N.25.c.3.9.	9.50 a.m.	OUDEZEELE – BERTHEN – BOESCHEPE – WESTOUTRE – MONT VIDAIGNE – LA HUTTE – SCHERPENBERG.	Road Junction 100 yds E. of SCHERPENBERG N.25.a.7.2.	N.17.c.5.4.	1. The head of Units will pass the starting point at times mentioned in column 3.
4th East Yorks.	- do -	10.0 a.m.	- do -	- do -	N.9.c.6.	2. 1st & 2nd Lines Transport will follow immediately behind Units.
4th Yorks.Regt.	- do -	10.10 a.m.	- do -	- do -	N.9.c.7.2.	
5th Yorks.Regt.	- do -	10.20 a.m.	- do -	- do -	N.17.a.3.1.	3. On arrival at place mentioned in Column 5, Units will march independently to billets mentioned in Column 6.
5th Durham L.I.	- do -	10.30 a.m.	- do -	- do -	N.9.a.6.5.	Column 6 shews in every case the Headquarters of Units.
2nd Field Coy. R.E.	- do -	10.40 a.m.	- do -	- do -	N.10.a.2.3.	
5 Coy. Pioneers	- do -	10.50 a.m.	- do -	- do -	N.1.d.4.2.	
Brigade Machine Gun Company.	- do -	11.0 a.m.	- do -	- do -	N.1.d.3.3.	

180TH INFANTRY BRIGADE.

SECRET.
Copy No. 10

Operation Order No. 22.

Ref. Maps Sheets
27, 28, & 36 S.W.

March 27th 1916.

1. The following moves will take place on the 30th & 31st March and 1st April.

    30th March.

    (a) The 4th Yorks. will relieve the 28th Bn. Canadian Regt. in billets at LOCRE, arriving there by 10.30 a.m.
    Transport will occupy 28th Bn. Canadian Regt. Lines.

    (b) The 4th East Yorks. will relieve the 27th Bn. Canadian Regt. in billets at LOCRE, arriving there by 11.30 a.m.
    Transport will occupy 27th Bn. Canadian Regt. Lines.

    After relief the 4th East Yorks. will pass to 5th Canadian Brigade Reserve, and the 4th Yorks. to 2nd Canadian Divl. Reserve.

    (c) The 150th Brigade Machine Gun Coy. will march direct to billets at M.24.d.5.7. arriving there by 11a.m.

    (d) 2nd Field Coy. R.E. and ½ Coy. Pioneers will march to billets at M.29.d.4.5. arriving there by 11 a.m.

2. **On the night 31st March/1st April.**

    (a) The 4th East Yorks. will relieve the 29th Bn. Canadian Regt. in right sub-sector trenches marching by DRANOUTRE ROAD.

    (b) The 4th Yorks. will relieve the 31st Bn. Canadian Regt. in left sub-sector trenches marching by KEMMEL SHELTER ROAD.

    All details of relief to be arranged direct between the C.Os. of Battalions concerned.

    (c) 150th Infantry Brigade Hd. Qrs. will close at X.17.d. at noon and will open at M.28.b.5.6. at 2 p.m. Command of the Brigade line will be taken over by G.O.C., 150th Infantry Brigade, as soon as relief is reported complete.

3. **On the 1st April.**

    (a) The 5th Yorks. will relieve the 31st Bn. Canadian Regt. in billets at LOCRE arriving there by 11.30 a.m. Transport will occupy 31st Bn. Canadian Regt. lines.

    (b) The 5th Durham L.I. will relieve the 29th Bn. Canadian Regt. in billets at LOCRE arriving there by 10.30 a.m. Transport will occupy 29th Bn. Canadian Regt. Lines.

4. **On the night 1st/2nd April.**

    5th Yorks. Regt. will relieve a battalion of 5th Canadian Brigade in KEMMEL SHELTERS.

- 2 -

5.   Acknowledge.

[signature]

Major,
Brigade Major,
150th Infantry Brigade.

Issued at 6 p.m.

Copy No. 1. Filed.
         2. Filed.
         3. 4th East Yorks.
         4. 4th Yorks.Regt.
         5. 5th Yorks.Regt.
         6. 5th Durham L.I.
         7. 6th Canadian Inf.Bde.
         8. 2nd Field Coy. R.E.
         9. 7th (Pioneer) Bn. D.L.I.
        10. 150th Bde.M.G.Coy.

50

Army Form C. 2118.

WAR DIARY of 150 Bde M.G. Coy
50th Division.
or
INTELLIGENCE SUMMARY.
APRIL.

(Erase heading not required.)

Vol 3

Place	Date	Hour	Summary of Events and Information	Remarks and references to Appendices
Sheet 28. In trenches about N.29.	APRIL 1st		Machine Gun School started today at 9. A.M. under Lt. N.B. Stephens. I went round trenches with Bde. Bombing Officer & tried and got into touch with Division on our Right but could not on account of there being a gap in trenches, also heavy shelling.	Appendix 1.
	2nd		A good deal of shelling today. Having obtained arms. [?] from Ordnance to Coy. Gunners we started on	
	3rd		First day arranged to "Barrage" STANBROEKMOLEN in case of an enemy attack. Billets and district heavily shelled with 5.9" from 4pm to 11pm. No casualties. One shell fell 5- from horse lines but did not explode. July 3 others fell 10- from H.Q. hut. Only one burst. Probable cause of shelling the 6" gun which is just across the road	Appendix 2.
	4th		Usual trench routine. A certain amount of shelling.	
	5th		Cold day. Otherwise as yesterday. 2nd Lt. Rose sick.	
	6th		Relieved teams in S.P.8 & 9 (?) 10 (?) 11 (?) 11.20. Lt. G.O. Dawson relieved 2nd Lt. C.H. ROSE who went straight to Hospital. Reconnoitered KEMMEL DEFENCES with Bde. Bombing Officer in evening. Lt. N.S.N relieved Lt. Dawson in POLKA F.M. so that latter could relieve Lt. ROSE. Bitter-shelled again today as change.	Appendix 3.
	7th		Usual trench routine. Fine day	

Army Form C. 2118.

WAR DIARY 150 Bn M.G. Coy
50th Division
INTELLIGENCE SUMMARY. April.
(Erase heading not required.)

Place	Date	Hour	Summary of Events and Information	Remarks and references to Appendices
Sheet 28.	April 9th		Trench routine. Interviewed Brigadier at night. 6" gun near billet busy all night.	
In trenches & Billet.	10th		Lt. G.B. PURVIS went on leave this morning. Lt. C Wood in charge of Coy. Working party for HOLLEBEKE FARM tonight.	
M24d4.8.	11th		Quiet day. Working party sent again to HOLLEBEKE Fm tonight to complete app to strong dugout. Battalion relief on April 13th/14th.	
	14th		Yeands relieved today by men from Bllt. A good deal of shelling & trench mortars during the day.	
	16th		Capt. B.M.R. SHARP returned from hospital today. Trenches took quiet visit. Lt G.B PURVIS re-called from leave on account of (General order to that effect) for everyone on leave.	
	17th		2nd Lt. C.H. ROSE returned from Hospital. Heavy shelling of trenches	
	18th		Lt. C. Wood relieved Lt. J.K.M Henderson La POLKA Fm. Stormy day.	
	19th		2nd Lt. C.H Rose relieved Lt DAWSON today. Still stormy. Nearby dugouts broken in	
			Left; somewhere about the SALIENT. 6" gun busy	Apps in
	22nd		2 Lt N.B. Stephens relieved Lt C. Wood today at School finished yesterday evening	5. 6.

WAR DIARY 150 Inf: Bde M.G. Coy 50th Division
INTELLIGENCE SUMMARY.
April

Army Form C. 2118.

Place	Date	Hour	Summary of Events and Information	Remarks and references to Appendices
Sheet 28. Trenches & Billet	24th		Capt ZEIGLER and 3 Officers of 176th Bde M.G. Coy came to reconnoitre our sector so as to be able to relieve us. Hot day some shelling	
	25th/26th		Capt Zeigler + 3 other Officers came to reconnoitre lines again today. Capt Zeigler remained. Half Company of 176 Bde M.G. Coy arrived about mid-day & were accommodated in the School. Hot day	
	27th		Other half of 176 M.G. Coy + remaining Officers arrived about noon. First half Coy + 3 officers relieved the 1st 3 guns which this Company had in the line + supports.	App. Y.
	28th		All limbers painted. Morning spent booking up, cleaning billets etc. Left for Rest Billet 10.30. Bayonets about 2 pm Very Hot.	App. Y.
Sheet 27. Rest Billet Q.35.A.7.4.	29		Day spent cleaning up, erecting Cook Houses etc as men were left by 176 Bde M.G. Coy	
	30th		Inspections etc in morning. Church Parade 3 pm. The first for 3 months	App. 8.

G. D. Purvis Lt.
150th Bde M.G. Coy

APPENDIX.

O.C.,

Brigade Machine Gun Coy.

1. ~~Two~~ Y/two Lewis Guns from both 5th Yorks. Regt. and 5th Durham L.I. will be sent up tonight to the Headquarters of the Right and Left Sub-sectors. These guns will be placed in positions in front lines selected by Os. C. sub-sectors and will be manned by the Battalions in the trenches.

2. On relief each outgoing Battalion will leave two Lewis Guns in its sub-sector for the use of incoming Battalion. The latter Battalion will find the crews for the guns.

3. Attached is the distribution of the Brigade Machine Gun Company's guns in Brigade Sector.

Major,
Brigade Major,
150th Infantry Brigade.

Headquarters,
150th Infantry Brigade.
1st April 1916.

APPENDIX 2.

SECRET.

DISTRIBUTION OF MACHINE GUNS.

4 Guns in School - 3 Vickers, and 1 Maxim.

Classes commence April 1st - 2 Officers 20 other ranks. i/c Lt.Stephens, Machine Gun Coy., and 2 N. C. Os.

Guns in Position.

```
        S. P. 8      - 2 - 1 Vickers & 1 Maxim.)
                                                ) Lieut.
        S. P. 9      - 1 - Vickers.             ) Dawson.
                                                )
        S. P. 10     - 1 - Vickers.             )

        S. P. 11     - 1 - Maxim                )
        S. P. 11 a.- 1 - Vickers                )
        (BEAVER HUT)                            )
                                                ) Lieut. Rose.
        Parrain Fme  - 1 - Vickers              )
                                                )
        LA POIKA     - 1 - Vickers              )

        VIERSTRAAT SWITCH - 1 - Maxim           )
                                                )
        FORT REGINA       - 1 - Maxim           ) Lieut.
                                                ) Messler.
        FORT VICTORIA     - 1 - Maxim           )
                                                )
        FORT EDWARD       - 1 - Maxim           )
```

Orders:- To work up to 20 belts per gun in position.

To get in defensive portions, safe accommodation for teams.

Teams - 3 per gun.

150th INFANTRY BRIGADE.　　　　　S E C R E T.

OPERATION ORDER No.23　　　　　Copy No. 6

Ref.Map.
Sheet 28 &　　　　　　　　　　　　5th April 1916.
Trench Map.

Appendix 3.

  On the night of the 7th/8th April the following reliefs will take place.

 (a) The 5th Yorks. will relieve the 4th East Yorks. in right sub-sector trenches.

 (b) The 5th Durham L.I. will relieve the 4th Yorks. (less 1 Coy) in left sub-sector trenches, marching by KEMMEL SHELTER Road,

2. At 9 p.m. on night 7th/8th April one company 4th Yorks. Regt. will pass under the orders of the O.C., 5th Durham L.I. and will be distributed as follows:-

  2 platoons KEMMEL CHATEAU.
  2 platoons PARAIN FARM.

 This Company will be under the orders of O.C. Left Sub-sector for tactical purposes. It may be relieved by arrangement between C.Os.

3. Each outgoing Battalion will leave behind two Lewis Guns for the use of incoming Battalions. The crews will be found by latter Battalions.

4. After relief the 4th East Yorks. will move into Divisional Reserve at LOCRE and the 4th Yorks. (less 1 Coy) will move to Brigade Reserve at KEMMEL SHELTERS.

5. All details of relief will be arranged between O.C.Battalions direct.

 Completion of reliefs will be reported to Brigade Headquarters by wire.

                R.S.Guy
                Major,
                Brigade Major,
                150th Infantry Brigade.

Copy No.1 Filed:
  2 4th East Yorks.
  3 4th Yorks.Regt.
  4 5th Yorks.Regt.
  5 5th Durham L.I.
  6 Brigade M.G.Coy.
  7 2nd Field Coy.R.E.
  8 72nd Infantry Brigade.
  9 149th Infantry Brigade.

Appendix 4.

Op 10

S E C R E T.

Copy No. 8

150TH INFANTRY BRIGADE.

OPERATION ORDER NO. 24.

April 13th 1916.

1. The following reliefs will take place within the Brigade on the night of the 15th/16th April.

2. (a) The 4th East Yorks. will relieve the 5th Yorks. in the Right Sub-sector.
On relief the 5th Yorks. will move into Divisional Reserve at LOCRE.

(b) The 4th Yorks. Regt. will relieve the 5th Durham L.I. in the Left Sub-sector.
On relief the 5th Durham L.I. will move into Brigade Reserve at KEMMEL SHELTERS.

3. Reliefs will commence as soon as it is dark.

4. All details of reliefs will be arranged direct between the Battalion Commanders concerned.

5. Completion of reliefs will be reported to Brigade Headquarters.

Acknowledge.

R.S. Guy

Major,
Brigade Major,
150th Infantry Brigade.

Issued at 12 noon.

Copy No.1. Filed.
2. 4th East Yorks.
3. 4th Yorks.Regt.
4. 5th Yorks.Regt.
5. 5th Durham L.I.
6. 2nd Field Coy. R.E.
7. Pioneer Coy.
8.✓ Bde.Machine Gun Coy.
9. 149th Infantry Bde.
10. 72nd Infantry Bde.
11. War Diary.

SECRET.

Copy No.

150TH INFANTRY BRIGADE OPERATION ORDER NO.25.

Ref. Trench Map.   17th April 1916.

1.   The following reliefs will take place within the Brigade on the night of the 22nd/23rd April.

2.   (a) The 5th Yorks. will relieve the 4th East Yorks. in the Right Sub-sector.

        On relief the 4th East Yorks. will move into Brigade Reserve at KEMMEL SHELTERS.

        (b) The 5th Durham L.I. will relieve the 4th Yorks. in the Left Sub-sector.

        On relief the 4th Yorks. Regt. will move into Divisional Reserve at LOCRE.

3.   Reliefs will commence as soon as it is dark.

4.   All details of relief will be arranged direct between the Battalion Commanders concerned.

5.   Completion of reliefs will be reported to Brigade Headquarters.

        Acknowledge.

                                        Major,
                                        Brigade Major,
                                        150th Infantry Brigade.

Issued at 12 noon.

Cop. No. 1. Filed.
    2. 4th East Yorks.
    3. 4th Yorks. Regt.
    4. 5th Yorks. Regt.
    5. 5th Durham L.I.
    6. 2nd Field Coy, R.E.
    7. Pioneer Coy.
    8. Bde. Machine Gun Coy.
    9. 149th Infantry Bde.
    10. 72nd Infantry Bde.
    11. War Diary.

SECRET.

appendix 6

O.C.,
Brigade Machine Gun Coy.

Reference 150th Infantry Brigade Operation Order No.25 of 17th April 1916.

After relief on the night of the 22nd/23rd April one Company of the 4th East Yorks. will pass under the command of O.C. Left Sub-sector, and will be accommodated in KEMMEL CHATEAU. This Company may be relieved under arrangements made direct between C. Os.

Please acknowledge.

Major,
Brigade Major,
150th Infantry Brigade.

Headquarters,
150th Infantry Brigade.
19th April 1916.

SECRET.
Copy No. 7

150TH INFANTRY BRIGADE OPERATION ORDER NO.26.

Ref.1/40,000
Sheets 27, & 28.
& Trench Map.

April 22nd 1916.

1. The 50th Division will be relieved by the 3rd Division between the 21st April and 2nd May, and proceed to Rest Area with Divisional H.Q. at FLETRE.

   From 12 noon on May 3rd the 50th Division will be in G.H.Q. Reserve and will be ready to entrain at Nine hours notice.

2. The following moves will take place between 27th and 29th April.

   <u>27th April.</u>

   (a) The 4th Yorks. Regt. will be relieved in billets at LOCRE by 11.30 a.m. by the 1st Gordons. On relief the 4th Yorks. Regt. will march to Rest Area.

   (b) The 4th East Yorks. (less 1 Coy) will be relieved at KEMMEL SHELTERS by 10th Royal Welsh Fusiliers, by 12 noon.

   On relief the 4th East Yorks. (less 1 Coy) will march to Rest Area. Battalions moving East of LOCRE & DRANOUTRE will do so by Companies at intervals of half a mile.

   <u>Night of 27th/28th April.</u>

   (c) 150th Infantry Brigade Machine Gun Coy. will be relieved by 76th Infantry Brigade Machine Gun Coy. under arrangements to be made direct between O.C., Companies.

   (d) 150/1 Trench Mortar Battery will be relieved by 76/1 Trench Mortar Battery under arrangements to be made direct between O.C. Batteries.

3. (a) <u>On the 28th April.</u>

   2nd Northbn. Field Coy. R.E. will be relieved by 1/1st E.R.Field Coy. R.E. at LOCREHOF, and forward, under arrangements to be made direct between O.C.Coys.

   On relief the 2nd Nbn. Field Coy. R.E. will move to Rest Area.

   (b) The Pioneer Company will rejoin 7th Bn. Durham L.I. in camp at LA CLYTTE under orders to be issued by O.C., that Battalion.

   (c) <u>On the night 28th/29th April.</u>

   The 5th Yorks. Regt. will be relieved in Right

/Sub-sector

- 2 -

Sub-sector trenches by the 10th R.W.Fusiliers.

On relief the 5th Yorks. will be in 76th Brigade Reserve at KEMMEL SHELTERS.

(d) 5th Durham L.I. and 1 Coy. 4th East Yorks. will be relieved in Left Sub-sector trenches by the 1st Gordons.

On relief the 5th Durham L.I. (and 1 Coy. 4th East Yorks.) will be in 3rd Division Reserve in billets at LOCRE.

All details of reliefs to be arranged direct between the C.Os. concerned.

(e) As soon as relief is reported complete, and G.O.C., 76th Infantry Brigade has assumed command of area, Brigade H.Q. will close at M.30.b.3.3. and will move to Q.35.b.2.2. (Sheet 27).

4. 29th April.

(a) The 5th Durham L.I.(and 1 Coy. 4th East Yorks.) will be relieved in billets at LOCRE by 11.30 a.m. by the 8th K.O. Regt.

On relief the 5th Durham L.I. (& 1 Coy. 4th East Yorks.) will march to Rest Area where the Company 4th East Yorks. will rejoin its Battalion.

(b) The 5th Yorks. Regt. will be relieved in KEMMEL SHELTERS by 11.30 a.m. by the 1st Suffolks. On relief the 5th Yorks. Regt. will march to Rest Area.

Battalions moving between East of LOCRE & DRANOUTRE will do so by Companies at intervals of half a mile.

5. All Units moving from this Brigade Area to Rest Area will march via BAILLEUL and METEREN. Details regarding billets have been communicated to O.C., Units by the Staff Captain.

6. Transport will march under the orders of O.C. Units.

7. Log-books, Defence Schemes, Orders, Maps, Photographs, and all useful information available relating to the 50th Division area will be handed over to relieving Units.

ACKNOWLEDGE.

Major, Brigade Major,
150th Infantry Brigade.

Issued at 6 p.m.

Copy No.1 Filed.
    2. 4th East Yorks.
    3. 4th Yorks.Regt.
    4. 5th Yorks.Regt.
    5. 5th Durham L.I.
    6. 2nd Field Co.R.E.
    7./Bde.M.G.Coy.

Copy No.8 150/1 T.M.Batty.
    9. 76th Inf. Bde.
    10. 72nd Inf. Bde.
    11. 7th D.L.I.(Pioneers).
    12. 50th Division.
    13. War Diary.

O.C. G "alarm post"

150th (Y & D)
No. BM 540
Date 30.4.16
INFANTRY BRIGADE

Brigade Machine Gun Coy.

appendise 8.

In the event of an alarm Battalions will fall in on their Battalion alarm posts with 1st Line Transport complete and await orders. An Officer will be sent to Brigade Headquarters for orders.

If ordered the Brigade will concentrate on Brigade alarm post i.e. main road between FLETRE AND CAESTRE, as f follows:-

    Head of 4th Yorks on road 200 yards west of FLETRE.
        4th East Yorks.
        5th Yorks.
        5th Durham L.I.

Head of Brigade Machine Gun Coy will be 200 yards north west of FLETRE on FLETRE-THIEUSHOUK Road and will march in rear of 5th Durham L.I.

2. Units will halt clear of the road and await further orders. Transport will march in rear of Battalions.

3. All Officers will reconnoitre Brigade Alarm Post and approaches thereto.

    Acknowledge.

Major,
Brigade Major,
150th Infantry Brigade.

Headquarters,
150th Infantry Brigade.
30th April 1916.

Army Form C. 2118.

WAR DIARY of 150 Bde M.G. Coy.
150 Inf Brigade
May 1916.

(Erase heading not required.)

Place	Date	Hour	Summary of Events and Information	Remarks and references to Appendices
In the Field	May 1st	—	All Spare Part Boxes inspected & made up of what aspects. Thunder shower in Evening	G.B.P.
"Busing"	3		Gun drill & usual routine work	G.B.P.
Nr THIEUSHOEK	5		Company went to Baths near Meteren. Dull day	G.B.P.
27 Q 35 d 7,5	8		Commenced having Coy Inoculated at No 3 Field Ambulance. (Northumbrian T.F.)	G.B.P.
	9		Lt. C. Wood returned from leave today	G.B.P.
	11		Lt G.W. Dawson went on leave. Lt G.B. Purvis took his class in Rangefinding	G.B.P.
	12		Rangefinding Class in morning. Divisional Inspection of Northolport Afternoon	G.B.P.
	13		Rained all day. Could do nothing	G.B.P.
	16		Capt B.M.R. Bluff went on leave today to Father who was dying. Command of Coy taken by Lt G.B. Purvis	G.B.P.
	17		Two officers went on Tour of Divisional Area. Saw Flying Ground, Sniping + M. Schools, Army Workshops R.E. & Ammunition Parks, C.C.C. etc. Very Instructive	G.B.P.
	20.		I rode to BAILLEUL - met CAPT. ZEIGLER, of 76 M.G. Coy & made preliminary arrangements about relief.	G.B.P.
	22.		Half Coy sent to Divisional Gas School for Instruction in Lower Respirator. Brigade-Coy Sports in afternoon. Sgt Baron A. took he arm at High Jump.	G.B.P.
	23.		Divisional Inspection by Gen Plumer. Presentation of Medals. Other half of Coy sent to Divisional Gas School for Instruction in Lower Respirators in Coy.	G.B.P. appx six

Army Form C. 2118.

WAR DIARY of 150 Bde M.G. Coy
150 Inf. Brigade
INTELLIGENCE SUMMARY. For May: 1916.

(Erase heading not required.)

Place	Date	Hour	Summary of Events and Information	Remarks and references to Appendices
	MAY.			
Resting	24th	—	Cleaning up. Packing up ready for move tomorrow	G.B.P.
Farm	25th	—	Dull morning with Rain. Cleaned up billets. Marched 6.15 pm from Regentrain after BAILLEU.	G.B.P.
Q35d4/5.			Very heavy cots: men billeted in Barn for night.	Appendices 2,3,4.
Intended 6:			Fine day. Rest of Coy arrived. Relieved 13 guns of 76th Bde M.G. Coy in old position	G.B.P.
in front of			from E6 to H.I.A. Very little work had been done in the last month.	
KEMMEL	29th	—	76th M.G. Coy moved off to their next billet in morning. 9 unarmoured trenches	G.B.P.
VILLAGE	29th	—	Working party at night putting in an Emplacement in VIA GELLIA C.T.	G.B.P.
	30th	—	Fine day. Leamo relieved tonight.	Appendix 5
	31st	—	Working party started second emplacement in VIA GELLIA. 2nd Lt N.B. Stephens	G.B.P.
			seriously wounded while indirect firing, about midnight.	
			Attached are also Amendment to Strategic Move Programme.	
			Operation Order No 21.	
			Also Operation Orders for relief of 150 Bde MG Coy by 76 M.G. Coy on	
			night of 27/28 April 1916. which were omitted from last month's Diary	
				G.B. Purvis Lt
			G.B. Purvis Lt	
			150 Bde M.G. Coy	

O.C.

Brigade Machine Gun Coy.

The Brigade will parade tomorrow in the field S. of CAESTRE - FLETRE Road for presentation of Distinguished Conduct and Military Medals.

Dress. Drill Order, with Smoke Helmets, worn over left shoulder.

2. Units will clear the entrance gate to the field Q.6.c.6.5. by the following hours and will form up in two lines of Battalions in Mass.

Brigade Signal Section.	By 9.35 a.m.
Bde. Machine Gun Coy.)	
150/1 Trench Mortar Bty.)	" 9.40 a.m.
4th East Yorks.	" 9.45 a.m.
5th Yorks.	" 9.50 a.m.
4th Yorks.	" 9.55 a.m.
5th Durham L.I.	10.0 a.m.

The Brigade Signal Section, Machine Gun Coy, and 150/1 Trench Mortar Battery will form up on the right of the Brigade.

Brigade Markers will meet the Brigade Major in the field at 9.15 a.m.

3. The following Officers only will be mounted when the Brigade is formed up.-

C.O's., Senior Majors, and Adjutants of Infantry Battalions.

4. The Brigade will "Present Arms" to the sound of a bugle. One "G" will call the Brigade to attention, a second long "G" followed by a short note will be sounded and Units will present arms on the last sound of short note. A rehearsal of this procedure will take place on parade tomorrow.

5. Platoons will be sized and equalized before coming on parade. Men for medals will parade separately without rifles.

6. Attached is rough sketch of parade.

Headquarters,
150th Infantry Brigade.
22nd May 1916.

Major,
Staff Captain,
150th Infantry Brigade.

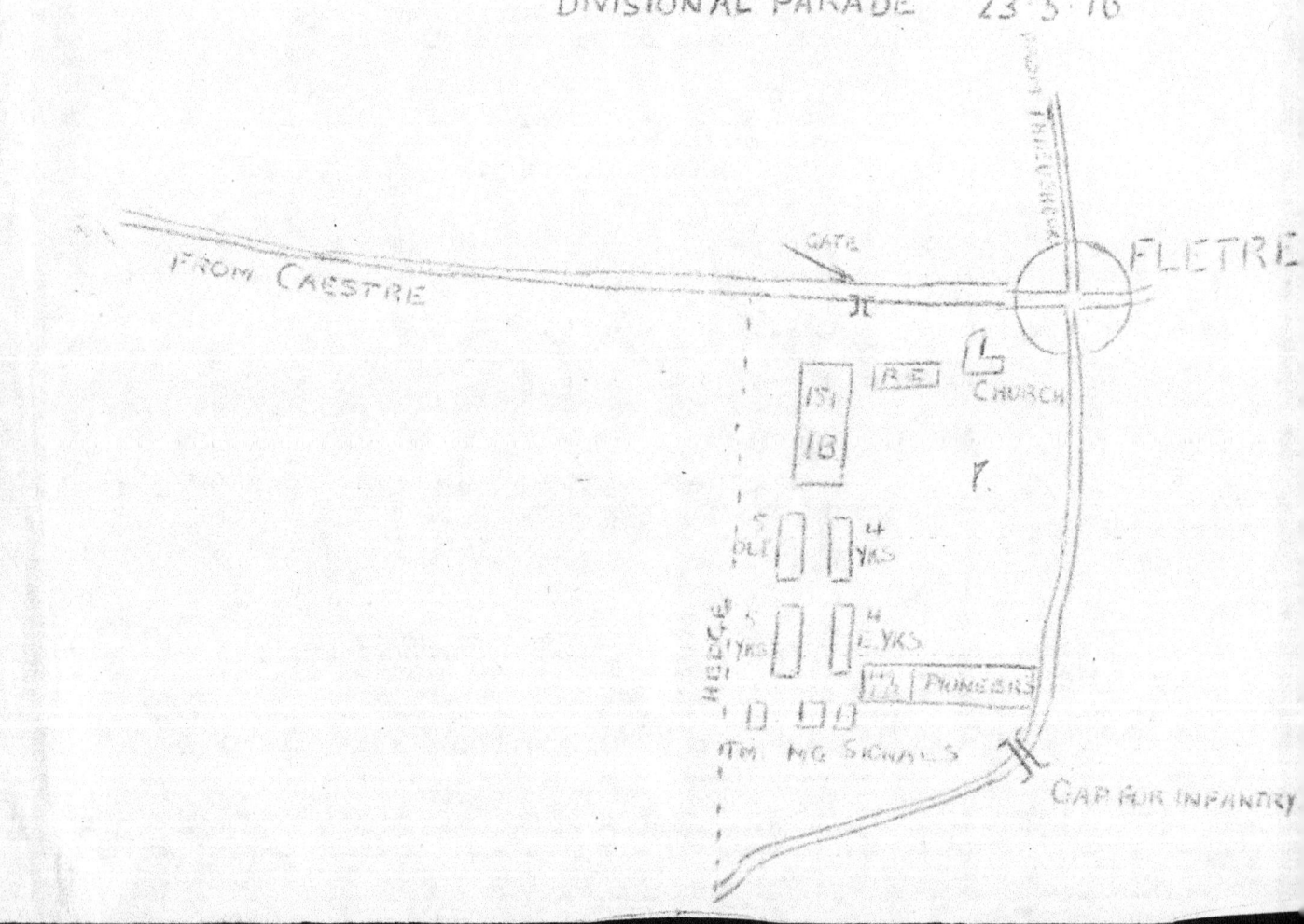

Appendix 2

SECRET.
Copy No. 6

150TH INFANTRY BRIGADE.

OPERATION ORDER NO. 28.

Reference 1/40,000
Sheets 27 & 28.
& Trench Maps.

1. The 50th Division will relieve the 3rd Division between the 23rd and 31st May 1916.

2. The 150th Infantry Brigade will relieve the 76th Infantry Brigade.

3. The relief will be carried out as follows :-

   May 26th.

   (a) The 4th East Yorks will relieve the 10th Battalion Royal Welch Fusiliers in billets at LOCRE before 11.0 a.m.

   (b) The 4th Yorks will relieve the 1st Bn. Gordon Highlanders in Kemmel Shelters before 11.30 a.m.

   Night of 26th - 27th.

   (a) The 150th Brigade Machine Gun Company will relieve the 76th Brigade Machine Gun Company.

   (b) The 150/1 Trench Mortar Battery will relieve the 76/1 Trench Mortar Battery.

   Arrangements for relief to be made direct between O.C. Companies and Batteries.

   Night 27 - 28th.

   (a) The 4th East Yorks Regt. will relieve the 2nd Bn. Suffolk Regiment in the right sector. On relief the 2nd Bn Suffolk Regiment will move into billets at LOCRE and will then be in 50th Divisional Reserve.

   (b) The 4th Yorks will relieve the 8th Bn. Kings' Own (R.L.) Regt. in the left sector. On relief the 8th Bn. Kings' Own (R.L.) Regt. will move into KEMMEL SHELTERS and will then be in 150th Brigade Reserve.

   (c) The 2nd Field Coy. R.E. will relieve the 1/1st East Riding Field Coy. R.E. at LOCREHOF and forward. Arrangements of relief to be made direct between O.C. Companies.

   (d) On completion of the relief the General Officer Commanding 150th Infantry Brigade will take over command of the sector. Brigade Headquarters will be at CURE HOUSE, LOCRE.

150TH INFANTRY BRIGADE. OPERATION ORDER NO.28. Continued.

May 28th.

    (a) The 5th Yorks will relieve the 2nd Bn. Suffolk Regt. in LOCRE before 11 a.m.

    (b) The 5th Durham L.I. will relieve the 8th Kings' Own (R.L.) Regt. in KEMMEL SHELTERS before 11.30 a.m.

4. All details of Battalion reliefs will be arranged between C.O's concerned.

5. Battalions moving East of LOCRE in daylight will do so by Companies at intervals of half a mile.

6. Battalions moving from Rest Area to KEMMEL SHELTERS will do so via., BAILLEUL - DRANOUTRE - CROSSROADS M.30.B.

7. Log Books, Defence Schemes, Orders, Maps, Photographs, and all useful information available relating to the 3rd Divisional Area will be handed over by Units of the 76th Infantry Brigade.

All Trench Stores will be taken over on relief and lists will be made out in duplicate; one copy being forwarded to Brigade Headquarters.

8. Bombers, Signallers, and Lewis Gun Detachments of the 4th East Yorks and 4th Yorks will relieve the specialists of the 2nd Bn. Suffolk Regt. and 8th Kings' Own (R.L.) Regt, respectively 12 hours before Battalion reliefs commence.

9. All Battalions will send on in advance on the day of relief one Officer and one N.C.O. per Company to take over billets and trench stores in daylight.

10. The Completion of all reliefs will be reported to Brigade Headquarters.

Acknowledge.

Copy No. 1. Filed.
    2. 4th East Yorks.
    3. 4th Yorks.
    4. 5th Yorks.
    5. 5th Durham L.I.
    6. Bde Machine Gun Coy.
    7. 150/1 Trench Mortar Battery.
    8. 2nd Field Coy. R.E.
    9. 72nd Infantry Brigade.
    10. 76th Infantry Brigade.
    11. 149th Infantry Brigade.
    12. O.C. Divisional Train. A.S.C.
    13 50th Division.
    14. War Diary.

Major,
Brigade Major,
150th Infantry Brigade.

Operation Orders No 2.   Secret
76th Coy Machine Gun Corps.   Copy No 3.
76th Inf Brigade

Map Ref.
Sheet 28
" 27

Appendix 3

1. The 76th Coy. M.G. Corps will be relieved in the line by the 150th Coy M.G. Corps (13 Guns) on the night of the 26th/27th May 1916. The relieving Company will march from rest. area on the night of the 25th/26th and will be accommodated in the Machine Gun School Field for that night.

2. Guides of the 76th Coy will be at Coy Headquarters. Sheet 28 M.24.D.4.7. at 8pm on the night 26th/27th inst to guide limbers + teams of the 150th Coy to their respective positions, they will leave camp at 8.30pm.

3. Orders issued to transport of the 76th Coy are as follows. —
 1 limber to be at LA POLKA Farm at 10.30 pm 26th/27th to collect 2 Guns + stores.
 1½ limbers to be at FARM PARRAIN at 11pm 26th/27th to collect 2 Guns + stores from SP. 11 + 1 Gun + stores from FORT REGINA
 1 limber to be at HALEYBROEK FARM at 10.30 pm. 26th/27th inst to collect 1 Gun + stores from HALEYBROEK
 1 Gun + stores from FRENCHMAN.
 1 limber to be at SPY FARM at 10.30 pm. to collect 2 Guns + stores.
 2 limbers to be at REGENT ST. Dug outs at 11pm 26th/27th inst to collect 1 Gun from SP. 10. 1 Gun from SP. 9. 2 Guns from SP. 8.
 No limbers will be allowed to pass LINDENHOEK, or KEMMEL Korner, until after dark

25.5.16.

4. All Gun positions will be handed over to the relieving Coy in a clean & tidy condition. Officers & N.C.O's. must explain everything in detail before leaving the position.

5. All maps, Schemes &c. will be handed over, or returned to Coy Headquarters & will be handed over to the O.C. the 150th M.G. Coy.

6. All Trench Stores will be handed over & lists will be made in duplicate & Signatures must be obtained for everything handed over.

7. Completion of relief will be reported to Coy Headquarters by wire.

8. Team on arrival at billets will be accomodated in M.G. School for the night, they will parade at 9 a.m. on the 27th inst. & will march via BAILLEUL — METEREN ~~Bailleul~~, ~~Meteren~~, to same billets as occupied when last at rest.

9. Acknowledge.

A. E. Ziegler Capt
Com 2/6th Coy
M.G. Corps

25/5/16

Copy No 1 filed
No 2 76th Bde
No 3 150th Bde M.G. Coy

Appendix 4.

(No 4)

150th Bde. M.G. Coy. Operation Order. (SECRET)

Map Reference. Sheet 28.S.W. 1/20.000.

1. 150th Bde. M.G. Coy will relieve the 46th Bde M.G. Coy on the night of May 26/27. 1916.

2. The positions to be taken over & order of relief as per attached table.

3. One guide will be supplied by 46th Bde. M.G. Coy. to be at Suicide Corner at 8.30 P.M. to guide Limbers to Fm. Parrain.

4. 2nd Lt. Moon will report at S.P.10 and 2/Lts Stephens & Spooner at Polka Farm at 5 P.M. on May 26th to take over trench stores.

5. Carrying parties will be arranged if possible from remaining half Company.

6. Limbers will not pass Lindenhoek Corner before 8.30 P.M.

7. Relief Complete will be telephoned from Polka Farm only to O/C 150th Bde. M.G. Coy.
S.P. 10. will not telephone, but send a message by carrying party.

Copy No. 1. Filed
2. 46th Bde M.G. Coy.
3. 150th Inf. Bde.
4. 150th Bde. M.G. Coy. War Diary.

May 25th 1916.

G.B. Purvis. Lt.
150 Bde M.G. Coy.

To Trenches May 26th 1916

Team	Destination	Officer	Number Limbers	Destination Limber
Sgt. Dawson Pte. Husby " Hogarth " Jefferson	Polka Farm	Lt. Stephens	1	Gun Position
" Harrison C. " Daubney " Lambert	Polka Farm	Lt. Dadd		Do
Cpl. Smith Pte. Martinson " Bennett	S.P. 11		1	Farm Parrain and thence by Tramway
Cpl. Dring Pte. Teale " Armitage	S.P. 11A			Do
Cpl. Windle Pte. Tillotson " Harrison R.	Fort Regina		½	Farm Parrain
L/Cpl. Butler Pte. Broderick " Parry	Halybrook Fm.	Lt. Spooner	1	Gun Position
Pte. Williamson R. " Harrison J. " Harker	Frenchman's Farm			Gun Position
Cpl. Perry Pte. Bulke " Kenworthy	Sky farm		1	Do
" Dixon H. " Dixon W. " Parvin	Do			Do
Sgt. Milburn Pte. Coates " Leyland " Barclay	S.P. 8		1	Regent St. Dugouts
Cpl. Anderson Pte. Patterson " McLeod	Do			Do
L/Cpl. Rymer Pte. Dickinson " Thompson G.	S.P. 9		1	Do
L/Cpl. Parker Pte. Gilbert " Jerome	S.P. 10	Lt. Moon		Do

May 25th 1916.

G. B. Purvis, Lt.
150 Bde M.G. Coy.

Operation Orders.
150th Inf. Bde. M. G. Coy.

24/5/16

Map Ref.
Sheet 27.
28.

Appendix 4A.

Copy No. 9

Relief. The Company will relieve 76th Bde. M.G. Coy. in Trenches on night of May 26/27th.

Move. The Company will parade at 6.15 P.M. May 25th and march by FLETRE – METEREN – BAILLEUL – LOCRE road to 76th Bde. M.G. School field.
As many men as possible will be accommodated in the Barn. The remainder will bivouac out in the school field.

Stores. All Q.M. Stores surplus clothing, etc. will be left at Q.M. Stores & be sent by Motor lorry on May 26th. Two journeys may be made if necessary.

Officer & Men remaining. Lt. Wood. C.Q.M. Sergeant, Storeman and six other privates will remain to load up lorry and clean up Camp Ground. The storeman will proceed with this load, all the others remaining till the second.

Guide. A Guide will be at corner in Fletre near Gas School at 6.55 a.m. meet Motor Lorry & show it the way to Company's Billet.

Cooks. One cook with 12 Dixies & necessary Rations to make Tea & Breakfast will go on ahead in Mess Cart & prepare tea for the men when they arrive. The other Cook will march with the Company.

S.A.A. 30.000 Rounds S.A.A. will be left behind for 76th Bde. M.G. Coy. when they arrive.

Chargers. Officers will be mounted.

Water. Men's Water Bottles to be full before moving.

G. B. Purvis. Lt.
for O/c 150th I.B.M.G. Coy.

(For May 30th 1916) Appendix 5. ~~No 6~~ May 30/5/16

Teams.	Destination	Officer
Sgt. Glover		
Pte Dodds	"Polka farm"	Lt. Dawson
" Dodgson		
" Foreman		
" Makepeace	Do	Lt. Carpenter
" Wallis		
Sgt Barnett		
Pte Swalwell	S.P. 11	
" Greenwood		
" Moore		
" Bayes	S.P. 11a	
" Hayton		
" Redshaw		
" Porter	Fort Regina	
" Parker		
Cpl. Acklam		
Pte Robson	Haleybrook farm	Lt. Spooner
" Kennedy		
" Peirson		
" Percy	Frenchman's farm	
" Cockfield		
Sgt. Cope		
Pte Sidgwick	Spy farm	
" Beautiman		
" Fox. J.		
" Fox. H.	Do	
" Powell		
Sgt. Gartham		
Pte Dixon J.	S.P. 8	
" Smith W.		
" Lowell		
" Smith G.	Do	
" Braul R.L.		
Cpl. Jacobs (sick to H May 31st) Cpl. G. Clark took his place June 1st		
Pte Bowman	S.P. 9	
" Dobinson		
Cpl. Fields		
Pte Hendry	S.P. 10	{ Lt. Stephens. W to H 31/5/16 Died of W 1/6/16 Lt C.H. Rose took his place at S.P. 10 on June 1st
" Pearce		

150th Infantry Brigade.

50th Division.
G.X.1403/16

In the Programme for Strategical Move of 50th Division by Railway Train from Second Army Area to Third or Fourth Army Area, issued on 30th April with 50th Divisional Letter G.X.1403/13

Amendments will be made on Sheet two for Trains 18, 19, 20:-

    Train 18.   CASSEL. No 4 Company Divisional Train will entrain NOT No. 3 Company.

    Train 19.   BAILLEUL. No 2 Company Divisional Train will entrain.

    Train 20.   GODEWAERSVELDE. No.3 Company Divisional Train will entrain NOT No. 4. Company.

No alteration in Field Ambulances.

(sd) H.W.B. Thorp. Major,
General Staff,
50th Division.

2nd May 1916.

-2-

O.C.

Brigade Machine Gun Coy.

Please make necessary amendment in the case of train 18 in the "Programme of Move" send you under My B.M. 588 of 1.5.16.

Major,
Brigade Major,
150th Infantry Brigade.

Headquarters,
150th Infantry Brigade,
3rd May 1916.

SECRET.

Copy No. 6

150TH INFANTRY BRIGADE OPERATION ORDER NO.27.

9th May 1916.

1. Reference V Corps G.X.5577 of 6. 4. 16, and 50th Division G.X.1439 of 24. 4. 16, and 26. 4. 16.

2. The 5th Yorks. Regt. will relieve the Battalion (6th Durham L.I.) of 151st Infantry Brigade at LA CLYTTE on May 12th 1916.

3. All arrangements to be made direct between Units.

4. Completion of relief to be reported to Brigade Headquarters.

Acknowledge.

Major,
Brigade Major,
150th Infantry Brigade.

Copy No.1. Filed.
    2. 4th East Yorks.
    3. 4th Yorks.Regt.
    4. 5th Yorks.Regt.
    5. 5th Durham L.I.
    6. Bde.M.G.Coy.
    7. 150/1 T.M.Batty.
    8. Brigade Transport Officer.
    9. 50th Division.
   10. 3rd Division.
   11. 151st Inf. Bde.
   12. 6th Durham L.I.
   13. No.4 Coy. A.S.C.
   14. War Diary.

Ref. Map
No 28 SW
1/20,000
+ French Map

Secret
Copy No 7

Relief Orders by Capt B. M. R. Sharpe
Cmdg 150 Bde M. G. Coy

1. The 150 Bde M. G. Coy will be relieved in the line by the 1/6th Bde M G Coy on night 27/28 inst.

2. Guides of 150 Bde M. G. Coy will be at Transport lines at 7 p.m. on night 27/28 to guide limbers and teams of 1/6th Bde M. G. Coy as under

	No of limbers	No of Guides	Destination of limbers	Remarks
a)	one	one	HALEYBROUCK FM	1 gun
			FRENCHMANS FM	1 gun
b)	one	one	SPY FARM	2 guns
c)	two	three	REGENT ST DUMP	2 guns - S.P.8 1 " - S.P.9 1 " - S.P.10
d)	one	one	LA POLKA FM	2 guns
e)	one	one	FM PARRAIN	2 guns S.P.11
f)	half	one	FM PARRAIN	1 gun FT RESINA

ref. 2/ This half limber will be met at SUICIDE CORNER by a guide to be found by 2nd Lt ROSE who will also provide a trolley for trench tramway at FM PARRAIN to SP 11, if available. Above limbers will move off in the order named from billets at 7.15 p.m. & will proceed via DRANOUTRE and LINDENHOEK CORNER & return by that route under their guides.

3/ Limbers of 150 Bde. M.G. Coy will proceed as above to same places and will not pass LINDENHOEK CORNER before 8.30 p.m. nor SUICIDE CORNER before 8.45 p.m. Limbers marked a, b, & c will take former route, d, e, & f the latter, all returning to transport lines via DRANOUTRE.

4/ 2 Officers of 76 Bde M.G. Coy will be at POLKA FM to take over stores from 2nd Lt ROSE and Lieut WOOD respectively at 3 p.m.

5/ S.O's will obtain a signature for all documents relating to positions, lines of fire etc. before completion of relief.

6/ Completion of relief will be reported to Coy Hqrs by wire.

7/ Teams on arrival at billets will be accomodated in the SCHOOL & will be met by a guide there.

8/ Acknowledge.

SECRET.
Copy No. 3

76TH BRIGADE MACHINE GUN COMPANY.

OPERATION ORDER NO.1.

Map Reference Sheet 28.S.W. 1/20,000.

1.   The 76th Brigade Machine Gun Company will relieve the 150th Brigade Machine Gun Company (13 guns) on the night of the 27/28th April 1916.

2.   The positions to be taken over and order of relief will be as per table attached.

3.   All guides will be furnished by the 150th Brigade Machine Gun Company and will be at Headquarters M.24.d.2.8. at 7 pm. - they will guide teams to their respective positions, and will accompany limbers back to Headquarters.

4.   2nd Lieuts.C.W.R. Ball and H. Briston will report to LA POLKA FARM at 3 pm. on the 27th instant and will take over Trench Stores &c.

5.   Completion of relief will be reported to O.C. 76th Machine Gun Company, Headquarters, 150th Brigade Machine Gun Company.

O.C. J.C. Ziegler Capt
76th Brigade Machine Gun Coy.

26.4.16.

Copy No. 1. Filed.
  "   2. 76th Brigade.
  "   3. 150th Brigade Machine Gun Coy.

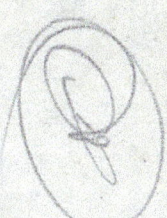

No of teams.	Positions to be taken over.	Map Ref.	Destination of Limber.	No. of Guides supplied.	Officers in charge.
No. 5. No. 6. Nos. 7 & 8.	FRENCHMANS FARM. HAZLEBROOK FARM. SPY FARM.	N.34.b.8.5.) N.34.b.4.9.) N.28.c.2.6.)	Gun positions.	Two.	2nd.Lieut.C.W.R.Ball. 2nd.Lieut.J.W.Dixon.
No 9.) " 10.) " 11.) " 13.) " 14.)	FORT REGINA. S.P.11. LA POLKA FARM.	N.28.b.3.7.) N.25.c.9.4.) N.25.d.3.5.) N.27.d.9.5.	FARM PARRAIN. LA POLKA FARM.	Four.	2nd.Lieut.H.Briston. 2nd.Lieut.E.M.Wood.
No.15.) No.16.)	S.P. No.8.	N.29.d.1.4.)	REGENT STREET DUG-OUTS.	Three.	2nd.Lieut.H.J.Carr.
No. 1. No.12.	S.P. No.9. S.P. No.10.	N.29.d.1.9.) N.29.a.6.3.)			

WAR DIARY of 150 Inf. Brigade M. G. Coy
150 Bde
INTELLIGENCE SUMMARY for JUNE Vol 5

Army Form C. 2118.

Place	Date	Hour	Summary of Events and Information	Remarks and references to Appendices
In trenches in front of KEMMEL VILLAGE	June 1	—	2nd Lt. N.B. Stephens died of wounds and was BURIED at BAILLEUL the morning. Working party continued on No 2 Emp'n in VIA GELLIA.	G.O.C. G.S.O.
	2		Another working party tonight.	G.S.O.
	3		Fine Day. 24th Division had a raid on our Right we helped to Barrage with M. gun fire. Was not to co-operate with them. The raid was not a success.	G.O.C.
	4		Table of relief attached app. No 1. Guns relieved tonight.	G.O.C.
	5		Working party at night.	
	6		Heavy rain all night. Had to return to Armstrong Hutt to Division today. Put in new loophold in emplacement in E2. As enemy were very close I made a	G.S.O.
	7		canvas screen painted like a parapet. This I altered round where the parapet was to be dug away — this hid the gap produced by taking out the old loophole. Very lights were sent very close to it — a parachute light, no doubt directed at it for the northern after through weefrunded to the screen removed a machine gun was turned on the place. Lt. C.Y.C. Stanger arrived today from M. G. Corps Base.	G.S.O.
	8th		Guns Relieved tonight. Table of relief. app. No 2.	M.O.

Army Form C. 2118.

WAR DIARY of 150 Bde M.G. Coy
150 Inf. Brigade
INTELLIGENCE SUMMARY for June

(Erase heading not required.)

Instructions regarding War Diaries and Intelligence Summaries are contained in F.S. Regs., Part II. and the Staff Manual respectively. Title pages will be prepared in manuscript.

Place	Date	Hour	Summary of Events and Information	Remarks and references to Appendices
In Trenches in front of KEMMEL VILLAGE	9th		Working party under Lt G.W. DAWSON started making "Shell + lid" in S.P.8.	G.B.P.
	10th		Quiet day, wet.	G.B.P.
	13th		Same received high 16/17th. German Gas attack on our Right. E.2 got half gassed, gun the wheels.	App 4/BP
	16th		I went to M.G. School to arrange billet for 73 M.G. Coy who were coming to relieve us. Passed information	App. 3/BP
	17th		73 M.G. Coy came this afternoon. Men & officers went upon the School transport in one limber.	G/BP
	18th		I went round trenches with O/C 73 M.G. Coy & got carried in a strafe of H.I.A. & tops of V.I.A.	G.B.P.
			GELLIA 2w casualties.	
	19th		73rd M.G. Coy relieved this Coy in trenches tonight, early quiet relief, no casualties.	Total strength of Coy on relief App 5. 6.7.8
	20th		Marched to Rear billets - thunderstorm, left at 11.30 a.m. arrived 12.30 at M.20.1.8. sheet 28.	
			Relieved 3rd M.G. Squadron in Kemmel Defences this morning with 6 guns.	Appendix 9.
	21st		Found 2 new billets near ST JANS CAPPEL as present billets adjoined by Cavalry. Two	
			farms 26. M.2 6. C 5.4. New quarters bad, most of them bivouacs out. Officer quarters good.	G.B.P.
	22nd		6 Guns on Kemmel Defences relieved by 3rd Motor Machine Gun Battery. Very trying day.	G.B.P.
	23rd		I rode out to 150 I/Bde at LOCRE to attend conference re French Raid which was to be carried out the	G.B.P. App 37
			&. arranged with H Q/C 73rd & Lieut 16 guns forming a barrage in conjunction with the Artillery	
	26th		Fine day. Selected party marched to LOCRE at 4 p.m. to take part in French Raid. Arrived 6.15 p.m.	G.B.P.

WAR DIARY
or
INTELLIGENCE SUMMARY.
(Erase heading not required.)

Army Form C. 2118.

Place	Date	Hour	Summary of Events and Information	Remarks and references to Appendices
KEMMEL TRENCHES	26th		Marked 6 trenches at 9pm. Saw 5 Enemy observation balloon brought down by our aircraft. Heavy rain about 10pm till 12 midnight. Strafe commenced 1.30pm & 2pm went on for 15 minutes Rd Upkerlin. 15 minutes more strafe. 6 guns were taken up by the company. 4 placed near Ft EDWARD 10. & 2 near Ft HALIFAX. During the strafe 6 guns got off 25,000 rds. QBP retaliation was very little. The casualties were little. In everything was so quiet the party returned straight to Billet.	
Billet	27		Arrived back 6.15AM. Packed up and moved to new billet at P.23.c.6.7.sheet 27.	QBP
28.M.26.C.5.4.	28th		Had to go a long way round in short cut was very bad going. Good billet. Filling up with 6th after strafe. 2/Lts CARPENTER & DODD with 25 men marched to LA QBP CLYTTE reported to 2nd field Coy R.E. for work.	QBP
	29		Usual company routine work.	QBP
	30		Route march.	QBP

E B Inman Lt
150th Bde M.G. Coy

Appendix 1.   June 4 - 1916

Team	Destination	Officer
Pte. Ashton " Bennett " Murrin	Polka farm	Lt. Dawson.
Cpl. Windle Pte Tillotson " Harrison R.	VIA GELLIA	Lt. Carpenter.
" Dixon H " " W. " Parvin	S.P. 11	
Sgt. Nichol Pte Kenworthy " Cockfield	S.P. 11	
L/cpl Parker Pte Gilbert " Dickenson	Fort Regina	
L/cpl Dring Pte Teale " Armitage	Haleybrook farm	Lt. Dadd.
L/cpl Rymer Pte Martinson " Lowe	Frenchman's farm	
" Coates " Layland " Barclay	Spy farm	
Cpl. Anderson Pte Patterson " McLeod.	D⁰	
Sgt. Dawson Pte Hutty " Howarth " Jerome	S.P. 8	
" Harrison C. " Daubney " Lambert	D⁰	
L/cpl Butler Pte Broderick " Parry	S.P. 9	
" Williamson " Harrison J. " Harper	S.P. 10	Lt. C.H. Rose.
	Destination	

Appendix 2. Thursday June 8th 1916

Team	Destination	Officer
Sgt. Gardham		
Jefferson	Polka Fm	Lt Rose
Dixon J		
Yowell		
Smith W	Do	Lt Skooner
Baul		relieves Lt Carpenter
Foreman		
Makepeace	Via Gellia	
Wallis		
Sgt. Pope		
Sidgwick	S.P. 11	
Beautiman		
Present Team for S.P.11 to remain. For S.P.11a Martinson, Pinchbeck, Hart. [Dixon H, Corvin crossed out] Via Gellia team stayed up.	S.P. 11a	
Cpl. Jacobs		
Dobinson	Fort Regina	
Bowman		
Cpl. Clarke		
Redshaw	E.2	
Porter		
Parker		
Cpl. Fields		
Hendry	Frenchman's Fm	
Pearce		
Sgt. Barnett		
Swalwell	Spy Farm	
Layland (to remain)		
Moore		
Charlesworth	Do	
Hayton		
Cpl. Acklam		
Metcalfe	S.P. 8	
Kennedy		
Dodds		
Dodgson	Do	
Burke		
Fox H		
Jewitt	S.P. 9	
Powell		
Pearson		
Percy	S.P. 10	Lt Dadd & Lt Hops
Gillyon		relieves Lt Dawson

Appendix 3.   June 13-1916

	Teams	Destination	Officer
Sgt	Glover		
	Lowe	Polka fm	Lt Carpenter
	Jerome		
	Dixon H		
	" W	"	Lt Hays.
	Parvin		
L/Cpl	Butler		
	Hutty	Via Gellier	
	Howarth		
	Ashton		
	Bennett	S.P. 11	
	Murrin		
Sgt	Dawson		
	Tillotson	" 11ᵃ	
	Harrison R		
Team to remain excepting one man who will be relieved by Pte. Cockfield		Fort Regina	
L/Cpl	Dring		
	Teale		
	Armitage	E 2	
	Daubney		
	Williamson		
	Harrison	Frenchman's farm	
	Harper		
Sgt	Nicol		
	Nicholson	Sky farm	
	Holliday		
	Harrison C.		
	Pugh		
	Lambert	"	
Cpl	Perry		
	Kenworthy	S.P. 8	
	Dickenson		
	Gilbert		
	Coates	"	
	Barclay		
	Moore Charlesworth } from Sky Hayton } farm	S.P. 9	
Cpl	Anderson		Lt Moon
	Patterson	S.P. 10	Lt Spooner
	McLeod		

appendix 4

150th Brigade Machine Gun Coy.

Disposition of Guns on 150th Infantry Brigade Front.

Ref. Map Sheet 28
1/20,000, Trench
Map MESSINES 1/10,000.

<u>Front Line Group</u>: H.2. One gun loophole emplacement covers front of SPANBROEKMOLEN.
H.1.A. nil. An emplacement to be built at Lewis Gun Position as soon as materials can be obtained.
VIA GELLIA.- Two loophole emplacements, one gun in the higher one. Fires to right across SPANBROEKMOLEN and covers "NO MAN'S LAND" between our front and Support trenches.
Men live in S.P.11.A.

<u>S.Ps.</u> S.P.8.   2 Guns.)
         " 9   1 "   )
         " 10   1 "   ) 6 guns.
         " 11   1 "   )
         " 11.A.   1 "   )

N.B.- All these (except new one S. of S.P.8) are bad. They are not shell or splinter proof and the loopholes large and no doubt located.
New concrete and steel emplacements should be put in.

1. S.P.8. New one - close girdered roof and sandbagged along hedge S. of S.P.8.

2. Old Colt Emplacement in S.P.8 not used. Gun is mobile in trench system for purposes of local defence. Open platform in S. part of S.P. from which fire can be brought to bear on SPANBROEKMOLEN in case of surprise attack.
Tripod is kept in position here and aiming mark provided.

<u>Dug-out</u>:- New strong steel girdered dug-out has been erected with good brick burster on top.

S.P.9:- Enclosed emplacement. Gun kept mounted.

<u>Dug-out</u>:- New close girdered dug-out has been erected.

S.P.10.- Emplacement as in S.P.9.
<u>Dug-out</u>:- Strong wooden frame and brick and sandbag roof. M.G. Officer's dug-out here.

S.P.11.- Two emplacements one open, one closed. Open one shoots to left and covers S.P.12 and next Brigade front. Covered emplacement shoots to right and fires towards S.P.11

S.P.11.A.- "BEAVER HAT". Fairly strong sandbag emplacement. Dug-outs for 3 teams here all fairly strong, shell slit near An indirect firing covered position on right of C.T. fires on to SPANBROEKMOLEN.
An open emplacement for indirect firing in front of these fires on to WYTSCHAETE and PECKHAM etc.
Either of these positions could be used for Barraging purposes in case of attack.

VIERSTRAAT SWITCH AND "FORT" GROUP:-

1. **LA POLKA FARM:-** 2 guns : functions as follows :-

    (a) Offensive - Position 200 yds S.E. of Farm.

    Tripods kept mounted here, also barrage as per table on rear of SPANBROEKMOLEN is fired from here in case of sudden attack.

    (b) Defence of VIERSTRAAT SWITCH - from left of Brigade Boundary to N.27.b.central. Map showing emplacements herewith.

    (c) Local Defence of KEMMEL approaches. Emplacements in LA POLKA FARM and houses in N.21.c. as per map herewith.

    (d) Anti-aircraft. 1 Gun on necessary occasions mounted immediately S. of LA POLKA FARM, on special mounting.

2. **VROILAND.-** 1 Gun. 3 Defensive positions.

    (a) Two open platforms running saps under wire for Planking Fort.

    (b) Pivot mounting position. (Open) an indirect fire covered position is also here for firing on to SPANBROEKMOLEN

3. **SPY FARM**   2 Guns - functions as follows:-
(Fort Victoria)

    (a) Offensive - fire can be brought to bear indirectly on from positions A. and C. (vide map) on to important places in enemy's front and support lines.

    (b) Local Defence :-

    1. REGENT STREET and Road parallel thereto from emplacements A.B. or D.

    11. Local Defence of FORT VICTORIA from positions B. or C. which are within it.

    Guns mounted normally at A. and B.

FRENCHMAN FARM.- One Gun. Covered emplacement with two loopholes. Pivot mounting. Very strong. Indirect fire from behind buildings.

Accommodation for teams of above:-

1. **LA POLKA FARM.-** 2 teams in Farm. Two strong dug-outs constructed near old Railway Truck in rear of farm. (The cellars are very poor).

2. **SPY FARM.-** 2 Teams in Farm buildings - shell-shelter, strong dug-out with brick burster in Fort. Also 2 shell slits.

3. **VROILANDHOEK FARM.-** 1 Team in Dug-Out in Fort. The farm building not habitable. New dug-out wanted here.

(11) **FRENCHMANS FARM.-** 1 team in building - shell shelter, cellar underneath same.

DISPOSITIONS OF COMMAND.

1. S.P.11 & 11A) 2 Officers. H.Q. LA POLKA FARM.
   LA POLKA.)
   VROILANDHOEK)
   VIA GELLIA.)

2. S.P.8.)   H.P. Two Officers.   S.P.10.
   S.P.9.)
   S.P.10.)   Reference above :-
   E.2.)
   SPY FARM)
   FRENCHMAN)
   FARM.)

DIVISIONAL RESERVE.

2 Guns in Divisional Reserve, stationed at Billet and used for training puposes.

Arrangements in Case of Probable Gas attack.

"Gas Alert" vide 50th Division Scheme herewith.

All Gunners wear TOWER satchel, and affix respirator on gas alarm sounding.

Arrangements in case of Surprise Attack (Raid).

(i) As many guns as possible laid indirectly on to area behind SPANBROEKMOLEN, which is a favourable area for enemy to concentrate men, and from which to launch attack, and is before our main tactical point "HILL 74".

Concurrently with our field guns opening fire, M.G. would form a barrage lasting for 15 minutes, by steady rate of short bursts.

(ii) All guns are distinctly mobile as the country offers favourable opportunities for surprise action.

Shell Slits have been made at all positions except FORT REGINA, all are not finished but are in process of construction.

Lt.

Cmdg., 150th Bde Machine Gun Coy.

Appendix 5.

Operation Order No. 32.
150th Bde. M. Gun Coy.

June 19th 1916.
Copy 4

Map Ref.   Sheet 28 S.W.   1/20,000
Trench Map.   MESSINES.   1/10,000

Relief (1) The 150th Bde. M.G. Coy. will be relieved in trenches by the 73rd " " " on the night of June 19th/20th - 1916.

Positions (2) The order of Relief & Destination of Limbers as per Table attached.

Guides (3) Guides will be supplied by the 150th Bde. M.G. Coy. one for each position. They will parade at 5-45 P.M. and march up to the 73rd M.G. Coy's Billet and report there. These men will remain to help to carry gear down to limbers.

Limbers (4) Limbers will not pass LINDENHOEK CORNER before 9-30 P.M. Each set of the 73rd M.G. Coy's Limbers will follow behind limbers of relieved Teams who will act as guides.

Officers (5) Two Officers of the 73rd Bde. M.G. Coy. will report at Polka Farm and S.P. 10. respectively at 3-30 P.M. on the 19th inst. and take over all Trench Stores for which receipts will be obtained and handed to the O/C 150th Bde. M.Gun Coy. on relief.

Relief Complete (6) Relief Complete will be telephoned to 150th Bde. M.Gun Coy. H.Q. from Polka Farm and S.P. 10. Code word used "HERRING" & code title.

Copies No. 1. Lt. Rose.
         2. 150th Inf. Bde.
         3. Lt. Moon.
         4. File
         5. Lt. Wood.
         6. 73rd Bde. M.G. Coy.
       x 7 War Diary

Lb.
150th Inf. Bde. M. Gun Coy.

Table referred to in Clause (2)　　　　June 19th 1916

Gun Position	Number of Limbers	Destination of Limber	No. of Guns
Polka Farm	ONE	Polka farm	Two
Polka Farm			
S.P. 11.	One	Parrain Farm	Three Guns
S.P. 11A.			
Via Gellia.	Half.		
Fort Regina	Half.	nearly to Ft. Regina	One
Frenchman's Farm.	Half.	Frenchman's Farm	One
Spy Farm.	One	Spy Farm	Two
Spy Farm.			
S.P. 8.	One	Regent St. Dugouts.	Four
S.P. 8.			
S.P. 9.	One		
S.P. 10.			
E.2.	Half.	Regent St Dugouts	One

App. 6

SECRET.

Copy No. 6

150TH INFANTRY BRIGADE OPERATION ORDER NO.52.

Ref. Map Sheets
27 & 28 & Trench
Map.

16th June 1916.

1. The 150th Infantry Brigade will be relieved by the 73rd Infantry Brigade 24th Division, the relief being completed by the night June 20th/21st 1916.

2. Movements will take place as follows -

(a) June 19th :-

   (i) The 5th Yorks.Regt. will be relieved at KEMMEL SHELTERS by the 2nd Leinsters, and will move to billets about HAEGEDOORNE (S.9.b.)

   (ii) The 5th Durham L.I. will move to bivouacs near LOCRE, location of which will be notified later.

(b) Night of June 19th/20th :-

   The 4th East Yorks. will be relieved in Right Sub-sector trenches by the 13th Middlesex Regt. On relief the 4th East Yorks. will move to YORK HUTS.

(c) June 20th:-

   The 5th Durham L.I. will move from bivouacs near LOCRE to billets about ST.JANS CAPPEL.

(d) Night of June 20th/21st :-

   The 4th Yorks.Regt. will be relieved in the Left Sub-sector trenches by the 2nd Leinster Regt.
   On relief the 4th Yorks. Regt. will move to BADAJOZ HUTS.

3. The 150th Brigade Machine Gun Coy. and 150th Light Trench Mortar Battery will be relieved by 73rd Brigade Machine Gun Coy. and 73rd Brigade Light Trench Mortar Battery on the night 19th/20th June under arrangements to be made direct between Os. C. Units.

4. All details of Battalion reliefs will be arranged between C.Os. concerned.

- 2 -

5. Battalions moving East of LOCRE in daylight will do so by Companies at intervals of half a mile.

6. Log Books, Defence Schemes, Orders, Maps, Photographs, and all useful information available will be handed over to Units of the 73rd Infantry Brigade.

All Trench Stores will be handed over on relief and lists will be made out in duplicate, one copy being forwarded to Brigade Headquarters.

7. Bombers, Signallers, and Lewis Gun Detachments of the 4th East Yorks. and 4th Yorks. Regt. will be relieved by the specialists of the 13th Middlesex Regt. and 2nd Leinster Regt. respectively, 12 hours before Battalion reliefs commence.

8. All Battalions will send on in advance on the day of relief one Officer and one N.C.O. per Platoon to take over billets and trench stores in daylight.

9. The completion of all reliefs will be reported to Brigade Headquarters.

Brigade Headquarters will remain at present billet after relief.

ACKNOWLEDGE.

[signature]

Major,
Brigade Major,
150th Infantry Brigade.

Issued at 4.0 p.m.

Copy No.1. Filed.
2. 4th East Yorks.
3. 4th Yorks.
4. 5th Yorks.
5. 5th Durham L.I.
6. Bde. Machine Gun Coy.
7. 150th Light Trench Mortar Batty.
8. 2nd Field Coy. R.E.
9. 72nd Infantry Brigade.
10. 73rd Infantry Brigade.
11. 149th Infantry Brigade.
12. O.C., 50th Div. Train A.S.C.
13. 50th Division.
14. War Diary.
15. O.C., 50th Div. Trench Mortars.

appendix 4 SECRET.

Copy No.2.

150th (Y & D)
No. BM 208
Date 15.6.16
INFANTRY BRIGADE

50th DIVISION OPERATION ORDER NO.36.

Ref.Map 1/40000 Sheets 27 & 28.   14th June 1916.

1. 150th Infantry Brigade, 50th Division, will be relieved by the 73rd Infantry Brigade, 24th Division, the relief being completed by the night June 20th/21st.

2. Movements will take place as follows:-

    (a) June 16th - 1 Battalion 150th Infantry Brigade, from WAKEFIELD HUTS to YORK HUTS, LOCRE.

    2 Battalions, 73rd Infantry Brigade to LOCRE. WAKEFIELD HUTS & BADAJOS HUTS.

    (b) June 19th/20th - 1 Battalion 73rd Infantry Brigade from LOCRE will relieve 1 Battalion 150th Infantry Brigade in Right Sector trenches.

    Battalion 150th Infantry Brigade in Right Sector Trenches will move to LOCRE.

    1 Battalion, 73rd Infantry Brigade, from LOCRE will relieve 1 Battalion 150th Infantry Brigade in KEMMEL SHELTERS. This Battalion on relief will move to billets about HAEGEDOORNE (S.9.b.)

    1 Battalion, 73rd Infantry Brigade moves from HAEGEDOORNE to LOCRE.

    (c) June 20th/21st - 1 Battalion, 73rd Infantry Brigade from KEMMEL SHELTERS relieves 1 Battalion 150th Infantry Brigade in Left Sector Trenches.

    Battalion 150th Infantry Brigade in Left Sector Trenches moves to LOCRE (BADAJOS HUTS).

    1 Battalion, 73rd Infantry Brigade, moves from ST.JANS CAPPEL to LOCRE.

    1 Battalion, 150th Infantry Brigade, moves from LOCRE to billets about ST.JANS CAPPEL.

    1 Battalion 73rd Infantry Brigade, from LOCRE moves to KEMMEL SHELTERS.

3. Details of the above reliefs will be arranged direct between Brigade Commanders concerned.

4. The G.O.C., 150th Infantry Brigade will remain in command of the front until relief is completed on night 20th/21st June.

5. That portion of the 50th Divisional Artillery, including the Medium Trench Mortars, covering the front of the 150th Infantry Brigade, will remain in their present position and come under the orders of the 24th Division when Infantry relief is complete on night 20th/21st June.

6. 2nd Field Company R.E. will remain in Right Section as a temporary measure.

- 2 -

Company, 7th Durham L.I. Pioneers, from Right Section will move to SCHERPENBERG on 20th June.

7. The Brigadier-General, Commanding 150th Infantry Brigade will remain in Command of the KEMMEL DEFENCES, with Headquarters at LOCRE, under the orders of G.O.C., 50th Division.

8. Completion of each stage of the relief to be reported to 50th Division Headquarters.

            (signed) D.FORSTER,
                     Lt.Col.,
                 General Staff,
                 50th Division.

Issued at 6.0 p.m.

- 2 -

O.C.,
Brigade Machine Gun Coy.

        Forwarded for information.

        Brigade Operation Order will follow later.

        Please acknowledge receipt.

                            Major,
                            Brigade Major,
                            150th Infantry Brigade.

Headquarters,
150th Infantry Brigade.
15th June 1916.

appendisc 8.

SECRET.

Copy No. 6

Ref. Map Sheets 27
& 28 & Trench Map.

AMENDMENT TO OPERATION ORDER NO.32.

17th June 1916.

Para 2.   5th Yorks. will move to Camp, N.13.d.7.3. (1st Entrenching Battalion and vicinity), Headquarters being at N.19.a.6.9., on 19th instant.

8th Durham L.I. will move into camp at N.1.a.3.1.

Machine Gun Coy. and 180th Trench Mortar Batteries will move into billets at N.20.a.1.8. [M.20.a.1.8] and M.14.b.2.2. respectively on relief.

ACKNOWLEDGE.

Major,
Brigade Major,
180th Infantry Brigade.

Appendix 9

Operation Orders, No. 33.
150th Bde. M. Gun Coy
(Copy No. 6.)

June 19th 1916.

Relief. Six guns of the 150th Bde. M. Gun Coy. will relieve No. 3. Squadron in KEMMEL DEFENCES on the night of 19/20 June, 1916.

Order of Relief. Order of Relief with Times, Guides, etc., will be as per Table attached hereto.

Reveille. Reveille on June 20th at 5.30 a.m.
Breakfast " " " 6 a.m.
Limbers to be packed, ready to move off, by men who came in after relief from trenches.

Parades. The men for Nos. 8 and 8B gun positions will parade at 7.30 P.M. on the night of June 19th and march via KEMMEL BARRIER and AU BOUEF BIGARRE Estt. to their position.
Limber will parade at same time and proceed via DRANOUTRE.
Sgt. Gardham will go with this Limber to act as guide.
Men for other gun positions will parade at 7 A.M. prompt. on June 20th 1916.

Relief Complete. Relief complete will be telephoned by Lt. Hoys. to Company Head Quarters.

Rations. Rations will be dumped at KEMMEL BARRIER each evening at 7. a.m.

Copy No. 1 Lt Dawson
2 Lt Hoys.
3 150th Bde. M.G. Coy.
4 150th Inf. Bde.
5 No. 3. Cav. M. G. Squadron
✓ 6 War Diary

Lt.
150th. B. M. G. Coy.

Table referred to in O. Order. No 3.   June 19/20 – 1916.

Position	No. of Guns	Off. in charge	Team	Guide at	Time of Guide	No. of Limbers	Destination of Limbers
No. 8.	one	Lt. Hays.	Sgt. Gardham, Martinson, Jewitt, Gillyon / Cpl. Fields, Pierson, Fox H., Makepeace	Dranoutre Road.	8.30 P.M night of June 19/20th	one	Dranoutre Road.
No. 8B.	one						
Mobile Guns.	one	Lt. Dawson.	Sgt. Pope, Hendry, Beauchman, Waltho / Peace, Powell, Hart.	Y.M.C.A. Hut. near Kemmel Shelters.	4.30 A.M. morning of June 20th	one	Y.M.C.A Hut.
	one						
16 A.	one		Cpl. Clarke, Yowell, Smith W., McDoyall / Cpl. Acklam, Boyes, Metcalf, Greenwood	Kemmel Barrier	4.30 A.M. morning of June 20th	one	KEMMEL BARRIER.
15.	one						

Operation Order No. 34

Appendix 10.   June 25/16

General Idea

1. The 150th Bde. M.G. Coy. in conjunction with 43rd M.G. Coy. Trench Mortars & Units of 150th Inf. Bde. will carry out a minor operation on the night of June 26/27 - 1916.

2. Six Vickers Guns & Teams will proceed to selected positions and assist in the Barrage Fire which will be opened after the Trench Raiding Parties have got into the Enemy Trenches.

Special Idea

1. <u>Teams</u> Six strong Teams as detailed on attached Table will parade at 4 P.M. ready to move off.

   <u>Limbers</u> Three full limbers will be packed, each containing the following:- Two Vickers Guns "Tripods with traversing dial, Spare part Wallets & Boxes. Twenty filled Belt Boxes per gun, Night firing attachment one per gun. Siege lamps one per gun if possible. Clinometers one per gun if possible, otherwise spirit-levels. Cleaning Rods. Spare Barrels, Belt Box Carrier, Condenser, etc. The men's packs, Oil Flannelette.

   Above three limbers & a Transport Corporal will parade at 4 P.M. on the 26th inst.

   One limber will proceed two hours before the above named three & will contain 24 hours Rations for Teams & Officers, etc. and Cooking utensils, Fuel.

   This limber will proceed by best Route to M.G. School Field near KEMMEL SHELTERS & the Cook will prepare Tea for teams on arrival.

<u>Rations</u> 24 Hours Rations will be taken for all men on the Expedition. Drivers are responsible that feeds for 24 hours are taken for their animals. Grooms will see that feeds are taken for Officers' Chargers. 24 Hours fuel Ration to be taken.

Guides Two guides of the 73rd M.G. Coy. will be met at Polka Farm & guide four guns to positions near V.C. Road and Alston House.

A third guide will take remaining two guns to positions in front of Hollebeke.

Limbers will move at Dusk, as follows:-

Two to La Polka.   One to Hollebeke Farm.

The two limbers will remain at La Polka farm while the one for Hollebeke will take cover behind Spy farm & remain there while the Strafe is on.

After the Strafe the guns will be packed on the limbers and the latter will return to School field and unlimber.

Teams will march back to School field independently and may either Bivouac for the few hours rest or go into the Barn to sleep.

Party will parade for Return on the morning of the 24th inst. at 10 A.M.

Details Servants of Officers taking part will also parade. L/Cpl. Brookes will proceed with advance limber - Pte H Johnson will also parade mounted, and will look after Officers' chargers.

Table referred to

TEAMS

No 1 Team	No 2	No 3	No 4
Sergt Gardham	Corpl Anderson	Lgt W. Barnett	Lgt E Glover
Pte Ashton G	Pte Y Brown	Pte R Boyes	Pte Bowman
" Armitage	" Cockfield	" Baul	" Dodds
" Broderick J	" Gilbert	" Cromack	" Foreman
" Harrison C	" Dixon W	" Holliday	" Fox J
" Hutty	" McLeod	" Porter	" Lowe J
" Tillotson	" Patterson	" Parker J.H.	" Pearce J

No 5 Team	No 6 Team	Officers for Teams
Lgt Pope	Sergt C Nicol	
Sect 4 { Beautiman / Peirson	Pte Burke	1 & 2 Teams 2/Lt Moon
3 { Swalwell W / Williamson J R	" Barclay	
	" Kenworthy	3 & 4 " 2/Lt Rose
	" Hayton	
2 { Layland / Thompson G	" Greenwood	5 & 6 " Lt Purvis
	" Makepeace	

Vol 6

War Diary

150th Brigade Machine Gun Coy

July 1916

Volume 6.

WAR DIARY of 1/150 BRIGADE MACHINE GUN COMPANY.

INTELLIGENCE SUMMARY for JULY 1916.

Army Form C. 2118.

Place	Date	Hour	Summary of Events and Information	Remarks and references to Appendices
Sheet 57.	July 1st	—	Men marched to L.O.E R.E for Baths. Received O.O. No 35 150th Bde Brigade	Appendix 1.
Billen	2nd	—	Officers went to 149 Bde M.G. Coy to reconnoitre trenches. Recalled & ordered to take over	
R.23.6.7.	3rd	—	Church Parade. I rode over to see O/C 149 Bde M.G. Coy to compleat arrangements for relief not	
			now take place. 4th Coy moved from billet at 10.30 A.M. to 149 Bde M.G. Coy Camp	
Sheet 22		—	at M.R.C. 7. R.– Relieved 11 guns of 149 Bde M.G. Coy & sent up 3 extra new	Appendix 2. 3.
M.R.6.c.4.8	6th	—	Capt Sharp returned from 9 days leave. 20/K Lin reinel trenches.	
Sheet	7th	—	The Coy took over new pieces of ground & extended our front to the right.	Appendix 4.
S. 3–4.5.	8th	—	Half 149 Bde M.G. Coy attached us reserve as all our guns were in the line. 5th York Regt made a very successful	
"	9th	—	raid the night. Appendices. Inter Company relief Tonight	Appendix 5. 6. 7.
"	10.	—	Quiet day. A lot of shelling at night. 73rd Bde made a raid. No prisoners	
"	11	—	17th Brigade M.G. Coy relieve S.P. 10 tonight. Our Lieu. goes to Poles turn	App. 8.
"	13.	—	Inter Company relief. 14th Minot of trenches wants to extent of right.	Appendix 9.
"	15.	—	Slight alteration in grouping of guns. Appendix.	App. 10.
"	17	—	Heavy bombardment tonight. Brutts inched raid. Inter Coy relief.	Appendix 11.
"	18.	—	Another bombardment & heavy M.G. barrage fire tonight 10 guns firing for an	
"	19	—	Quiet day. Brocks very busy at night. 50th Divin quite artillery was cutting	

Army Form C. 2118.

WAR DIARY of 159 Machine Gun Coy.
or
INTELLIGENCE SUMMARY for JULY.
(Erase heading not required.)

Instructions regarding War Diaries and Intelligence Summaries are contained in F.S. Regs., Part II. and the Staff Manual respectively. Title pages will be prepared in manuscript.

Place	Date	Hour	Summary of Events and Information	Remarks and references to Appendices
Intrenches	July 21st	—	Men out of trenches went on minie-lature range in morning. No casualties in trenches from Blunt day.	appendix 1,2
	22nd	—	Guns relieved in Right Sector by 151 M G Coy	3.
	24th	—	One man killed by shrapnel, one sgt wounded by M.G. Fire. A great deal of trench mortaring during the	
	25th	—	one man wounded by forward bullet. Changed a Maxim-Vickers for 2 Vickers Relief.	14.
	26th	—	One man killed by M G Fire in C.T. one man wounded by M.G fire in knee	
	27th	—	Enemy very quiet indeed, practically no shelling, trench mortars or rifle fire.	
	28th	—	Lt. Luttring with two guns & teams sent to KEMMEL SHELTERS late in division reserve	15.
	29th	—	Inter Coy relief tonight. No casualties	
	30th	—	Church Parade. Enemy still very quiet & inoffensive. Changed room of teams who will not be relieved on 2/9th.	
	31st	—	2 C.M held on Pte Makepeace. No casualties, weather very hot. Enemy quiet.	appendix 16

July 31st 1916.

E R Purvis Lt.
15th Bde M.G Coy

Appendix 1.

SECRET.

Copy No. 7

150th INFANTRY BRIGADE OPERATION ORDER NO.33.

Ref. Map Sheet 28.   1st July 1916.
and Trench Map.

1. The 150th Infantry Brigade will relieve the 149th Infantry Brigade between the nights 2nd/3rd and 4th/5th July 1916.

2. Relief will be carried out as follows :-

    Night of 2nd/3rd July.

    The 150th Brigade Trench Mortar Battery will relieve the 149th Bde. Trench Mortar Battery under arrangements to be made direct between C.Os.

3. Night of 3rd/4th July.

    (a) The 5th Yorks. will relieve the 7th N.F. in Right Sub-sector trenches.

    (b) The 5th Durham L.I. will relieve the 4th N.F. in Left Sub-sector trenches.

    (c) The 4th East Yorks. will relieve the 5th N.F. in Brigade Reserve at 'R.O.Farm' (N.15.a.1.0)

    (d) The 4th Yorks. will relieve the 6th N.F. in Divisional Reserve at M.17.d.central.

4. Night of 4th/5th July.

    The 150th Bde. Machine Gun Coy. will relieve the 149th Bde. Machine Gun Coy. under arrangements to be made direct between C.Os.

5. All details of Battalion reliefs will be arranged between C.Os. concerned.

6. Log Books, Defence Schemes, Orders, Maps, and Photographs, and all useful information available will be handed over by Units of the 149th Infantry Brigade.

    All Trench Stores will be taken over on relief and lists will be made out in duplicate, one copy being forwarded to Brigade Headquarters.

7. Bombers, Signallers, and Lewis Gun detachments of the 5th Yorks. and 5th Durham L.I. will relieve specialists of 7th N.F. and 4th N.F. respectively at 2 p.m. on 3rd instant.

- 2 -

8. All Battalions will send on in advance on the day of relief one Officer and one N.C.O. per Platoon to take over billets and trench stores in daylight.

9. The Completion of all reliefs will be reported to Brigade Headquarters.

10. On completion of relief G.O.C., 150th Infantry Brigade will take over command of the line.
Brigade Headquarters will be at BRULOOZE (M.24.b.5.9) after 9 p.m. on 3rd instant.

Acknowledge.

Major,
Brigade Major,
150th Infantry Brigade.

Issued at 9 p.m.

Copy No. 1. Filed.
2. War Diary.
3. 4th East Yorks.
4. 4th Yorks.Regt.
5. 5th Yorks.Regt.
6. 5th Durham L.I.
7. 150th Bde.Machine Gun Coy.
8. 150th Trench Mortar Batty.
9. 149th Inf.Bde.
10. 73rd Inf. Bde.
11. 250th Bde. R.F.A.
12. 50th Division.
13. 50th Div. Trench Mortars.
14. 50th Div.Train A.S.C.
15. 1st Field Coy. R.E.

Appendix 2

Copy No 2

149th INFANTRY BRIGADE, MACHINE GUN Coy.
No ......
Date 3/7/16

Secret

Map Ref
Sheet 28 S.W.2
1/10000.

Operation Orders No 33

1. The 149th Bde. M.G. Coy. will be relieved by the 150th Bde M.G. Coy. in the sector of trenches J.3 N to L.15 inclusive on the night of 4/5th July 1916.

2. Guides.
(1) A Guide for J.4, SP.12 and Fort Royal will be at bottom of Rossignol C.T. (N.22.A.5.8) at 10.30 p.m.
(2) A Guide for SP.13 Rear, K.1A, L.5, L.7 Left, L.15, and Farm Brykerie will be at M.G. Farm (N.11.C.1.8) at 10.30 p.m.

Each guide will be in possession of a chit stating the position for which he is a guide.

3. All S.A.A, Defence Schemes, Standing orders, Trench Stops

Range cards, Vermoral Sprayer Solution, Very Lights, Bombs, Pistol Mountings, Mineral Jelly and Gas Blankets will be handed over by N.C.Os at each position and Section Officers will ensure that each N.C.O prepares a proper list of stores at each position in duplicate and retains one copy with relieving N.C.Os receipt endorsed.

4, A complete list on the official form of all Trench stores handed over in the Brigade Area will be prepared and signed by Lt Cowen and the officers relieving at M.G Farm

5, 4 Limbers (for teams 9 to 16) will be at M.G Farm and 2 limbers (for teams 5.6.7 and 8) at bottom of Rossignol C.T. at 11.30 p.m and on loading up limbers at Rossignol will proceed under Lt Mawson to new billet at Sheet 27 K19a1.3 and limbers at M.G Farm under Lt Cowen to the same place.

6. Section officers will be responsible that all emplacements and dug-outs are handed over in a clean condition.

7. Completion of relief to be reported to Coy H.Q. by wire.

8. Acknowledge.

Copies N° 1 147th Inf. Bde
2 150th Bde M.G.Coy ✓
3 ⎫
4 ⎬ Section
5 ⎭ Officers
6
7 War diary
8 File

J.R. Wittin
Capt
Comdg

148th
INFANTRY BRIGADE,
MACHINE GUN Coy.

Operation Orders No 35.   SECRET.
              Appendix 3.   Copy 5

Map Ref.
Sheet 28 S.W. (2) 1/10,000

Relief.   The 150th Bde M.G. Coy. will relieve 149th Bde M.G. Coy. in Billets & Trench Sector J 3 to L 5 inclusive, on the night of 4/5th July 1916.

Move.   No. I Section with four guns, one S.A.A. limber and a limber with Rations, discs, etc., for the whole Company will move off from this Billet, Sheet 27. R.23. c.6½. 4. at 9-30 A.M. and march to the 149th Bde. M Gun Coy. billet and relieve four Reserve Guns there. A Cook will proceed with this Section.

The Cook will prepare Dinner for the whole Company on arrival.

Nos. II, III and IV Sections will clean up the Billet and move off at 10-30 A.M. leaving a party of four men to act as loading party for Surplus Stores.

Rations   The A.S.C. Wagon will move with this Column to new Billet & dump the Rations there.

Tents, etc.   All Tents, Offrs' Valises, Mess Stores, etc. will be sent on an empty S.A.A. limber. Anything which cannot be taken will be dumped by Q.M. Stores & collected on the second journey.

Teams.   Teams will be supplied with Chits shewing which position they are to go to. Guides will also have similar Chits. Teams will meet their guides at 8-30 P.M. & will then go up to their positions where they will leave their Kits & return to

O.O. No. 35 Continued

return to Dumps where they will wait for limbers.

Order of Relief. Order of Relief. Guides, Limbers, Position of Officers, etc, as per attached Table.

Relief Complete. Relief Complete will be reported to Company Head Quarters by wire.

Acknowledge.

G. B. Purvis. Lt.
150th Bde M.Gun Coy.

Copies.
1. 150th Inf Bde.
2. 149th Bde M.G. Coy.
3. Sect. Offr.
4. C.S.M.
5. War Diary
6. File
7. Sect. Offr
8.

Scheme Referred to in O.O. 35   4/4/16.

Teams	Position	Maxim or Vickers	Guides at - No.	Guides at - Place	Guides at - Time	Limbers at - No.	Limbers at - Place	Limbers at - Time	Officer in Charge	Remarks
1 Cpl Acklam Kennedy Baird Moore Roper	J.H.	V.	1	Bottom Rossignol C.T.	Pm 8-30	½	Bottom Rossignol C.T.	Pm 10-15		
2 Cpl Verardon McDougall Rogers	Fort Royal	M.	1	N.22.a.5.8.	8-30	½	N.22.a.5.8.	10-15	Lt Rose	
3 Cpt Kersley Redshaw Parker Williamson	S.P. 13 Rear	V.	1			½				
4 Harmon Harber	K.I.A.	V.	1			½				
5 Halliday Cronaldi Dixon	L. 5.	V.	1	M.G. Farm		½	M.G. FARM	Pm 10-15		
6 Cpl Anderson Pattyson McLeod	L.Y. Left	V.	1	N.11.C.1.8.	8-30	½	N.11.C.1.8		Lt Spooner	
7 Sept Kimmeri Colefield Laybourd	L.1.S.	V.	1			½				
8 Corp Arthur Kinworthy Dickinson	Farm BRYKERIE	M.	1			½/1				
9 Sgt Nicol Nicholson Guth	M.G. Farm	V.	No Guide			1				
10 Gilbert Coates Lansberry Beaumont T.	Do	M.				1½	M.G. FARM N.11.C.1.8.	Pm 10-15	Lt Dawson	
11 Sept Parker Dixon W Parram	Do	M.				1				

Amendment to O/Order No 35 of 4/4/16

Teams	Position	Maxim or Vickers	Guides at			Limbers at			Officer in Charge	Remarks
			No.	Place	Time	No.	Place	Time		
L.Y. Left will not go to L.7. Left but as per Column 2.	No 11 Emplacement Subsidiary Line	V.	1	M.G. FARM.	P.M. 8.30	½	On main road opposite M.G. Farm	P.M. 10.30	⎫	
Pte. Ashton. G.G. Hart Pinchbeck	No 12 Emplacement Subsidiary Line	M.	1	Do	Do	½	Do	Do	⎬ Lt Moon	Men live at M.G. Farm. All year except spare parts to be kept at Emplacement.
Thompson G. Burke Nutt. C.	M.G. Farm	M.	No Guide	—	—	½	M.G. Farm	Do	⎭	
Armitage Pennington W M°Kenzie Wilson	Fort Halifax	V.	Lt Moon	—	—	½	Bottom of Rossignol C.T.	Do	Lt Rose.	

Appendix 4.   8/7/16.

Op. Order No. 26.   SECRET.
                                            Copy No. 9

1. The following alterations in dispositions will be made today the 8th July 1916, as far as possible in daylight, remainder after dusk.

(a) Lt. Dawson will take over from Lt. Moon & will be in charge of positions BRICKSTACK, No. 11, and No. 12. Lt. Dawson's H.Qrs. will continue to be at M.G. FARM.

(b) 2/Lt. Moon will move four guns & teams as follows:—
    1 gun each to S.P.11 and S.P.11a.
    1 "   to VIA GELLIA, No. 1 position.
    1 "   to S.P.10. A Handcart to be borrowed from T.M.B. to move guns.
    2/Lt. Moon will be in charge of S.P.11, S.P.11a, and VIA GELLIA No. 1.   H.Qrs. at LA POLKA FARM.

(c) 2/Lt. Rose will arrange to send guns from FORT ROYAL to H.3. immediately. This gun will be under his command.
    2/Lt. Rose will move gun & teams from FORT HALIFAX to FORT ROYAL by night, where it will remain.

(d) 2/Lt. Carpenter will report to 2/Lt. Rose to assist in control of his group, by 4 P.M.

(e) 2/Lt. Dodd with one limber, 2 guns & teams will be at LA POLKA FARM as soon as possible and will be in Mobile Reserve to the extended Brigade front. The limber, teams & driver will remain there until further orders.

2. Arrangements for taking over from 1/3rd Bde. M. Gun Coy. will be made direct between Group Commanders concerned. All Stores, etc. must be taken over correctly.

3. Acknowledge in writing for orderly.

4. Report Relief Complete by wire.

Copy No. 1 O/C 2nd Bde.
         2 O/C 1/3rd M.G. Coy.
         3 Orderly Off.
         4
         5
         6
         7
         8 Transport Off.
         9 War Diary
        10 File
        11
        12

                                G. B. Barrett Lt.
                                1/5 Bde M.G. Coy

War Diary
appendix 5

150th (Y & D)
No. B.M.652
Date 9.7.16
INFANTRY BRIGADE

SECRET.
50th Division.
G.X.2116.

150th Infantry Brigade.

For information.

The G.O.C. 149th Infantry Brigade will hold in readiness half the 149th Brigade Machine Gun Company (i.e. 8 guns with personnel etc.), and one Section (i.e. four Stokes Mortars with personnel etc.) of 149th Light Trench Mortar Battery to proceed to KEMMEL SHELTERS early on Sunday morning 9th July, for duty as local reserve to 150th Infantry Brigade.

The Machine Guns and Mortars of 149th Brigade at KEMMEL SHELTERS will continue their training at that place, and will not be moved forward except in case of emergency.

Copy of this letter is sent direct to 149th Brigade Machine Gun Company and 149th Trench Mortar Battery for information, to save time; all orders for move of these Units will be issued by G.O.C. 149th Brigade.

(sd) H.W.B.THORP, Major,
General Staff,
8th July, 1916.   50th Division.

-2-

O.C.

To 150th Infantry Brigade.

Moves mentioned in 50th Division letter G.X.2116 dated eight will take place on Sunday ninth AAA Hours and details to be arranged direct between Brigades AAA Letter 2116 sent to you by six p.m. D.R. AAA Addressed 149th and 150th Bdes AAA acknowledge

8.7.16.   From: 50th Division.

-3-

O.C.
    Bde. Machine Gun Coy.

For information and action.

Major,
Brigade Major,
150th Infantry Brigade.

Headquarters,
150th Infantry Brigade.
9th July, 1916.

Appendix 6.

Ref Map
Sheet 28
1/40.000.

Operation Order No. 31

Secret

1. Sections A. B. G and H under 2 Lts Taylor and Horsley will parade with limbers packed ready to move off at 9 am on the 9th July 1916 and will proceed to KEMMEL SHELTERS (N 20 D 3.4) via WESTOUTRE and LOCRE for duty as local reserve to 150th Infy Bde.

2. On arrival at KEMMEL SHELTERS sections will come under the orders of G.O.C. 150th Infy Brigade to whom Lt Taylor will report arrival in person.

3. Subject to any orders of the G.O.C 150th Infy Brigade and to the necessary reconnoitring of the positions in the area to be occupied, training of the sections will be continued at KEMMEL SHELTERS as the guns will not be moved into position except in case of emergency.

4. Lt Armstrong (Range-finder) with Barr & Stroud Instrument

and Pte Richardson (cook) with necessary dixies will accompany Sections.

5. Arrival at New billet to be reported by wire to 149th Infy Brigade and to Company H.Q.

Acknowledge.

Copies No 1. 149th Infy Brigade
2. 150th Infy Brigade (As Information)
3. Section Officers
4. War diary
5. File.

149th INFANTRY BRIGADE, MACHINE GUN Coy.

July 8th 1916

160th Bde. M.G. Coy.
Local Relief for night of July 9/10 1916.   O.O. 37.

TEAMS.	POSITION.	OFFR I/CHARGE.	REMARKS.
Corp. Guild Laycock Percy.	J.4.		Appendix. 7.
Present Team remains	FORT ROYAL.		
Sergt. Pope Cox H. Cox J.	S.P.13. Rear.	Lt. Young. relieves Lt. Rose. 2/Lt. Carpenter. lives at S.P.12.	
Pierson Ramm Jewitt	K.1.A.		
Sgt. Butler Brodrick Yeal.	H.3.		
Beauteman Pearce Makepeace	L.5.		
Corp. Jacobs. Bowman Dodgson.	L.1.S.	Lt. Dawson will relieve Lt. Spooner. July 10th 1916 morning after Strafe.	
Foreman Wallis Powell.	F.M. BRYKERIE		
Team remains.	No. 11. Emp. Subsidiary Line	Lt. Spooner	Vide. Lt. Dawson's relief.
Team remains.	No. 12. Emp. Subsidiary Line		
Team remains.	VIA BELLIA.		
Hutty Howarth Gibson Metcalf.	S.P.10	Lt. Moon.	
Corp. Windle Harrison R. Jerome.	S.P.11A		
Corp. Clark Swalwell Barclay	S.P.11		G.B. Purvis Lt. 160 Bde M.G. Coy
Team remains.	POLKA. FM.	Lt. Dadd.	
Team remains Charlesworth relieves Corp. Windle	POLKA. FM.		Corp. Windle to take charge of S.P.11A

Appendix 8

Op Order No 38.

Copy No 5

1. __Relief__. The M.Guns in S.P.10 will be relieved on night of July 12/13 - 1916 by the 14" M.G. Coy.

   The 14" M.G. Coy will take over all Sector to the South of WYTSCHAETE - KEMMEL ROAD.

   The M.Guns from S.P.10 will go to POLKA FARM on relief & remain there in Brigade Reserve under orders of 2/Lt R.C. MOON.

2. __Guides__. A guide will be at LINDENHOEK Cross Roads at 9.30 pm to guide Team up to S.P.10.

3. __Carrying Party__. A carrying party of 1 N.C.O and six men will be supplied from Camp & report at Emplacement S.P.10 at 9 P.M. July 12th.

4. __Relief Complete__ will be telephoned to Coy H.Q. by 2/Lt R.C. MOON.

July 12th/916.

G. B. Purvis Lt
for O/C 150 Bde M.G. Coy.

Copy No. 1. 14th Bde M.G. Coy
     2. 150th Inf Bde
     3. War Diary
     4. File
     5. "
     6. Lt R.C. Moon

150th Bde M.G. Coy.
LOCAL Relief for night of July 13/14 O.O. 39.

TEAMS	OFFR. in charge POSITION.	REMARKS.
Cpl. Perry, Kenworthy, Dickenson	J.4.	Appendix 9.
Armitage, Tillotson, Makepeace	Ft. Royal	Team from S.P. 13 Rear
Sgt. Barnett, Holliday, Cromack, Dixon. 9.	S.P. 13 Rear	Lt. Turing 2/Lt. Carpenter
Dodds, Dobinson, Robson	K.I.A.	
L/Cpl. Parker, Dixon W., Lambert	H 3	
Thompson, Nutt, Jefferson	L. 5.	2/Lt. Dadd relieves Lt. Dawson
Corp. Jacobs, Bowman, Dodgson	L.I.S.	Team Remains.
Corpl. Acklam, Kennedy, Baul	FME. BRYKERIE	
Redshaw, Porter, McDougal	No. 11 Emp.l Subsidiary line.	Lt. Spooner.
Foreman, Wallis, Powell	FME. BRYKERIE	Team Remains
Cpl. Windle, Harrison, Jerome	VIA GELLIA	from S.P. 11ᴬ
L/Cpl. Rymer, Cockfield, Layland	S.P. 11	2/Lt. C.H. Rose
Williamson, Harrison, Harker	S.P. 11ᴬ	
Sgt. Nicol, Nicholson, Pugh	POLKA FM.	
Moore, Boyes, Hayton	"	2/Lt. Moon
Huttly, Howarth, Metcalf	"	Team Remains

Copy No. 1

Appendix 10.

SECRET.

The following alterations in dispositions will be made on the night of the 15/16 July.

1. A gun from the BRYKERIE will be sent up each night at 9 P.M. and will be accommodated in L.6.S. and will be available for action in that trench if necessary and will specially protect the open left flank of it in case of a raid.
   This gun will be under the tactical command of the Officer in charge at L.1.S., and will come back to the BRYKERIE by day.

2. One gun at LA POLKA will always be detailed to proceed to YOUNG St. position at any time in case of emergency and to occupy the right hand open emplacement there.
   A shellproof Dugout to be built under the orders of 2/Lt. C.H. Rose, immediately; and when it is completed this gun will be stationed at YOUNG St.

Smut Sharp. Capt
O/c 150th Bde. M.Gun Coy.

Copy No. 1 File.
        2 150th Bde. H.Q.
        3 2/Lt. Moon
        4   "   Rose.
        5   "   Spooner.
        6   "   Dadd.

Appendix 11

150th Bde. M.G. Coy. O.O.r No. 40.
Local Relief for night of July 17/18 - 1916.

TEAMS.	POSITIONS.	OFF.R i/c.	REMARKS.
Pte. Moore, Boyes, Houghton	J. 4.		
Armitage, Tillotson, Makepeace } Team remains	Ft. Royal.	Lt. Dawson relieves Lt. Turing	at S.P. 13 rear.
Sgt. Gardham, Ashton, Bennett, Gillyon	S.P. 13. Rear.		
Cpl. Clarke, Hart (Pugh crossed out), Barclay. — is Dawson's Servant pro tem	K.I.A.	2/Lt. Rose relieves 2/Lt. Carpenter	at S.P. 12.
Martinson, Daubney, Harrison. C.	H. 4.		
Nicholson to Hospital, Gilbert, Coates, Brown T.	L. 5.	2/Lt. Moon relieves 2/Lt Dadd	at L.I.S.
Corp. Anderson, McLeod, Patterson, Linchbeck	L. I. S.		
Sgt. Pope, Rayne, Langston	BRYKERIE. FM.		
Hewitt, Yot. J. } from L.I.S., Charlesworth.	No. 11. EMPLACEM.T. Subsidiary Line.	2/Lt. Dadd relieves 2/Lt. Spooner	Lt. Spooner goes down to Coy. H.Q.
Redshaw, Porter, McDougall } from No. 11. Emp	BRYCKERIE. FM. goes to L.6. at Night.		
L/Cpl Rymer, Cockfield, Layland } from S.P. 11.	VIA. GELLIA.		
Williamson, Harrison, Harper } from S.P.11.A	S.P. 11.	Lt. Turing relieves 2/Lt. C.H. Rose	at Polka
Corp. Perry, Kenworthy, Dickenson } from J.4.	S.P. 11.A.		
L/Cpl Parker, Dyson. W., Lambert } from H.4.	POLKA FARM		
Thompson, Nutt, Jefferson } from L.5.	"	2/Lt. Carpenter relieves 2/Lt. R.C. Moon	at Polka.
L/Cpl Butler, Broderick, Teale	"		

Appendix 12

148th Bde. M.G. Coy. 2nd Relief

Local Relief on night of July 29th 1916

TEAMS.		POSITIONS.	REMARK
Cpl. ~~Fielder~~ McLeod, Patterson	Fields from L.I.S.	J.4	
Martinson, D'Aubrey, Harrison G.	from H.4	H. Royal.	L. Dawson
Cpl. ~~Reed~~ Glover, Charlesworth (from No. 11), Raine, Langston	from Brykerie	S.P. 12 Rear.	
Corpl. ~~_____~~ L/Cpl Parkers., Bird, Kennedy.		K.I.A.	2/Cockroll
~~Ashley~~ Armitage, Bennett, Gibson	from S.P. 12	H. 4.	
Holliday, Cromack, Dixon, Howarth		L. 5.	
Corp. Windle, Jerome, Metcalfe, Huthy		L.I.S.	
Cpl. Barrett, Shepherd P., Pugh, Wilcox 10.4		BRYKERIE FARM.	Cpl from K.I.A.
Cpl. Clarke, Barclay, Brown	from K.I.A.	No. 11 Cpl.'s Subsidiary Line.	Lt. N. Dahl
Gilbert, Coates, Brown 4	from L.5	BRYKERIE FARM goes to L. 6. at Night.	
L/Cpl. Butler, Broderick, Yeale	from H.S. position	VIA GILLIA	
Beautiman, Powell, Robson		S.P. 11	H. Laring
Cpl. Jacobs, Bowman, Bell P.S.		S.P. 11A	
Corpl. ~~_____~~ Anderson, Sedgwick, Watts J.		POLKA FM.	
Dodds, Dodson, Thomas W.		POLKA FM.	

G.B. Ruxie Lt.
148th M.G. Coy.

Appendix 13.

150th Bde. Machine Gun Coy. - Op. O. No. 42

1. Relief of Guns as follows will take place on night of 23rd/24th July 1916. Times & details as arranged with O/C 151st Bde. M.G. Coy. and between group Commanders concerned:—
   LA POLKA .... 2 Guns.
   S.P. 11A (BEAVER HAT) .... 1 "
   S.P. 11. .... 1 "
   VIA GELLIA. .... 1 "

2. On completion of relief guns & teams will be disposed as follows:—
   Two guns from POLKA FARM to Camp.
   One gun (L/Cpl. Butler) to FT. HALIFAX and to be under orders of Group Commander at S.P. 12.
   Two guns to M.G. FARM for disposition on the left flank.
   2/Lt. Carpenter to Camp.
   Lt. Turing to S.P. 13.
   Lt. Dawson to M.G. FARM.

3. Disposition of Reserve Guns at M.G. FARM will be subject to arrangements made by O/C Company with 6th Canadian Inf. Bde. M.G. Coy.

4. <u>Left Forward Group.</u>
   Position at L.5. is now vacated and a gun will be permanently at L.6.S.
   Two Guns will be stationed at BRYKERIE from July 23rd 1916 inclusive.

5. Completion of Relief as in (1) will be wired to M.G. FARM. (L.7)

6. Acknowledge.

G. B. Purvis. Lt.
for O/C 150th Bde M.G. Coy.

Copies. S. Offrs.
150th Inf. Bde. (for Information)
151 Bde. M.G. Coy.

Appendix 14.

150th Bde. M.G. Coy.   O.O 43.
Local relief for Night of July 25th 1916.

Teams	Positions	Offr. i/c	Remarks
L/Cpl Rymer, Cockfield, Lambert, Layland.	L.I.S.	Lt. Hoys relieves Lt Spooner	lives at L.I.S
Sgt. Gardham, Redshaw, Porter, McDougall	L.Y.L.		
Williamson, Harrison, Harper	S.P. 13. rear.	Lt. Dadd	S.P. 13.
Moore, Hayton, Greenwood.	K.I.A.		
Sidgwick, Hendry	H.5.		
Fox H, Fox G., Watt G., Makepeace	H.4		
Tillotson, Jefferson, Jewitt, Dixon W.	Ft Royal		
Nutt, Hart.	Ft Halifax		
Sgt. Pope, Foreman, Dickenson, Kenworthy	BRYKERIE FM.		
Nicholson, Pinchbeck, Burke	Do.		
Cpl Anderson, McLeod, Patterson	No. 11 Emp. Subs. lines.	Lt Dawson	M.G. Farm
Team remains	M.G. Farm		
Do.	M.G. Farm Windermere Dugouts		
Do.	M.G. Farm Windermere Dugouts		

G. B. Purvis Lt
for O/C. 150 Bde M.G. Coy.

Note Spooner to S.P. 12.

Appendix 15

100. Bde. M.Gun Coy. Op. Order No. 45.

Relief of Teams night of July 29/30 - 1916.

TEAMS	POSITION	Offr i/c	REMARKS
L/Cpl. Parker. S. Gilbert Barron Pugh	L.I.S.	Lt. Turing relieves Lt. Hoys & Lt. Dadd	Lt. Turing lives at S.P.13 during daytime L.I.S. at night.
Corp. Fields Dodds Dodgson	✕ L.Y.L.		Lt. Hoys down to Coy. H.Q.
Holiday Cromack Dixon. G.	✕ S.P.13 rear.		Lt. R. Dadd to M.G. FARM.
Sgt. Barnett Brown T Bame Langston	K.I.A.		
Corpl. Windle Howarth Charlesworth	H.5.	Lt. Carpenter relieves Lt. Spooner ※ See footnote.	
Corp. Clarke Kennedy Wilcox Cpl. H. (from Brykerie)	H.4		
Corp. Perry Shepherd Brown. S.G.	PT. ROYAL		
Corp. Jacobs Rowman Bell. A.	BRYKERIE FARM.		
Tillotson } from Jefferson } Pt. Royal Thomas	Do.	Lt. R. Dadd relieves Lt. Carpenter	Lt. C.H. Rose remains
Sgt. Nicol Patterson Baul	No. 11 Emp. Subs. Line.		
Redshaw } from Porter } L.Y.L. McDougall	M.G. FARM. WINDERMERE DUG OUTS.		
Nicholson } from Pinchbeck } Brykerie Burke	Do.		

※ Lt. Spooner will proceed as soon as possible to Reserve Battalion H.Q. at Sheet 28. M.19.c.9.2 and take charge of (2) two guns & teams in Divisional Reserve there.

✕ These two teams after relief will carry steel slit frames up to G.H. under C.S.M. Frames will be at Turners Town Dump about 11 P.M.

Armitage
Bennett } will relieve Holiday
Cromack } Divisional Reserve during afternoon
Gillyson Dixon

Appendix

O.O. 46
1/150th Machine Gun Coy.

July 30 – 1916

"The following reliefs will take place to-day the 30th inst.:–

NAME	POSITION	REMARKS
Pte. Harrison R.	to H.4	relieves Fox
" Dobinson.	BRYKERIE F.M.	" Jefferson.
Ptes. Foreman, Dickinson, Kenworthy }	to KEMMEL SHELTERS.	
L/Cpl. Butler's Team to relieve { Redshaw, Porter, McDougall }	from KEMMEL SHELTERS at M.G. FARM	WINDERMERE Dugouts.
{ Redshaw, Porter, McDougall }	Come down to Camp –	

G. B. Purvis Lt.
150th M.G. Coy

30/7/16.

VOLUME 7.

WAR DIARY of 150. Machine Gun Company Army Form C. 2118.
or
INTELLIGENCE SUMMARY.
(Erase heading not required.) MONTH of AUGUST.

Vol 7

Place	Date	Hour	Summary of Events and Information	Remarks and references to Appendices
In the trenches in front of VIERSTRAAT.	Aug 1st.	—	Everything very quiet in the trenches, practically no minenwerfer shelling. Enemy aeroplanes very busy.	G.B.Q.
"	2nd.	—	Weather exceedingly hot. Inter Company relief carried out. Oft from 59 Laheri inspected trenches & limits of sector.	G.B.Q. Appendix I
"	3rd.	—	Teams which were out resting carried out practice attack on Dummy trenches in Conjunction with 1/4 Kings Right Staffs. Mortars. Still very quiet in the line. 4 enemy aeroplanes which came over driven back by heavy A.A. Gun Fire. Teams at KEMMEL SHELTERS relieved.	G.B.Q. Appendix II
"	4th.	—	Company paid out. Dull day, not so hot.	G.B.Q.
"	5th.	—	Quiet day. An officer from 58th M.G. Coy came to arrange about relief of Company.	G.B.Q.
"	6th.	—	Men went to Baths at DRANOUTRE. Afterwards washed limbers 58th M.G. By. limbers came in to Camp Hill in evening. 13 of their guns went up to M.G. Farm preparatory to relief.	G.B.Q.
"	7th.	—	Guns at M.G. Farm & reserve position came out this morning. Half Company marched away to rest Billets near THIEUSHOEK in evening. 58th M.G. Coy relieved the rest of the Company in trenches at night.	G.B.Q. Appendix IV
2 Billet St Jean Fm	8th.	—	Remainder of Company left SCHERPENBERG CAMP at 1.30 A.M. and marched via MT ROUGE to THIEUSHOEK. Transport went by more direct road.	G.B.Q.
THIEUSHOEK	9th.	—	Day spent cleaning up, reducing stores etc. Hot Day	G.B.Q.
"	10th.	—	Left THIEULLET with full transport at 7pm & marched to BAILLEUL WEST STATION and entrained there with 150 T.M. Battery and 150 Brigade Headquarters in two trains for DOULLENS. Left station at 1 A.M. 11th. Train very crowded	G.B.Q.

Volume 7.
Sheet 2.

Army Form C. 2118.

WAR DIARY of 150 M.G. Coy.

INTELLIGENCE SUMMARY. AUGUST.

Place	Date	Hour	Summary of Events and Information	Remarks and references to Appendices
In train travelling				
DOULLENS.	11th		Arrived about 8.45 AM. Detrained and marched to AUTHERS, via HEM. Hilly road & 15 m march	6.9.P.
In Billet at AUTHEUX	12th		had an easy day owing to having had very little marching previously. Poor Billet. Men Bivouac'd out.	6.9.P.
			Fine day. Men resting. Brigade Staff called for all Company & Battalion Commanders in Brigade	6.9.P.
	13th Sunday		1st Showery day men doing equally gun drill	6.9.P.
	15th	11 AM	Reveille 1 AM, whole company moved off at 3.45 am by moonlight and marched to FLESSELLES, via Appendix I	Appendix I 6.9.P.
FLESSELLES	16th		cool march. Officers Billet in Chateau men in ? of same. Showery day	Appendix VI 6.9.P.
MOLLIENS AU BOIS			Company moved to MOLLIENS au Bois leaving FLESSELLES at 8.30 am arriving at 11 am	Appendix VI 6.9.P.
			Bivouaced in stubble field. Heavy rain at night. Very poor village	6.9.P.
MILLENCOURT	17th		Reveille 2.30 am moved at 4.30 am and marched to MILLENCOURT via VILLERS BOCAGE	6.9.P.
			Men bivouac'd in Field, officers in an Orchard with 5th Bn YORK REGT Officers	
"	18th		Commenced training today. Some rain. 19th More rain today delayed work to extent of	6.9.P.
"	20th		Church Parade in afternoon. Usual training in morning	
	21st		Company Staff ride in afternoon 22nd Continued Training. 23rd Training, went into	
	24th		Company staff rode in morning while men were at the Battd. Brigade practised attack on	
			village on ridge beyond in evening fairly successful. Return ? to begin with	
	25th		Hot close day. O/C Coy went to see demonstration of Contact Patrol work in morning	
			Heavy rain in afternoon	

VOLUME 7
Sheet 3

WAR DIARY of 150 Machine Gun Coy.
INTELLIGENCE SUMMARY. Month of AUGUST.

Army Form C. 2118.

Place	Date	Hour	Summary of Events and Information	Remarks and references to Appendices
MILLENCOURT	26th		Dull Showery day. 5th Bn Durham L.I. had Practice attack. Our section was on return from the Coy.	App.
	27th		Company marched to BUIRE sur L'ANCRE for Battle, got very wet. C/S E parade imported owing to non arrival of	App VIII
	28th		Company cleaned up camp & ground, which was flooded yesterday & continued training. two officers, Lt PURVES & 2nd Lt DADD went to reconnoitre 15th Division trenches in front of MARTINPUICH.	App
	29th		Showery day. Some sections on Range. 1 section attached 5th Yorks Reg. for Battalion attack.	App
	30th		Very heavy rain. Lecture for Coy. a C.O. of "Buire" flooded.	App
	31st		Inspection & Harangue by Brigadier in morning. Moved camp to new site. Brigade promised attack on Redoubt in evening. the same as 27th Contest machine worked well.	App

L.B. Purvis Lt.
O.C. Company
150 Machine Gun Company

Appendix I
War Diary

150th M. Gun Coy.   O.O.46

Local Relief of Teams on August 2nd 1916.

Teams	Position	Offr in charge	Remarks
L/Cpl Moore, Hayton, Redshaw, McDougall	L.I.S.	2/Lt Rose	S.P. 13.
L/Cpl Martinson, Daubney, Harrison C.	L.Y.L.		
Sgt. Anderson, Coates, Cockfield, McLeod	S.P. 13 rear.		
L/Cpl Pearson R., Sidgwick, Wallis	K.I.A.		
L/Cpl Rymer, Dixon, Nutt	H.5.	2/Lt Carpenter	S.P. 12.
Jefferson, Metcalf, Hart, Hutty	H.4.		
Williamson J., Harrison J., Harper J.	2/Lt Royal.		
Sgt. Pope, Fox H., Fox J.	Brykerie Fm.		
Beautiman, Powell, Watt.	Do.		
Cpl Acklam, Greenwood, L/Sgt Rayland A.	No. 11 Cmpl. Subs. line.	Lt Swing, 2/Lt Moor	M.G. Farm.
Sergt Gardham, Pte Lambert, Rest of team relieved tomorrow	Windermere Dugouts		
Team relieved tomorrow.	Do.		

G. B. Purvis Lt
150 Bde M. G. Coy.

APPENDIX. II

O.O. 46ᵃ

War Diary. 150 M.G. Coy.

August 3rd 1916

The following Reliefs will take place to day :-

L/Sergt Fields
Pte Dodds   } to KEMMEL SHELTERS
 " Dodgson

Ptes. Armitage
     Bennett   } from KEMMEL SHELTERS } TO { WINDERMERE DUGOUTS
     Gillyon

One Team from WINDERMERE DUGOUTS
                    Down to Camp.

G. B. Purvis Lt
150" M Gun Coy

3/8/16

Appendix III

war diary

Operation Order 44.

Ref. Sheet 28 S.W. 1/20,000
and Trench Map.

SECRET.
August 4th 1916.

150th Brigade Machine Gun Coy.
No. .... Copy R.
Date ....
50th Division

(1.) The 150th Machine Gun Coy. will be relieved by the 58th " " on the 7th and night 7/8th inst.

(2.) Limbers of the 58th Coy. will take to M.G. FARM (N.16.b.4.4) during night of 6th/7th 13 Guns. They will be guided by a N.C.O. of the 150th M.G. Coy. and an unloading party will be detailed by Lt. TURING at M.G. FARM.
The limbers will return to Coy. H.Q. before dawn.

(3.) On the 7th inst. the following reliefs will take place :-

<u>i</u> Divisional Reserve N.19.d.9.2.   } Guide at Coy. H.Q.
  (1 Off: 2 Guns & limber)   } at 9-30 A.M.

<u>ii</u> Brigade Reserve
  M.G. FARM. (N.16.b.4.4)   2 Guns } Guide for party
  No. 11 Position   1 " } at 58 Coy's. Camping
  Fort Royal   1 " } ground at 9-30 A.M.
* S.P. 13.   1 " } to M.G. FARM.
* K.I.A.   1 " } 1 Guide for gun
                                      } at M.G. FARM.

* Rossignol C.T. will be used.

2

Guides for remaining positions will be at M.G. FARM at 9 P.M.

One guide will be at 58th M.G. Coys. Camping Ground at 8-15 P.M. to guide party to M.G. Farm.

Four limbers of the 150th M.G. Coy. will be at M.G. Farm at 10-30 P.M.

(4) Lt. Turing will detail carrying parties to each position to assist both incoming & outgoing teams.

(5) The guns relieved from trenches during the morning will proceed by means of hand-carts to R.E. FARM where two limbers will await them. These are to be loaded by 2 P.M. and will proceed to Coy. H.Q. via MILLEKRUISSE and LA CLYTE.

The hand carts will be taken by men detailed from the teams via KEMMEL to the O/C 150th Trench Mortar Batty. at KEMMEL SHELTERS and left there, & remainder under 2/Lt. MOON will proceed to Coy. H.Q.

(6.) All Stores will be handed over as per Lists prepared at each position between gun team commanders & between Section Offrs. concerned for all the positions under their control.

Lt. Turing will hand over at M.G. FARM. All signed Lists to be handed in to Coy. H.Q. on arrival.

(7.) Completion of each relief will be reported by wire to Coy. H.Q. using the code word "DITCH" to indicate completion.

(8.) Lt. Turing will remain at M.G. FARM. until all limbers of 150th M.G. Coy. have left.

The working party will be marched to Coy. H.Q. by C.S.M. after loading limbers.

B m R Sharp. Capt.
Cmdg. 150th M. Gun Coy.

Appendix /

To - All Officers. War Diary.
150 M.G. Coy.
August 6th 1916

Transport - Distribution of loads

(1) On the occasion of the present move & until further orders, each Section Commander will be allotted 2-4 horsed wagons which will be loaded as per Schedule. He is responsible for these wagons at all times on the move & that they are correctly packed. Points to be observed are:-

    I.   Greasing of wheels.
    II. Shoeing of animals.
    III. Set of spare shoes carried for each animal.
    IV. Buckets & picketing gear carried for every wagon.
    V.   No packages tied to the outside of vehicles.
    VI. Cover lashed down & not chafing against the wheels.
    VII. The limber hook & swingle-tree hooks kept greased.
    VIII. The wrapping round the axles wetted each morning.
    IX. No unauthorised men to ride on the vehicle.

Per Section.

(1.) **Fore half** — 4 Guns in Cases with Spare barrels and auxiliary mounting
                4 Tripods
                4 Sets Spare Parts
                Oil Tins
                Condensers
                2 Water Drums
                16 Belt Boxes

    Rear half. 40 Belt Boxes.

(2.) **Fore half** — 24 Belt Boxes
                2 Belt filling machines
                2 Boxes S.A.A.
                1 Off'rs Valise.
                1 Set Packsaddlery

    Rear half — 10 Boxes S.A.A.
                 1 Off'rs Valise.
                 1 Set Packsaddlery.

Balance of gear belonging to Gun divided on No 2 Limber.

2

March discipline.

Sections will march in column of route at the head of the Transport except where the tactical situation demands otherwise.

Sections will be at horse interval apart, the Section Commander being at the head & 2nd in Command of Section in the rear of their Section.

Strictest attention will be paid to march discipline which at present hardly exists. Straggling & opening out are very noticeable faults. On the 10 minute halt being given all men fall out on the right of the road without further orders & take off their equipment. They should fall in & stand at ease immediately the whistle is again sounded. Drinking of water from water bottles should be discouraged. Men are not allowed to break ranks, when halted or not, to go into estaminets & houses. Any man falling out must be given a signed note by Officer at rear of his Section & will not be allowed to leave the column unless seriously ill.

4/8/16

War Diary
appendix V
150 MG Coy.

SECRET.
=========

Copy No. 6

150TH INFANTRY BRIGADE OPERATION ORDER NO.38.

13th August, 1916.

1. The 50th Division is to be transferred at midnight 14th/15th August, 1916, from G.H.Q. Reserve in Reserve Army to 4th Army, 3rd Corps, and will march on 15th August from the BERNAVILLE AREA to Area C. about VIGNACOURT.

2. The 150th Brigade Group will march on 15th August as per time-table attached and will billet on night 15th/16th at VIGNACOURT Area East. VILLERS - BOCAGE & FLESSELLES.

   Brigade Group includes 3rd Northumbrian Field Ambulance, No.4 Coy. A.S.C., and 1st Field Coy. R.E.

3. Each Unit will move with its 1st Line Transport.

4. The baggage wagons of all Units will report to O.C., Baggage Section of No.4 Coy. A.S.C., at 6 a.m. on the road running East and West half a mile North of the starting point.

5. Units marching from and through AUTHEUX must be clear of FIENVILLIERS by 4.30 a.m..

   All Units are to be South of the line ST. OUEN - LAVICOGNE by 10.a.m.

6. During the march the usual halts for 10 minutes in every hour will be observed by troops and 1st Line Transport. All will halt at 10 minutes Before the clock hour and will march on at the hour. Watches will be synchronized at the starting point.

7. The Trench Mortar Battery will march independently under separate arrangements.

8. The times of starting have been arranged so as to leave a gap of about ¼ mile between Units. Every Unit must, therefore, keep a steady pace of 120 to the minute, to avoid closing up or losing distance.

9. Special parties will be called for to go on ahead for taking up billets.

ACKNOWLEDGE.

Copy No. 1 Filed.
   2. 4th East Yorks.
   3. 4th Yorks Regt.
   4. 5th Yorks Regt.
   5. 5th Durham L.I.
   6. 150th Machine Gun Coy.
   7. 150th Trench Mortar Battery.
   8. 1st Field Coy. R.E.
   9. No.4 Coy. A.S.C.
   10. 3rd Northumbrian Field Ambulance.
   11. 50th Division.
   12. 50th Divisional Train.
   13. War Diary.

F. de C. Boys.

Captain,
Brigade Major,
150th Infantry Brigade.

U N I T.	Starting Point	Hour	Route	Destination.
Brigade H.Q.) Signal Section)	Cross Roads ¾ mile N. of 'N' of BERNEUIL.	5.30 a.m	CANAILLES, HAVERNAS, FLESSELLES.	FLESSELLES.
5th Durham L.I.	do.	5.40 a.m	do	VILLERS-BOCAGE.
Bde. achine Gun Co.	do	6 a.m.	do	FLESSELLES.
4th East Yorks.	do	6.10 a.m	do	do
4th Yorks.Regt.	do	6.20 a.m	do	do
5th Yorks.Regt.	do	6.30 a.m	do	VILLERS-BOCAGE.
No.1 Field Coy. R.E.	do	6.39 a.m.	do	FLESSELLES.
3rd Nbn.Field Amblce.	do	6.48 a.m.	do	do
No.4 Coy. A.S.C.	do			

50TH DIVISION. QX/3666/14. 13/8/16. 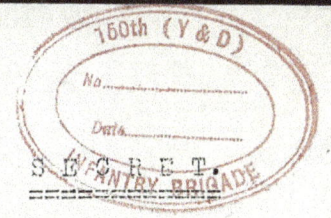 S E C R E T.

BILLETS FOR NIGHT 15th/16th AUGUST, 1916.   AREA "C".

```
Divisional Headquarters                         VIGNACOURT.
    Divisional Signal Company                       "
    C.R.E.                                          "
    Divisional Train (H.Q. & 1 Coy)                 "
    Sanitary Section                                "
    Mobile Veterinary Section,                      "
    Salvage and Drainage Sections.                  "
    7th (Pioneer) Bn. D.L.I.                        "

Divisional Artillery
    Headquarters                                VIGNACOURT.
    Two Brigades                                BOURDON.
    Two Brigades                                BETHENCOURT ST. OUEN.
    Divisional Ammunition Column                BOURDON.

149th Infantry Brigade
    Headquarters                                NAOURS.
    Four Battalions Infantry                        "
    Machine Gun Company                         WARGNIES.
    Trench Mortar Battery                           "
    1st Field Coy. R.E.                             "
    1st Field Ambulance.                            "
    One Company Divisional Train                    "

151st Infantry Brigade
    Headquarters                                VIGNACOURT.
    Four Battalions Infantry                        "
    Machine Gun Company                             "
    Trench Mortar Battery                           "
    2nd Field Coy. R.E.                             "
    2/2nd Field Ambulance                       OLINCOURT.
    One Company Divisional Train                    "

150th Infantry Brigade
    Headquarters                                FLESSELLES.
    3 Battalions Infantry                           "
    1 Battalion        "                        VILLERS-BOCAGE.
    Machine Gun Company                         FLESSELLES.
    Trench Mortar Battery                           "
    7th Field Coy. R.E.                         VILLERS-BOCAGE.
    3rd Field Ambulance.                        FLESSELLES.
    One Company Divisional Train                    "
```

                                                Colonel,
                                    A.A. & Q.M.G., 50th Division.

H.Q., 50th Div.
13th Augt. 1916.

O.C.

150th Machine Gun Coy.

Reference this office B.M.262 of to-day and Operation Order No.38.

All hand-carts of Units will report at starting point laid down in time-table to Captain Wilkinson, O.C., 150th Trench Mortar Battery at 3.30 a.m. on 13th August, 1916.

R de C Bryce
Captain,
Brigade Major,
150th Infantry Brigade.

Headquarters,
150th Infantry Brigade.
13th August, 1916.

Appendix VI

War Diary 150 M.g. Coy

Operation Order No. 48
150 Machine Gun Coy.

SECRET.

Aug. 14/15. 1916

1. Company will parade in "full marching order" at 6 P.M. today the 14th for Inspection.

   Rations, less Breakfast, will be issued & are to be carried in the pack or haversack and are for consumption on the 15th August.
   S.A.A. in pouches must be complete.
   Section Commanders will read out orders concerning March Discipline.
   Water Bottles are to be filled from water-cart.

   "Roll Call" to-night (the 14th) at 6.30 P.M.
   "Lights Out"   "   "   " 7.30 "

2. All Limbers will be packed & ready to move off by 3 A.M. tomorrow the 15th inst.

3. Reveille (August 15th) 2 am   O/off: 2/Lt Spooner.
   Breakfast   "   2-30 "   O/Sgt. Sergt. Pope.

   Parade in front of Coy. H.Q. at 3.15 A.M.
   Move off   3.30 "

   All ground to be thoroughly cleaned & latrines filled in by 3 am. when O/Officer will report same.

4. Packs to be marked with owners No. Rank, Name & Unit in indelible pencil on the back.

   B.M.R. Sharp. Capt.
   Comdg. 150th M.G. Coy.

war diary 150 MG Coy
Appendix VII

SECRET.
=======

Copy No. 6

150TH INFANTRY BRIGADE OPERATION ORDER NO.39.

Reference Map $\frac{1}{100,000}$
Sheets LENS No.11 and
AMIENS No.17.

15th August, 1916.

1. The 50th Division will march on Wednesday 16th August, 1916 to the Area VILLERS-BOCAGE-PIERREGOT - HIRVAUX and MOLLIENS AU BOIS with Artillery about MONTIGNY.
   On 17th August the 50th Division will move into the Third Corps Reserve Area.

2. The 150th Infantry Brigade Group, less 3rd Field Ambulance, will march on 16th August as shewn on attached march table.

3. Each Unit will march complete with first line transport. Supply wagons will march with No.4 Coy. A.S.C. Baggage wagons will report to O.C., Baggage Section of No.4 Coy. A.S.C., at 10.45 a.m. at the Church VILLERS BOCAGE.

4. During the march the usual halts for 10 minutes every hour will be observed by troops and 1st line transport. Watches will be synchronized at the starting point.

5. The Trench Mortar Battery will march independently under separate arrangements.

6. The times of starting have been arranged so as to leave a gap of about $\frac{1}{4}$ mile between Units. Every Unit must, therefore, keep a steady pace of 120 to the minute to avoid closing up or losing distance.

ACKNOWLEDGE.

Captain,
Brigade Major,
150th Infantry Brigade.

Copy No.1 Filed.
2. 4th East Yorks Regt.
3. 4th Yorks Regt.
4. 5th Yorks Regt.
5. 5th Durham L.I.
6. 150th Machine Gun Coy.
7. 150th Trench Mortar Bty.
8. 1st Field Coy. R.E.
9. No.4 Coy. A.S.C.
10. 3rd Northumbrian Field Ambulance.
11. 50th Division.
12. 50th Divisional Train.
13. Brigade Signalling Officer.
14. Brigade Transport Officer.
15. 149th Inf. Brigade.
16. 151st Inf. Brigade.
17. War Diary.

U N I T.	Starting Point.	Hour.	Route.	Destination.
Brigade Headquarters) Signal Section.)	Bend in road one Mile East of VILLERS BOCAGE.		VILLERS BOCAGE.	MOLLIENS AU BOIS.
Bde. Machine Gun Coy.	ditto.	10.15 a.m.	ditto.	ditto.
4th East Yorks Regt.	ditto.	10.24 a.m.	ditto.	ditto.
4th Yorks Regt.	ditto.	10.35 a.m.	ditto.	ditto.
5th Yorks Regt.	ditto.	10.45 a.m.	ditto.	ditto.
5th Durham L.I.	ditto.	11.5 a.m.	ditto.	ditto.
No.1 Field Coy. R.E.	ditto.	11.15 a.m.	ditto.	ditto.
No.4 Coy. A.S.C.	ditto.	11.24 a.m.	ditto.	ditto.

S E C R E T.

Copy No. 6

150th INFANTRY BRIGADE OPERATION ORDER NO. 40.

Reference Map $\frac{1}{100,000}$
Sheet LENS No. 11 and
AMIENS No. 17.

16th August, 1916.

1. On Thursday 17th August, the 50th Division will move into the Third Corps Reserve Area.

2. The 150th Infantry Brigade Group, less 3rd Field Ambulance, will march on 17th August as shewn on attached march table.

3. Each Unit will march complete with first line transport. Supply wagons will march with No. 4 Coy. A.S.C. Baggage wagons will report to O.C. Baggage Section of No. 4 Coy. A.S.C. at 5 a.m. at the Church MOLLIENS AU BOIS, facing South.

4. During the march the usual halts for 10 minutes every hour will be observed by all units. Watches will be synchronized at the starting point.

5. The Trench Mortar Battery will march independently under separate arrangements.

6. The times of starting have been arranged so as to leave a gap of about $\frac{1}{4}$ mile between units. Every unit must therefore keep a steady pace of 120 to the minute to avoid closing up or losing distance.

ACKNOWLEDGE.

E.de C. Boys.
Captain,
Brigade Major,
150th Infantry Brigade.

Copy No. 1. Filed.
2. 4th East Yorks Regt.
3. 4th Yorks Regt.
4. 5th Yorks Regt.
5. 5th Durham L.I.
6. 150th Machine Gun Co.
7. 150th Trench Mortar Battery.
8. 1st Field Coy. R.E.
9. No. 4 Coy. A.S.C.
10. 3rd Northumbrian Field Ambulance.
11. 50th Division.
12. 50th Divisional Train.
13. Brigade Signalling Officer.
14. Brigade Transport Officer.
15. 149th Infantry Brigade.
16. 151st Infantry Brigade.
17. War Diary.

UNIT.	Starting Point.	Time.	Route.	Destination.
Brigade Headquarters) Signal Section.)	Cross Roads half a mile North of I of MONTIGNY.	5 a.m.	MONTIGNY, BEHENCOURT, BAIZIEUX, HENENCOURT.	MILLENCOURT
4th Yorks Regt.	--ditto--	5.7 a.m.	--ditto--	--ditto--
5th Yorks Regt.	--ditto--	5.18a.m.	--ditto--	--ditto--
5th Durham L.I.	--ditto--	5.29 a.m.	--ditto--	--ditto--
4th East Yorks Regt.	--ditto--	5.40 a.m.	--ditto--	--ditto--
150th Machine Gun Coy.	--ditto--	6 a.m.	--ditto--	--ditto--
No.1 Field Coy. R.E.	--ditto--	6.9 a.m.	--ditto--	--ditto--
No. 4 Coy. A.S.C.	--ditto--	6.18 a.m.	--ditto--	--ditto--

Appendix IX
War Diary

150th M.Gun Coy.
Brigade Scheme 31-8-16

(1) Scheme with minor alterations is as for 27/8. See copy in Officers' Mess.

(2) Dispositions of Sections as follows:—
No. 1 to be in reserve & form barrages from about V.27.c.6.4
  barrages = No. A. from V 24 central to W. 19 central.
  No. B. W. 19 central to W. 26. a.0.0
to be worked out for guns & kept in readiness. Four frames & 4 tripods will be drawn from No. 4 Section.
Remaining sections disposed as follows:—
No. 2 to 4th East Yorks
No. 3 to 5th Durham L. Inf
No. 4 to 5th Yorks.

Nos 3 & 4 Section Comdrs. will report to respective Battalion H.Q. at 3 P.M. for orders.
No. 2 will report to O/C 4th East Yorks on road near Coy. H.Q. at 4·45 P.M.

Section Comdrs. Nos 3 & 4 will arrange to have their guns & gear dumped on the respective Battalion Dumps by 4·30 P.M. Limbers can then return to Transport lines until end of practice.

(3) Memoranda for Scheme of 27th inst. applies.
Ref.(2) Each Section will leave its own signallers & should get into visual communication with Battalion H.Q. through which messages should be transmitted. Each gun should have a periscope with it & numbers should keep heads down when in position.

(4). H.Q. Signallers will establish a Telephone between No 1 Section & Coy. Head Quarters.

(5) Officers will take servants with them to act as orderlies.

(6) Gun Bags. Nos 2 & 4 will draw 1 gun bag per gun & use same. All belt-boxes should be carried in Sand-bags.

Time Table.

4 P.M. Limbers parade on road as before
4 "   Officers synchronise watches at Coy. H.Q.
4.30   C.S.M. sent to obtain carrying party.
4.45   All troops in position lying down.
5.15   Outer batts. light P bombs on flanks, centre battn. red flares.
       Section Comdrs. should then complete their reconnaissance for gun positions
5.15. Carrying party goes up to Battn. Dumps leaving 2 men at each Dump as orderlies.
5.30   Each Team sends two men for rations.
5.30 to 6.30 P.M.
       Contact patrol machines will appear.

Appendix: VIII
150 M.G. Coy War Diary.

150th Inf. Bde. Scheme.
Orders for 150th M. Gun Coy.   24/8/16

(1) Coy. will parade with limbers at 3-45 P.M. in Fighting Order on Road N. of Orchard, each Section with its own limbers, tools carried down the braces of equipment. Order of March 1, 2, 3, 4.

(2) Coy. H.Q. & limbers will be at East Corner of MILLENCOURT (near waterpipe)

(3) O/C. Coy will be with Brigade H.Q. which will be at V.29.d.8.3. Two cyclist orderlies will be with O/C. Coy and two with Coy. H.Q. under Lt. Purvis. C.S.M and C.Q.M.S. will be at Coy H.Q. & will be allotted duties by Lt. Purvis

(4) Nos. 1 and 2 Sections will send two orderlies each to be with O/C. Coy.

Memoranda:

(1) Consolidation & fire direction & control will be actually practised. No exposure that would not be possible under fire is to be made.

(2) Section Comdrs. should try to get messages of some sort back to Coy. H.Q. even if no occasion arises.

(3) Each Section Comdr. should explain the Scheme & operations as fully as possible to his Section

(4) Forward positions (Shell-holes) etc. should be selected if possible.

(5) Flares for Contact patrol machine should be got from Battalion to which attached & must be lighted from any isolated or forward position. This should be strongly impressed on the men.

(6) All gear should be carried up by teams such as Very pistols, etc.

Time Table.

P.M.

3.45 Parade on Road N. of orchard. Section Comdrs. explain Scheme to Sections.

4.15 Move to assembly point (Coy H.Q.)
Nos. 3 & 4 Sections commence to carry to Battalion Dumps.

4.30 Synchronize watches. Nos. 1 & 2 Sections send orderlies to O/C. Coy. No. 2 Section gets into position.

5. P.M. C.S.M. reports to Lieut. Feetam Brigade Staff at D5 central for carrying party of 40 men.

5.30 All guns, teams, etc. to be in position at Battalion Dumps & ready to commence the operation.
Section Comdrs. report to Battalion Comdr.

6.0 Assault takes place. No. 2 Section commences Barrage on line A and continues at normal rate for 20 minutes. Carrying parties to Battn. dumps go forward under C.S.M. leaving 2 men at each dump.

6.15 Each Team sends back 2 men to Battn Dump for Rations & with a Report to O/C. Coy. which is taken back by the two men left on the Dumps.

6.30 No. 1 Section joins 4" East Yorks under orders from O/C Coy.

7.15 No. 2 Section opens intense barrage on line "B" for fifteen minutes.

about 7.30 P.M. Contact Patrol Machine will appear, flares to be lighted when it sounds a succession of "A"s on Klaxon horn.

150th. INFANTRY BRIGADE

50th. DIVISION

150th. MACHINE GUN COMPANY

SEPTEMBER 1916.

VOLUME 8.

Army Form C. 2118.

WAR DIARY of 150 Coy: Machine Gun Corps

INTELLIGENCE SUMMARY for SEPTEMBER, 1916.

(Erase heading not required.)

Vol 8.

Instructions regarding War Diaries and Intelligence Summaries are contained in F.S. Regs., Part II. and the Staff Manual respectively. Title pages will be prepared in manuscript.

Place	Date	Hour	Summary of Events and Information	Remarks and references to Appendices
In Billets at MILLENCOURT	1st Sept.		Company continued training. Weather changeable	G.H.Q.
	2nd		Usual Parades and gun drill in the afternoon. Cold + wet. Lectures to Company re coming Parade.	G.H.Q.
	3rd		Brigade Church Parade near Transport lines under Chaplain KEYMER. Divisional General present.	G.H.Q.
	4th		The Brigade practised attack on Redoubt as before Battalion in composition Section of the	G.H.Q.
	5th		Company changed round. No 1 with 6th York Regt. No 3 with the York Regt. No 1 doing advance firing Heavy Rain during night. Company went to bathe in morning. Officers rode round and reconnoitred ground for Coy. training scheme for the evening. In the evening Brigade carried out Staff scheme.	G.H.Q.
	6th		Organise reorganised. Parades as usual	G.H.Q.
	7th		50th Division practised attack on flagged course about a mile beyond BAIZIEUX. Glorious day. Dinners in the field after the "attack".	G.H.Q.
	8th		Morning spent packing up ready to move. Afternoon entered balance in men's pay books.	G.H.Q.
	9th		Company marched from MILLENCOURT at 9.30 A.M. via ALBERT to where transport was to meet us. arrived at MAMETZ WOOD at 1.15 pm. accommodated in old German Dugouts. Two sections moved up to Dugouts in support. The one section went to Dugouts in front line trenches. Very thick fog 9.14 morning. Two officers reconnoitred the front line trenches.	G.H.Q.
	10th		Guns under Lt Hoys visited other two guns in O.G.1 line.	G.H.Q.
	11th		Arranged that remainder of Company in O.G.1 line. Company H.Q. near Brigade H.Q. in North edge of MAMETZ WOOD.	G.H.Q.

# WAR DIARY of 1/150 Coy. MACHINE GUN CORPS

INTELLIGENCE SUMMARY — SEPTEMBER 1916

Army Form C. 2118.

(Erase heading not required.)

Place	Date	Hour	Summary of Events and Information	Remarks and references to Appendices
MAMETZ WOOD	Sept. 11th 12th 13th		LT. G.W. DAWSON proceeded to 137th Company as 2nd in Command. LT. L. GILL M.G. Company in Swansea Trench, 3 Guns. LT. MATVYOR reported for duty. Fairly quiet day. No change in dispositions. Enemy aeroplane brought down by A.A. fire. 4 guns sent to R.O.Y.L.I. Redoubt for indirect fire. Corpl. Jacobs wounded rifle. Stores drawn from Brigade dump for the attack on 15th 1916.	G.B.O. G.S.O. G.S.O.
	14th		LT. L. GILL M.G. Coy. knocked out by crumps in SWANSEA TRENCH. One killed, 4 wounded. Gun and gun team knocked out by crump in SWANSEA TRENCH. Gun recovered. (W) SERGT. BARNETT was received Military Medal for his act. Stores read and ready for tomorrow.	G.M.O. appendices 2, 3, 4.
In trenches S. MARTIN PUICH	15th	6.20	Attack commenced with heavy artillery barrage. 6.25. Tanks go over 4 points to position. 6.35 first objective gained. All objectives gained by the Brigade but some delay caused by HIGH WOOD not being captured. Early enough. Casualties heavy. 1 officer killed, 4 other ranks killed, 7 other ranks wounded. Six guns went over with 8 in support. One gun in action. Two fell in enemy shell fire, and another gun knocked out by shells. A great deal of equipment lost owing to casualties in Lewis carrying party and also the lack of knowledge of what was beyond them. The gun got to the Sugar Camilla, a lot of education done. Enemy Germans. Heavy enemy barrage all through the day. Continued consolidating positions gained yesterday. Quiet and quiet. In early morning everything was quiet except for a few (crumps) on MARTINPUICH. Two enemy shelled all of near part of area very heavy. Casualties 1 officer wounded, other ranks killed 3, wounded 12.	G.M.O. Appendices 5 G.M.O.
	16th			
	17th		Two guns moved forward along MARTIN trench & MARTIN alley. Letter trench very much crumped during the day and gun withdrawn from SUNKEN road. Carried out a Relief of M.G. gun teams in SUNKEN Road. LT. TYLOR relieved LT. MOON in SUNKEN ROAD. 3 other ranks wounded.	G.M.O. G.M.O.
	18th		Bombing attack but got no reinforcements. B.19 R.V.E. trench not occupied by us. Two guns shell in this trench.	

VOLUME 8 (7h)

WAR DIARY of 150 COY. MACHINE GUN CORPS.
INTELLIGENCE SUMMARY

Army Form C. 2118.

(Erase heading not required.)

Place	Date	Hour	Summary of Events and Information	Remarks and references to Appendices
In captured trenches S.W. of MARTINPUICH	18th		TRUE trench was heavily shelled. It began to rain in afternoon. One gun in TRUE trench relieved by 69th M.G. Coy. It rained all night. Very soft trenches began to fall in. Guns in KOYLI Redoubt and INTERMEDIATE trench withdrawn. A draft of 20 returned to M.G. Base.	9/M.D.
	19th		69th Coy. M.G. Corps relieved guns in SUNKEN ROAD and MARTINS trench. Limbers sent up to INTERMEDIATE LINE. Everything in Coy H.Q. late owing to rain mud. Germans made counter attack on TRUE TRENCH about an hour after. Guns got out.	9/M.D. 6.
In Quarry Field of MAMETZ WOOD	20th		Fine day. Spent day clearing up & reorganising teams. Cleaning guns & equipment. A draft of 16 men arrived from M.G. Base.	9.B.P. 9.B.P.
	21st		Continued cleaning up & organising the sections.	
In trenches in front of EAUCOURT L'ABBAYE	23rd		Two sections of this Coy relieved 2 sections of 1/149 Coy in positions in support. Limbers utilised stores from BAZENTIN & PETIT for Dugout as always well Head Quarters	9.B.P.
	24th		No 1 Section relieved 4 guns of 149 Coy early this morning. Remainder of Coy moved from MAMETZ WOOD to QUARRY N of BAZENTIN-MAMETZ Road; two other men wounded.	7, 8, 9. 9. B.P.
	25th		As Germans had evacuated the trenches which the Brigade was attacked, the Brigade only had to walk in & occupy the objective. Division R & L had to attack which they did with rifles in conjunction with the French. Two guns sent up under 2/Lt CARPENTER & met forward positions in which French & ROSE & NO 3 section relieved No 1 Section in TRUE COPSE & CRESCENT ALLEY. Night attack by infantry to capture a German trench. Owing to intense Artillery barrage this attack was covered by fire of	9/M.D. appendix 10
	26th		16 machine guns. Enemy successful trenches not permanently remained French at Dawn. This attack was covered by fire of 9. B.P.	
	27th		Today 1st Division made an attack to capture trenches not obtained by night attack. 16 Machine guns again formed barrage fire behind German trenches and whilst any enemy were seen to mount to their barrage of Artillery fire received heavy casualties. Arrangements made to relieve by 157 M.G. Coy. two teams in Coy at 7/M.D. in morning on stretcher & wounded.	9/B.P.
	28th		Artillery relieved in morning by two section of 157 Coy today. Remainder of Company moved into Billeting Huts in E.R. in MAMETZ WOOD. QUARRY Etc W of H in MAMETZ WOOD. Fine day. Some rain in Evening at about 12.	9/M.D.

WAR DIARY of 150 COY. MACHINE GUN CORPS

VOLUME 8. IV.

INTELLIGENCE SUMMARY

Place	Date	Hour	Summary of Events and Information	Remarks and references to Appendices
Lduguts inclsd MAMETZ WOOD.	28.		Remaining section relieved at CRESCENT ALLEY a trench. Very dark night. Consequently slow relief. Last gun home by 1.30 A.M. 29th.	G.B.P.
	29th		Miserable wet day. could not obtain much cleaning info. As orders were received to be in readiness to move forward it was arranged between Coy 14.9.160 to remain in their present H.Q.S.	G.B.P.
	30th		Fine bright day. Cold. Men go for baths at BECOURT in parties of 40 per hour.	G.B.P.

G. B. Purvis, Lieut.
q. 150 M-G. Coy.
October 1st 1916

APPENDIX I

150 MG Coy War Diary

SECRET.
=========

Copy No. 6

150TH INFANTRY BRIGADE OPERATION ORDER NO.41.

Ref. Map 1/40,000
Sheets 57D. & 62D.
& Trench Map.

8th September, 1916.

1. The 149th and 150th Infantry Brigades will take over the present right sector of the 15th Division from SUTHERLAND ALLEY inclusive to about S.2.b.6.1.

    The whole relief to be completed by noon on the 10th September.

2. The 150th Infantry Brigade front will extend from S.3.c.8.9 to about S.2.b.6.1.

3. The relief will be carried out in accordance with the attached table.

    Distances of 200 yards will be kept between Companies on the march. In addition, when marching through and East of ALBERT distances of 200 yards to be maintained between platoons.

4. The 4th East Yorks and 5th Yorks will from their arrival at SHELTER WOOD come under orders of G.O.C., 44th Inf. Brigade until he hands over to G.O.C., 149th Infantry Brigade.

    The G.O.C., 149th Infantry Brigade will assume command of the whole Division Sector on completion of the relief of the left Battalion of the 44th Infantry Brigade on the morning of the 10th September, handing over Command of the left portion of the front to the G.O.C., 150th Inf. Brigade at 4.0 p.m. on the same day 10th.

5. All details of Battalion reliefs will be arranged between C.Os. concerned

6. Orders for Machine Gun Coy. and Trench Mortar Battery will be issued later.

7. Battalions will report completion of reliefs to Brigade headquarters by messenger.

8. From 4 p.m. on the 10th September the Headquarters of 150th Infantry Brigade will be in O.G.LINE at about S.13.b.3.10.

    ACKNOWLEDGE.

John C. Boys.

Captain,
Brigade Major,
150th Infantry Brigade.

Copy No. 1. Filed.
2. 4th East Yorks Regt.
3. 4th Yorks Regt.
4. 5th Yorks Regt.
5. 5th Durham L.I.
6. 150th Machine Gun Coy.
7. 150th Trench Mortar Bty.
8. 1st Field Coy. R.E.
9. No.4 Coy. A.S.C.
10. 3rd North'n Field Ambulance.
11. 50th Division.
12. 50th Divisional Train.
13. Brigade Signalling Officer.
14. Brigade Transport Officer.
15. 149th Infantry Brigade.
16. 151st Infantry Brigade.
17. War Diary.

Date 1916.	UNIT.	To move to.	Route.	Remarks.
Sept.8th.	4th East Yorks.	SHELTER WOOD Area.	MILLENCOURT - ALBERT - BECOURT.	Pass V.29.d.6.2. at 4 p.m.
Sept 9/10th	4th East Yorks.	Trenches of 150th Inf.Brigade Sector S.5.c.8.8 - S.5.b.6.1. 2nd Bn - S.267.3		
Sept.9th.	5th Yorks Regt.	SHELTER WOOD Area.	MILLENCOURT - ALBERT - BECOURT.	Pass V.29.d.6.2 at 4 p.m.
Sept.10th.	5th Yorks Regt.	O.G.Line.		Morning.
Sept.10th.	4th Yorks Regt.	SHELTER WOOD Area.	MILLENCOURT - ALBERT - BECOURT.	Pass V.29.d.6.2 at 8 a.m.
Sept.10th.	5th Durham L.I.	BECOURT.	ditto.	Pass V.29.d.6.2 at 11 a.m.

relief complete by 11 p.m.
SAA- staff

12 men. 2 limbers
10 per gun.

early morning

150 MG Coy War Diary
APPENDIX 2

SECRET.

Copy No. 8

150TH INFANTRY BRIGADE (PRELIMINARY) OPERATION ORDER NO.42. IN ACCORDANCE WITH 50TH DIVISION PRELIMINARY OPERATION ORDER.

Reference Map 1/40,000.
Sheets 57c., 57d., 62d.
and Trench Map.

14th September, 1916.

1. (a) The Fourth Army in conjunction with the French and the Reserve Army is going to renew the attack on Friday 15th September.

    (b) The 50th Division will attack with the 47th Division on its Right and the 15th Division on its left.

2. The 150th Infantry Brigade will attack with three Battalions in front line and one Battalion in Reserve in accordance with a time-table to be issued later.

    The 149th Infantry Brigade will be on the right and a Brigade of the 15th Division on the left.

3. The boundaries have been issued to Battalions and are marked on the maps.

4. The place of assembly and objectives are as follows:-

UNIT.	Place of assembly.	1st Objective.	2nd Objective.	Final Objective.
4th East Yorks.	S.3.a.2.5. to S.2.b.9.5.	S.3.a.4.8. to S.3.a.1½.8.	M.33.c.9½.8. to M.33.c.6.8.	M.33.b.4.6. to M.33.a.3.6.
4th Yorks.	S.2.b.9.5. to S.2.b.5.5.	S.3.a.1½.8. to S.2.b.8.8.	M.33.c.6.8. to M.33.c.1.7.	M.33.a.3.6. to M.33.c.1.7.
5th Yorks.	S.2.b.5.5. to S.2.b.1.5.	S.2.b.8.8. to S.2.b.3.9.	M.33.c.1.7. to M.32.d.3.5.	M.33.c.1.7. to M.32.d.3.5.

In reference to the map issued -

The 4th East Yorks will, therefore, finally seize and hold the STARFISH LINE facing North.

The 4th Yorks will, therefore, finally seize and hold the MARTIN ALLEY facing West.

The 5th Yorks will, therefore, finally seize and hold the TANGLE NORTH facing North.

(2)

Special orders are being issued to Machine Gun Coy. and Trench Mortar Battery.

Each line when captured will be consolidated and garrisoned.

The 5th Bn. Durham L.I. will be reserve in front of BAZENTIN LE PETIT and will move up at zero hour to the original front line.

A Company of the Pioneer Battalion (7th D.L.I.) will be in position at an hour to be notified later, in the New Intermediate Trench, to be employed under orders of Brigadier General Commanding 150th Infantry Brigade, in digging forward communication.

5. (a) ARTILLERY. The attack will be prepared by a bombardment during the two or three day's prior to the day of the assault.

The artillery programme will be issued later.

(b) The actual assault will be assisted also by the fire of both light and medium Trench Mortars.

The C.R.A., will arrange for the three medium T.M. Batteries to be in position.

(c) There will be an artillery officer at each Infantry Brigade H.Q. and at each H.Q. of the assaulting Battalions.

(d) The whole of the Divisional Artillery will work to a set programme which will be issued later.
This programme will not be departed from except for some urgent reason without reference to Divisional H.Q.

(e) Preparations will be made for at least 3 Batteries to move forward as the attack progresses, and also for a certain number of F.O.O's. to move up at once to the high ground to obtain a view of the 2nd and 3rd Objectives.

6. Prisoners will be brought back by escorts found by the assaulting Battalions to Brigade H.Q. where they will be taken over.
As soon as prisoners have been handed over, the escorts will return at once to their former positions as quickly as possible.

7. WOUNDED. Wounded will be brought back as follows:-

To Advanced Collecting Post at S.8.a.1.4. and about X.12.c.9.5.

At the Advanced Collecting Posts the personnel of the Field Ambulances will remove the lying down cases to the Advanced Dressing Station at FLATIRON COPSE (S.14.c.5.2) and CONTALMAISON.
Walking Cases will all go to CONTALMAISON.

8. STRAGGLERS Straggler Posts will be established about S.15.a.0.9. and THE CUTTING.
Stragglers will be handed over to the rearmost Battalion of the Reserve Brigade at SHELTER WOOD.

9. (a) DUMP. An Advanced Divisional Dump for ammunition of all kinds except Artillery Ammunition will be established at ~~~~~~~~~ S.14.b.1.8.

(b) An Advanced R.E. Dump will be established at the end of JUTLAND ALLEY about S.2.d.9.7. and about S.14.b.9.9.

(3)

10.   Headquarters will be established as follows by 6 p.m. on the 14th September:-

    Advanced Div. H.Q. .... RAILWAY COPS.X.28.b.2.1.
    149th Inf.Bde. .... QUARRY. S.8.b.9.1.
    150th Inf.Bde. .... O.G.1, S.7.d.2.1.
    151st Inf.Bde. .... HAMETZ WOOD, X.24.b.9.8.

<u>ACKNOWLEDGE.</u>

E.J.de.C. BOYS,
Captain,
Brigade Major,
150th Infantry Brigade.

Copy No. 1. Filed.
       2. War Diary.
       3. Brigade Commander.
       4. 4th East Yorks.
       5. 4th Yorks Regt.
       6. 5th Yorks Regt.
       7. 5th Durham L.I.
       8. 150th M.G.Coy.
       9. 150th T.M.Battery.
     10. 50th Division.
     11. 50th Division.
     12. 149th Inf. Brigade.
     13. 151st Inf. Brigade.

TABLE OF MOVES. 14th September, 1916.

4th East Yorks Regt. — To have all Companies clear of O.G.1 by 12 Midnight 14th/15th September and to be assembled by 3 a.m.

4th Yorks Regt. — To leave SHELTER WOOD 8 p.m. and report at Brigade H.Q. when extra Stores will be issued and given out - To move to place of assembly after issue.

5th Yorks Regt. — To have all Companies clear of O.G.1 by 12 Midnight 14/15th September and to be assembled by 3 a.m.

5th Durham L.I. — To leave BECOURT at 8 p.m. and report at Brigade H.Q. - To be over O.G. Line at 12 Midnight - Draw Stores and issue to men - Move to area between SWANSEA TRENCH and 6th AVENUE at Zero Hour.

Pioneer Company. — Arrive in Intermediate trench 5 a.m., send an Officer and Orderly to Brigade Headquarters.

150 MG Coy. War diary
Appendix. 3.

SECRET.

150TH INFANTRY BRIGADE OPERATION ORDER NO. 43.

Copy No. 8

Reference Map 1/40,000
Sheets 57c., 57d., 62d.
and Trench Map.

14th September, 1916.

In reference to 150th Infantry Brigade Operation Order No. 42 of to-days date.

1. No alteration.

2. The time-table is issued herewith.

 The 45th Inf.Brigade of the 15th Division will be on the left.

3. No alteration.

4. Places of assembly and objectives remain the same.

 The advance will be as follows:-

 Assaulting Battalions will advance in 3 waves from the EYE TRENCH to the 1st Objective. At the same time the 4th wave will move up from SWANSEA TRENCH to the EYE TRENCH.

 While consolidating the 1st Objective the 4th wave will come up from the EYE TRENCH and join their Companies at the earliest opportunity.

 The advance from the 1st Objective to the 2nd will be in 4 waves. It is imperative that the 2nd objective be seized, consolidated and held, and the 2nd waves are to be specially retained in it as a garrison.

 3rd wave

 The advance from the 2nd Objective to the final will, therefore, be in three lines.

 This final Objective held and consolidated will mark a very great success.

 The 5th Bn.Durham L.I. will share in each Advance - supporting the assaulting Battalions trench by trench.

 The O.C. will keep two Companies in hand. Special lines of advance have been arranged.

 Machine Gun Company. -

 4 Guns will go forward under special orders to Sunken Road, M.33.c.

 2 Guns will go forward under special orders to Sunken Road, M.33.a.

 6 Guns cover the advance of both Brigades from about S.2.b. & d.

 Headquarters and 2 Guns are in Reserve at Brigade H.Q.

 Trench Mortar Batteries.-

 No more guns to be employed than can be kept supplied with ammunition.

 4 Guns are detailed to support the advance of the Left Battalion, of which two will go forward.

(2).

2 Guns are detailed to support attack on HILL 154 and afterwards establish themselves in Sunken Road about M.33.c.2.5.

2 Guns in Reserve off PIONEER ALLEY, about SEVENTIETH AVENUE.

ACKNOWLEDGE.

Captain,
Brigade Major,
150th Infantry Brigade.

Copy No. 1 Filed.
2 War Diary.
3. Brigade Commander.
4. 4th East Yorks.
5. 4th Yorks Regt.
6. 5th Yorks Regt.
7. 5th Durham L.I.
8. 150th M.G.Coy.
9. 150th T.M.Battery.
10. 50th Division.
11. 50th Division.
12. 149th Inf.Brigade.
13.   Inf.Brigade.

150 M.G. Coy. War diary
appendix 4

SECRET.

Copy No. 8

ADDENDUM No.1 to 150TH INFANTRY BRIGADE OPERATION ORDER NO.42.

Reference Map 1/40,000
Sheets 57c., 57d., 62d.
and Trench Map.   14th September, 1916.

In reference to 150th Infantry Brigade Operation Order No. 42 of to-day's date.

1. No Alteration.

2. The time-table is issued herewith.

    The 45th Infantry Brigade of the 15th Division will be on the left.

3. No alteration.

4. Places of assembly and objectives remain the same.

    The advance will be as follows:-

    Assaulting Battalions will advance in 3 waves from the EYE TRENCH to the 1st Objective. At the same time the 4th wave will move up from SWANSEA TRENCH to the EYE TRENCH.

    While consolidating the first objective the 4th wave will come up from the EYE TRENCH and join their Companies at the earliest opportunity.
    The advance from the 1st Objective to the 2nd will be in 4 waves. It is imperative that the 2nd objective be seized, consolidated and held, and the 2nd waves are to be specially retained in it as a garrison.
    The advance from the 2nd objective to the final will, therefore, be in 3 waves. Magnetic bearings have been issued.

    This final objective held and consolidated will mark a very great success.

    The 5th Bn. Durham L.I. will share in each advance - supporting the assaulting Battalions trench by trench.
    The O.C., will keep two Companies in hand. Special lines of advance are being arranged.

MACHINE GUN COMPANY.-

   4 Guns will go forward under special orders to Sunken Road, M.33.c.

   2 Guns will go forward under special orders to Sunken Road, M.33.a.

   8 Guns cover the advance of both Brigades from about S.2.b. and d.

   Headquarters and 2 Guns are in Reserve at Brigade Headquarters.

(2).

TRENCH MORTAR BATTERIES.-

No more guns to be employed than can be kept supplied with ammunition.

4 Guns are detailed to support the advance of the Left Battalion, of which two will go forward.

2 Guns are detailed to support attack on HILL 154 and afterwards establish themselves in Sunken Road about M.33.c.2.5.

2 Guns in Reserve off PIONEER ALLEY, about SEVENTIETH AVENUE.

5. No alteration - Details of barrage have been issued to all Units.

6. No alteration.

7. No alteration.

8. No alteration - A control post of 1 N.C.O. and 3 men will be found by 5th Bn.Durham L.I. on PIONEER ALLEY about K.O.Y.L.I.REDOUBT and junction of SOMME ALLEY and SIXTH AVENUE East.

9. No alteration.

10. No alteration.

11. Battalion Headquarters will be at :-

    4th East Yorks. - SWANSEA TRENCH.
    4th Yorks Regt. -   "   "
    5th Yorks Regt. -   "   "
    5th Durham L.I. - O.G.1.

up to Zero Hour 15th September.

Provisional arrangements are made for forward moves, as follows:-

4th East Yorks to 2nd Objective about SUNKEN ROAD, about M.33.c.9.9.& 3rd Objective about M.33.a.8.8.

4th Yorks Regt.to 2nd Objective about M.33.c.5.8.

5th Yorks Regt.to TANGLE NORTH about M.32.d.6.4.

5th Durham L.I.to SWANSEA TRENCH about S.2.b.4.1.

12. All Units to report to Brigade H.Q. their arrival in Battle Positions, by runner.

ACKNOWLEDGE.

Copy No.1 Filed.
    2 War Diary.
    3 Brigade Commander.
    4 4th East Yorks.
    5 4th Yorks Regt.
    6 5th Yorks Regt.
    7 5th Durham L.I.
    8 150th M.G.Coy.
    9 150th T.M.Bty.
  10 50th Division.
  11 50th Division.
  12 149th Inf.Brigade.
  13 45th Inf.Brigade.
  14 151st Inf.Brigade.

Captain,
Brigade Major,
150th Inf.Brigade.

War Diary. Appendix 5

Preliminary Operation Order No. 50   SECRET
by Capt Sharp commanding 150th M.G. Coy.

(1.) The 150th Inf. Bde. will attack on Sept 15/16 with 45th Inf. Bde on its left and 149th Inf. Bde. on its right.

(2.) The following Machine Guns will be attached to the assaulting battalions: 4th Yorks 2 guns of No 2 Section
            5th "   2 "   No 3 "

These half sections under the Officers detailed & composed and equipped as ordered, will be in positions to which they have been assigned in fourth wave of the attacking battalions, by   on the 15th.

(3.) Objectives of M. Guns will be as follows:
No 1. Half Section i to establish itself on hill 155 (Square M.33.C.5.2.) in front of first objective.
      ii establish itself junction of 4th East Yorks & 4th Yorks.
No. 2. Establish itself on left of 4th Yorks and fire across its front to the right.
No. 3. Establish itself on right of 5th Yorks and fire across its front to the left (Square   )

These positions will depend on the position of the Infantry & every effort must be made to seize & consolidate high ground from which covering fire can be obtained and to deny to the enemy sunken roads.

(4.) 2 guns of No 1, 2 guns of No 3 and 4 guns of No 4 will cooperate by indirect fire from positions assigned to them. 2 guns of No 2 will be in reserve at Coy. H.Qrs.
All above guns will be prepared to move at once to any part of the Brigade front. Two Orderlies per half section will be at Coy. H.Q.

(5.) Supply arrangements as detailed, i.e. 1 N.C.O. & infantry carrying party on each Battalion Dump.

(6.) Coy. H.Q. will be as at present N.W. Cr of Maneta Wood. Reports & demands for reinforcements & stores should be sent via Battalion Dumps to Coy H.Qrs. Every effort should be made to send back a brief report on the situation & position of guns, as early as possible.

(7.) Zero hour will be.
(8.) Acknowledge.

                                        M.E. Sharp Maj.

150 M.G Coy. WAR DIARY. Appendix 6.

Provisional Orders for Relief of the 150th M.G. Coy.
by M.G Coy of the 23rd Division.

(1.) Company will be relieved by the 69 M.Gun Coy.
on the morning of the 19th Sept. 1916

(2.) Guides. 2/Lt. Moon will send one guide.
    Lt Wood " " one "
    2/Lt. Rose " " Two guides (one for
      Martins Alley & one for Starfish Trench gun)

These guides will be at the Dump (C.S.M)
at INTERMEDIATE TRENCH.

(3.) All outcoming Guns & Gear will be carried to
the dumps where the limbers will be brought
up to if the state of the ground permits.

The following carrying parties will be sent
from the dump by C.S.M. at
to assist in removing Belt Boxes.
  2/Lt. Moon 10 men.
  Lt. Wood 20 "
  2/Lt. Rose 10 "

All limbers & teams will report to Coy. H.Qrs
on completion of the relief.

Officers concerned will report completion of
relief of their positions by telephoning from
the dump.

Lt. Rose's teams should endeavour to bring out
as many German belt boxes (empty) and
empty Belts as possible.

(4.) It is most important that all Belt Boxes
be brought out.

(5.) Acknowledge.

         R.M.A.Sharp. Maj
         150 M.G Coy

150 M.G.Coy. WAR DIARY
Relief Orders. Appendix SECRET.
7

Ref. Trench Map 1/10,000.

(1.) The 150th M.G. Coy. will relieve the 149th M.G. Coy in trenches on 23rd Sept. and morning of the 24th.

(2.) The following Guns will be relieved on the 23rd inst.

Section	Officer	Position	Guides
No. 2	2/Lt. Moon	Four guns. Intermediate Trench S.3.c.2.5.	3 P.M. One guide at C Dump. (S.14.a.4.6) to guide all Limbers & Teams to Intermediate Trench position
No. 4	Lt. Turing	One gun, junction of Bethel Sap and Eye Trench S.3.b.2.6. One gun Hook Trench S.3.b.4.8. Two guns Sunken Road M.33.d.2.4.	At Intermediate Trench position.

These Teams will parade at 2-30 P.M. Move off 2-40 P.M.

The following Guns will be relieved on the 24th inst:-

Section	Officer	Position	Guides
No. 1	Lt. Taylor	One Gun Prue Trench M.34.a.9.5 (about) 1 Gun Prue Copse. M.34.b.1.9 (about)	One guide at junction Intermediate Trench & Road S.3.C.8.4. at 4 A.M. for Sunken Road, where there will be one guide per gun at 5 A.M.
No. 1	2/Lt. Dadd	2 Guns Crescent Alley N. of Prue Trench	

No. 1 Section will parade at 2-15 A.M. Move off 2-30 A.M.

(3.) Your guns (No 3 Section) in Reserve at Coy. H.Qrs. (Quarry S.8.b.9.2)

(4.) Company H.Qrs. will move at 9-30 a.m. on the 24th to above.

(5.) Forward dump will be at or near M.G. Position in Intermediate Trench as in (2.)
Spare belts S.A.A. will be here. Rations will be dumped each day here.
C.S.M. will be in charge & a carrying party will be kept which will carry rations to teams.

(6.) Completion of Relief will be reported by runner to forward dump.
All messages will be so sent.

(7.) Acknowledge.

M.M.R.Shap, Major.
Comdg. 150th M.Gun Coy.

Copy No 2. 150 M.G Coy Secret

WAR DIARY

Appendix 8

Map Ref
Trench Map   Operation Order No 48.
57C. SW.

1/ The 149th M.G Coy will be
relieved ˣin trenches by the 150th M.G Coy on
the night and morning of the
23/24th Sep.

2/ The 150th M.G Coy will take
over the Gun positions now
occupied by the 149th M.G Coy,
with the exception of the Guns
in HOOK TRENCH and CLARKES TRENCH
which will vacate their position
at 3 pm on the 23rd inst without
being relieved and proceed to
limbers at INTERMEDIATE LINE.

3/ Guides will be provided by
the 149th M.G Coy as follows:—
(1) 1 Guide at X Roads S11 B 1-8 at
3 pm on the 23rd inst
(2) Guides for BETHELS SAP, SUNKEN RD
and INTERMEDIATE LINE at S3 C 2-2
at 3-30 pm on the 23rd inst.
(3) Guides for CRESCENT ALLEY and
PRUE TRENCH at S3 C 2-2 at 4 am

on the 24th inst.

4. All teams will hand over SAA and flares but will bring out all belt boxes and other M.G. Equipment.

5. Teams on relief will proceed to limbers at INTERMEDIATE LINE

6. All guides and carrying parties will be provided from Coy H.Q.

Acknowledge.

[signature]

Major.
Comdg 149 M.G. Coy.

Copy No 1. 149 Inf Bde
2. 150 M.G. Coy
3. ⎫
4. ⎬ Section
5. ⎭
6. ⎫
7. ⎬ Officers
8. War diary
9. File

Appendix 9.

WAR DIARY. 150 M.G. Coy.

S E C R E T.

Copy No. 8

150TH INFANTRY BRIGADE OPERATION ORDER NO.43.

Reference Map 1/40,000
Sheets 57c., 57d., 62d.
and Trench Map.

23rd September, 1916.

1. The 150th Infantry Brigade will relieve the 149th Infantry Brigade on the night 23rd/24th September 1916.

2. The 4th East Yorks with one Company of 4th Yorks attached will meet guides at about S.3.d.0.9. at 7.30 p.m. and take over PRUE and STARFISH TRENCH, as shewn on map issued to those concerned.

   The 5th Durham L.I. with one Company of 5th Yorks attached will meet guides at S.3.d.0.9. at 8.30 p.m. and take over PRUE and STARFISH TRENCH as shewn on map issued to those concerned.

   The 4th Yorks less one Company will support the 4th East Yorks and take over the area about M.33.d. East of "TYNE".

   The 5th Yorks less one Company will support the 5th Durham L.I. and take over the area S.33.d. West of the BOW.

   All arrangements possible will be made by O.Cs. concerned.

   The 150th Machine Gun Coy. and 150th Trench Mortar Battery will relieve 149th Machine Gun Coy. and Trench Mortar Battery under arrangements to be made by the respective O.Cs.

3. **Dress:-** Fighting order with great-coats, Water and rations for next day to be taken so as to avoid movement in daylight in forward trenches.

4. Completion of relief to be reported by code to Brigade H.Q. Relief to include the gaining of touch with flanking Brigades or Battalions.

5. Brigade Headquarters will close at O.G.1 and open at the QUARRY at S.8.d.8.9 at a time to be notified later.

ACKNOWLEDGE.

Captain,
Brigade Major,
150th Infantry Brigade.

Copy No. 1 Filed.
    2. War Diary.
    3. Brigade Commander.
    4. 4th East Yorks Regt.
    5. 4th Yorks Regt.
    6. 5th Yorks Regt.
    7. 5th Durham L.I.
    8. 150th M.G.Coy.
    9. 150th T.M.Bty.
  10. 149th Inf.Brigade.
  11. 151st Inf.Brigade.
  12. 50th Division.
  13. 50th Division.
  14. 69th Inf.Brigade.
  15. 7th Durham L.I.

150 M.G. Coy WAR Diary
Appendix 10.

SECRET.

Copy No. 5

150TH INFANTRY BRIGADE. OPERATION ORDER NO.45.

1. Tonight the 150th Infantry Brigade will in conjunction with the 1st Division seize the German trench from about M. 28. b. 3. 7. to about M. 28. a. 0. 8.

   The 2nd Sussex Regt. will be on our right and will conform to our advance under orders from 2nd Infantry Brigade 1st Division.

2. The attack will be carried out as follows -

   4th Yorks. Regt. on the right will assault German trenches from M. 28. b. 3. 7. to M. 28. a. 8. 6.

   Battalion H. Qrs. at PRUE or STARFISH LINE.

   5th Yorks. on the left will assault the German trenches from M. 28. a. 8. 6. to M. 28. a. 3. 7.

   Battalion H.Q. at PRUE or CRESCENT ALLEY.

   Magnetic bearing of each attack is true North.
   Magnetic variation is about 13 degrees.

   Both these Battalions will enter the German trenches ~~at 11 p.m.~~ tonight, a preliminary alignment having been made along a tape line running from M. 28. a. 0. 3. to M. 29. a. 0. 3. advance from this tape line to be simultaneous at 11. 0 p.m. Officer on the inner flank from each battalion to ensure this latter point.

   Formation :-

   Attack in three lines in company column in single rank, four companies on line, 20 yards between companies, the fourth platoon in each company remaining in PRUE TRENCH to act as carrying party.

   The 4th East Yorks. will support the 4th Yorks. in the right attack moving into the PRUE TRENCH and STARFISH line at 9.45 p.m. Battalion H.Q. STARFISH.

- 2 -

The 5th Durham L. I. will similarly support the 5th Yorks. Regt. moving into the PRUE and STARFISH Lines at 9.45 p.m. Battalion H.Q. SUNKEN ROAD.

Of these two Battalions the latter will form a defensive flank in close support of the 5th Yorks. up CRESCENT ALLEY to M. 28. a. 0. 3.

3. Artillery barrages and howitzer fire have been arranged for and are known to those concerned. There will be no marked artillery fire previous to the attack. A time table is attached.

The Machine Gun Coy. will push forward two guns with each front line Battalion and help to hold the position when gained.

The Trench Mortar Battery will push forward guns on each flank -

One to a shell hole about M. 28. d. 2. 5.
One up CRESCENT ALLEY to about M. 28. a. 0. 3.

4. Dumps will be established at the junction of RUTHERFORD ALLEY and PRUE TRENCH and at the junction of CRESCENT ALLEY and PRUE TRENCH, from which the two right and two left battalions will draw as required. These dumps will be established by 9.30 p.m.

5. Medical Officers will establish medical aide-posts as far forward as time and circumstances admit.

6. Tactical considerations of the operation are added as a special memo.

7. Synchronising of watches will take place at 7 p.m. and 9 p.m. by telephone.

E.J. de C. Boys,
Captain,
Brigade Major,
150th Infantry Brigade.

26th September 1916.

TIME TABLE.

11 p.m.   The 4th East Yorks. and 5th Yorks. Regt. will move from the tape in conjunction with the 1st Division.

11.5 p.m.   4.5" Howitzers will bombard M. 23. c. 0. 6., Old Quarry (M. 22. d. 3. 1) and trench to M. 27. b. 9. 9. to M. 21. d. 6. 4. and trench junction M. 22. a. 2. 0.

This will assist in synchronising the advance from the tape.

11.10 p.m.   A light barrage by the Divisional Artillery will be established 350 yards beyond the trench captured. Special points for Artillery are - continuation of CRESCENT ALLEY, and a barrage from M. 22. c. 2. 9. to M. 21. d. 5. 1.

N O T E S.

1. Your front is being taped at 9.30 p.m.
   Stakes are being driven in at every 45 yards (Company front) with intervals of 20 yards between Companies. The left and right of each Battalion being marked by larger stakes, e. g. :-

   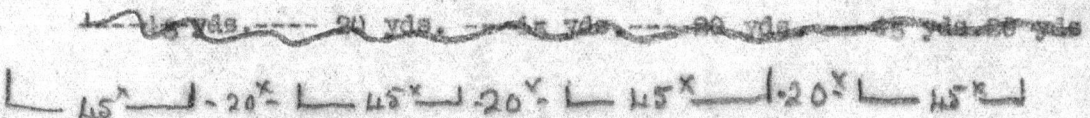

2. When the tape is laid, i.e., at 9.30 p.m. the Brigadier General Commanding wishes O.C. Battalions to send forward a few men to lie on it and prevent the possibility of German Patrols taking it away.

3. Do not forget visual signalling and runners back.

4. With reference to conference with C.O's. this afternoon, please note that the starting off time has been changed to 11 p.m. so as to move in conjunction with the 1st Division on our right. Reference Operation Order para.2, underlined.

5. Password will be "NEWCASTLE".

TACTICAL CONSIDERATIONS. REFERENCE OPERATION ORDER 4, PARA. 6.

As soon as the trench is captured blocks must be established at M. 28. b. 2. 8. in CRESCENT ALLEY towards EAUCOURT L'ABBAYE (4th Yorks.) and M. 28. a. 2. 7. North side of the road (5th Yorks.)

In case the attack on the right does not succeed a block will also have to be established about M. 28. b. 3. 6.

Trenches gained to be consolidated at once, and advanced posts pushed out into shell holes.

A communication trench is to be dug forward from about M. 28. d. 2. 7. by a party of Pioneers and 4th Yorks. Regt. will try and join up from about M. 28. b. 3. 7.

The Pioneer Company 7th Durham L. I. will be assembled about STARFISH LINE and RUTHERFORD ALLEY by 9. 30 p.m. tonight and will push forward at the first opportunity.

150 M.G. Coy.
WAR DIARY
Appendix 11.

SECRET.

Copy No. 5

150TH INFANTRY BRIGADE OPERATION ORDER NO.46.

27th September 1916.

1. The 151st Infantry Brigade will relieve the 150th Infantry Brigade on the ~~morning of the~~ 28th instant.

2. The 9th Durham L.I. will relieve the 4th East Yorks. whose guides will be at the junction of PRUE TRENCH and RUTHERFORD ALLEY at 4 a.m.

The 8th Durham L.I. will relieve the 5th Durham L.I. whose guides will be at the junction of PRUE TRENCH & CRESCENT ALLEY at 4 a.m.

Relief will commence by sending up small parties at a time, who will take over important points and come temporarily under the command of Units already holding those points. All arrangements to be made by C. Os. concerned.

4th Yorks. will be relieved by 6th Durham L.I.

5th Yorks. will be relieved by 5th Border Regt.

Times to be notified as soon as the front reliefs are complete. *These 2 reliefs may commence 12 noon 28th inst*

The 150th Machine Gun Coy. and 150th Trench Mortar Battery will be relieved by ~~149th~~ 150th Machine Gun Coy. and ~~149th~~ 150th Trench Mortar Battery under arrangements to be made by O. Cs. concerned.

3. All units will return to the location of the relieving Units.

4. Completion of relief to be reported to Brigade H.Q.

Acknowledge. *A full 24 hours are allowed for this relief.*

E de C Bray Captain,
Brigade Major,
150th Infantry Brigade.

Copy No. 1. 4th East Yorks.   8. 151st Infantry Bde.
       2. 4th Yorks. Regt.   9. 70th Infantry Bde.
       3. 5th Yorks. Regt.   10. 50th Division G.
       4. 5th Durham L.I.   11. 50th Division Q.
       5. 150th Machine Gun Co.   12. 2nd Infantry Bde.
       6. 150th T. M. Bty.   13. Bde. Transport Officer.
       7. 149th Infantry Bde.   14. Bde. Signalling Officer.
                                  15. Filed.
                                  16. War Diary.

150 M.G. Coy
WAR DIARY.

appendice 12

SECRET.
Copy No. 7

150TH INFANTRY BRIGADE OPERATION ORDER NO.47.

28th September, 1916.

1. On the 29th September the 149th Infantry Brigade will relieve the 150th Infantry Brigade in the O.G.LINE.

   On completion of relief the 150th Infantry Brigade will be in Divisional Reserve in MAMETZ WOOD and QUADRANGLE TRENCH AREA with Headquarters in MAMETZ WOOD.

2. The 4th Yorks will be relieved by 5th Northumberland Fusiliers.
   " 5th Yorks " " " " 6th Northumberland Fusiliers.

   Reliefs to commence at 9 a.m. under arrangements to be made by O.Cs. concerned.

   4th East Yorks will be relieved by 4th Northumberland Fusilier.
   5th Durham L.I. " " " " 7th Northumberland Fusiliers.

   150th Machine Gun Coy. and 150th Trench Mortar Battery will be relieved by 149th Machine Gun Coy. and Trench Mortar Battery.

   Time of Reliefs ~~to commence~~ and arrangements to be made between O.Cs. concerned.

3. Completion of reliefs to be reported to Brigade Headquarters.

4. Brigade Headquarters will close at O.G.LINE and open in MAMETZ WOOD at 3 p.m.

   ACKNOWLEDGE.

   Captain,
   Brigade Major,
   150th Infantry Brigade.

Copy No.1 Filed.
   2. War Diary.
   3. 4th East Yorks.
   4. 4th Yorks Regt.
   5. 5th Yorks Regt.
   6. 5th Durham L.I.
   7. 150th M.G.Coy.
   8. 150th T. M.Bty.
   9. 149th Inf.Brigade.
   10. 151st Inf.Brigade.
   11. 50th Division "G".
   12. 50th Division "Q".
   13. Bde.Transport Officer.
   14. Bde.Signalling Officer.
   15. Staff Captain.

VOLUME No. 9.

WAR DIARY of 150 MACHINE GUN COMPANY Army Form C. 2118.
for the Month of **OCTOBER**

INTELLIGENCE SUMMARY

Vol 9

Place	Date	Hour	Summary of Events and Information	Remarks and references to Appendices
In Reserve in MAMETZ WOOD.	1st		151 Inf. Brigade attacked the FLERS LINE 150 Inf. Brigade being in reserve. Took Bn in CLARKE'S TRENCH. Two sections of this Company were attached to the Infantry No 1 & 4 E.YORK. Regt. No 2 to 4 YORK.APP. & DUKES Regt. Very wet rainy night. An attack was a success these sections were not required.	G.R.P. 1 and 2.
In GERMAN DEEP DUGOUTS.	2nd		Very cold rainy day. Nos 1 & 2 sections returned from CLARKE'S TRENCH. Remnants of this Company being relieved tomorrow.	G.R.P.
BILLETS in ALBERT.	3rd		Packed limber and Company marched to BILLETS in ALBERT. Transport all moved to FRICOURT. Ball transport lines, as gun limbers had been up at MAMETZ Wood. Rainy day	P.B.Q.
BAIZIEUX.	4th		Company left ALBERT at 9 a.m. and marched to BAIZIEUX via MILLENCOURT. Transport follows Rainy day to start fairs up later. Men in tents. Bivvie Shelters. Officers in Billets. Everything muddy.	G.B.A.
Camp near the WOOD.	5th		Commenced Cleaning - overhauling guns & gear. Company Paid out in the afternoon.	G.B.P.
	6th		Washed limbers, issued Clothing & Spare Parts etc.	G.R.P.
	7th		Brigadier General inspected Transport this morning	G.B.Q.
	8th		Men went to BAIZIEUX for Bath. Church Parade in afternoon. Wet morning.	G.B.Q.
	9th		Company Parade. Cloudy day but no rain.	G.B.Q.
	14th		LT. ROSE left for GRANTHAM amidst general regret. Parades & Lectures.	G.B.Q.
	15th		Church Parade in morning. At night - Sunday practised marching on bearings making a night attack. Very good exercise	G.M.P.
	16.		Company went to Bath in BAIZIEUX in morning. Paid out in the afternoon.	G.B.Q.
	18.		Wet morning. Officers reconnoitred ground for Brigade outpost Scheme in afternoon.	G.B.Q.
	19.		Very wet morning. Brigade outpost scheme which should have taken place in the morning was postponed till the afternoon which although cold & windy was fine	G.R.P.

VOLUME 9. (ii).

WAR DIARY of 150 MACHINE GUN COMPANY
INTELLIGENCE SUMMARY
for the Month of OCTOBER

Army Form C. 2118.

(Erase heading not required.)

Place	Date	Hour	Summary of Events and Information	Remarks and references to Appendices
In Camp at BAZIEUX WOOD.	20th		Fine bright day. Usual Parade in the Morning. 1st Lt A.E. COMMINS arriving just in time from M.G. Base Depot.	9.30 P.
	21st		Usual Parades	9.30.
	22nd		Brigade Commandant Inspection at 10 a.m. Divisional Inspection at 10.30 A.M Company Church Parade at 11 A.M. 2nd Lt. A.H. MORRISON arrived from M.G. Base Depot.	B.P.
BILLETS in MILLENCOURT.	23rd		Company packed civilians and moved to MILLENCOURT where they were billeted in the Village	9.30 P.
BAZENTIN LE GRAND.	24th		Left MILLENCOURT at 1 pm for BAZENTIN LE GRAND via LA BOISELLE & CONTALMAISON. Latter part of march much impeded by very large quantity of traffic on the road. No accommodation except the shell torn huts in wing shelters which were lit of the wire was in most difficult to do	9.30.
In Trenches near LA BUTTE de WARLENCOURT	25th		Two Sections Nos 1 & 2 moved up to Trenches in early morning & relieved 27th Company Machine Gun Corps. Still day. Two casualties wounded, a cook killed.	9.30
	26th		No 3 section moved up to trenches leaving at 2.30 A.M & went to Company H.Q. in support. One man killed today. No 4 section moved up to M9 17 at 2.3 & is in support.	9.30.
	27th		Moved Company Headquarters this morning to the QUARRY. Rifle & Lewis Gun Groupings as follows: Rifle Group No 1 Sunken Rd. a Butler for 57d S.W. M. 28 a. 8.5 MG Rd. Gun now in position on each Snug Dugout. Four for which there Mill Two one officer Smyt Trench & the Hoops one eagl. Change Trench two. Headquarters at Seven Elms Farm.	9.30.
	28th		Remainder of Hill Boxes sent up today and distributed to teams. Enemy shelled heavily in the evening. No casualties	9.30.
	29th		Rained a good amount of promiscuous shelling. No casualties	
	30th		Attack a Tempt to retake Butte wounded till 9am. At Kenyon rain in the afternoon again a bit of shelling	9.30.
	31st		Fine day. 4am HB great walls [?] trench & Kitchen Trench & Kitchen Road Bayonet wire opened fire on Road but men seattered. Q Headquarters M.G. C.P. at 2.30 Could not see if casualties produced but men scattered. 9. Gordon Y.C. Lt. 1/5 G.H. Sergt.

SECRET.

APPENDIX I.   Copy No. 7

150TH INFANTRY BRIGADE OPERATION ORDER NO.48.

150 Coy. M.G. Corps
WAR DIARY.

30th September 1916.

1. The 50th Division is going to attack on the 1st October the two lines of trenches between M. 22. b. 3. 4. and M. 21. b. 8. 4.

    The 47th Division is to prolong the attack to the right & the 23rd Division to the left.

2. The 151st Infantry Brigade is to lead the attack, the 149th Infantry Brigade in Support and 150th Infantry Brigade in Reserve.

3. Zero hour will be 3.15 p.m.

4. Artillery programme attached.

5. The units of 150th Infantry Brigade will be distributed as follows, time to be notified later :-

    4th East Yorks.)   CLARKS - SWANSEA TRENCH - NEW INTERMEDIATE
    4th Yorks.Regt.)   LINE.   4th East Yorks. on right, 4th Yorks.
)   on left - Each with headquarters in CLARKS
)   TRENCH.
    5th Yorks.Regt.)   O. G. 1 right.
    5th Durham L.I.)   O. G. 1 Left.
    150th M. G. Coy.)   Special orders to be issued later.
    150th T.M. Bty.)

6. "D" Divisional Dump is to be established at the end of the Tramline about M. 34. b. 0. 6.

    An R. E. Dump will also be established at about M. 34. b. 0. 6.(Close to PRUE COPSE).

7. Every man to be in fighting order complete and in possession of a YELLOW FLARE.

8. A. D. of M. S. will arrange for an Advanced Dressing Station at M. 27. b. 7. 2. on the main MARTINPUICH ROAD near CRESCENT ALLEY.

                                    John C Boys
                                    Captain,
                        Brigade Major, 150th Infantry Brigade.

Copy.No.1. Filed.   7. 150th M.G.Coy.
       2. War Diary   8. 150th T.M.Bty.   13. 149th Inf
       3. 4th East Yorks.   9. Brigade Sig.Officer.   14. 151st "
       4. 4th Yorks.   10. Brigade Transport Officer.
       5. 5th Yorks.   11. 50th Division.G.
       6. 5th Durham L.I.   12. 50th Division Q.

ARTILLERY PROGRAMME.

1. The Artillery will begin deliberate bombardment of the objectives at 7.0 a.m. 1st October.

    The Infantry will advance to the attack at Zero, at which hour the Artillery Barrage will begin.

2. This barrage will begin fifty yards short of the German front line, and will rake back at "Plus Two Minutes" on to the German front line.

3. The Barrage will lift off the German front line at "Plus four minutes" and will establish itself one hundred and fifty yards beyond an East and West Line drawn through M. 22. b. 5½. 4½.

4. At "Plus Thirty Minutes" the barrage will lift clear of the line M.23.a.6.7. - M. 23.a.2.8. - M.22.b.4½.8. - M.16.c.1.3½. - M.15.d.7.8.

    At this hour the 47th Division will push forward to the German trenches in M.23.a.2.8. and 50th Division to the work in M. 22. a. 8. 8.

5. The 23rd Division will push forward strong patrols into LE SARS and to the QUARRY in M. 15. d. 7. 8.

6. At "Plus one hour and thirty minutes" the artillery will lift on to the line of trenches running North West from the BUTTE DE WARLENCOURT, and patrols will be pushed forward by 50th and 23rd Divisions due North; and an outpost line will be formed on the line M. 23.a.2.8. - M.16.a.9.1. - Round the Village of LE SARS - QUARRY in M.15.d.7.8.

7. A Contact Patrol will fly over the objective from Zero onward. YELLOW FLARES will be shewn when called for at Four p.m., Five p.m. and Six P.M. on 1st October.

8. All ground gained must be consolidated at once. The main line of resistance being from M.23.central - trenches in vicinity of M.23.a.2½.5. - round the Hill - thence to FLERS Line.

ZERO HR. GREENWICH 2-15

****

SECRET
BM 557

O.C.

150th Machine Gun Coy.

With reference to Operation Order No.48 para. 5.

All Units will be in position by 1 p.m. 1st October.

The 4th East Yorks and 4th Yorks Regt marching to CLARKS and SWANSEA TRENCH by the following route, 4th Yorks leading:-

> Along road running through S.13.b. and S.14.a & b. thence Northward to the Cemetery then by path through S.8.b., S.9.a, S.3.c, to CLARKS and SWANSEA TRENCH.

100 yards interval between platoons and Companies.
200 " " " Battalions.

After arrival at their destination troops are forbidden to move in the open before the operations commence.

It is important that no observation of the above movement should be known to the enemy.

Captain,
Brigade Major,
150th Infantry Brigade.

Headquarters,
150th Infantry Brigade.
30th September, 1916.

BM/48

SECRET.

O.C.

150th Machine Gun Coy.

Reference Artillery programme issued with 150th Infantry Brigade Operation Order No.48.

1. Para 4 will be amended to read :-

"4." At "Plus thirty minutes" the Barrage will lift "clear of the line M.22.b.4½.8. - M.16.c.1.3½. - "M.15.d.7.8.

"At this hour the 50th Division will push "forward to the work in M.22.a.8.8. and the 23rd "Division will push forward strong patrols into "LE SARS and the Quarry in M.15.d.7.8."

2. At the end of para.3 add :-
"Eastward of point M.22.b.5½.4½. the Barrage will "lift on to a line one hundred and fifty yards "beyond the FLERS SUPPORT LINE and then rake back "at the rate of thirty yards a minute to a line one "hundred and fifty yards beyond the green line".

Captain,
Brigade Major,
150th Infantry Brigade.

Headquarters,
150th Infantry Brigade.
30th September, 1916.

"A" Form.
MESSAGES AND SIGNALS.

Army Form C.2121 (in pads of 100).
No. of Message

| TO | L.H |

Sender's Number.	Day of Month.	In reply to Number.	
*BM563	1		AAA

Please detail a section of M.G. Coy to report to O.C. IR and a section to report to O.C. DF in Clarks trench at 1pm today aaa Addressed LH repeated IR and DF

From CE
Place
Time 9.10am

APPENDIX II WAR DIARY.

SECRET

Operation Order No 51   Copy No 11

Ref. French Map 1/10000

(1.) 50th Div. will attack the FLERS line & support from M.22.b.3.4. to M.21.b.8.4. inclusive.
The 47th Div will prolong the attack on the right and the 23rd Div on the left.

(2.) The 151st Inf. Bde. will lead the attack
149th " in support.
150th " in reserve.

(3.) Zero hour will be 3-15 P.M. (note Summer time ends Oct. 1st when clocks will be put back at 1 A.M.)

(4.) Dispositions of Battalions as follows:—
4th East Yorks & 4th Yorks
in CLARKS, SWANSEA & new INTERMEDIATE trench
4th East Yorks on Right. Batn H.Q. in CLARKS TRENCH.
5th Yorks & 5th D.L. Inf. in O.G. line.
150th M. Gun Coy. ½0 at present, limbered up and ready to move off in fighting order.

(5.) D. Dump (S.A.A. etc) end of tram line,
M.34.c.o.6. (near PROVE COPSE)

(6.) Section Officers will read and initial Artillery programme.

(7.) In the event of guns being ordered forward it is probable that one section would be attached to each 4th East Yorks and 4th Yorks Reg.
Nos 1 and 2 Sections would be detailed for this purpose. They would move via road with limbers to CARDIFF DUMP and there report to Battalion H.Qrs.

Page (2) Op. 51.

The attached carrying party would be distributed half to each section.

Composition of teams would be as for operations on the 15th Sept. 1916. Section Comdrs would have their limbers on Road at the end of RUTHERFORD ALLEY to form their dumps, leaving a N.C.O. and four other Ranks in charge of each limber & maintaining communication via it.

Guns would be carried in the canvas gun cases issued.

(8.) Yellow flares will be carried by each man instead of red flares.

(9) Coy. H.Q. will be as at present.

NOTES.

(1.) There is a tramway up to PRUE COPSE commencing at end of RUTHERFORD ALLEY. Latter C.T. is now continued up to QUARRY. M.22.d.3.1. MARTIN'S ALLEY might be useful.

(2.) The Div front has inclined left, its left end resting on South end of LE SARS. Right being the MARTINPUICH — WARLENCOURT ROAD.

(3) The country in front of over the final objective will be covered by our own outposts, as there are no other known German trenches for about a mile excepting S.P's.

Routine Orders for October 1st 1917

(1) O/Off. 2/Lt. C.H. Rose.   O/Sgt.
(2) Breakfast. 8 A.M.
    Dinners   1 P.M.
    All surplus food carried in mess tin.
10 A.M. Parade in fighting order ready to move if required. Guns will be inspected by Section Comdrs and Sections will then dismiss stand by.

Copies 1 to 9 S.O's
       10 150th Bde.
       11 Diary
       12 File.

Matthews D. Major
Comdg. 150th M. Gun Coy.

VOL. 10. NOVEMBER 1916.

WAR DIARY of S./150 COY. MACHINE GUN CORPS Army Form C. 2118.
INTELLIGENCE SUMMARY 50TH DIVISION.

Vol 10

Place	Date	Hour	Summary of Events and Information	Remarks and references to Appendices
In Trenches in front of BUTTE de WARLENCOURT	1st		Fairly quiet day as regards shelling. 1 direct hit by Whizzbang on Coy. H.Q. Rained in morning but cleared up & observation of Enemy working on GREVILLERS line too far away for the strafe of m.g.	C.M.G.O. appendix 1
	2nd		Attack on GIRD LINE postponed from yesterday. 151 Bde ordered for today but countermanded on account of the ground. Two 3rd Army relieved by 151 Bdy M.G. Coy. Two divisions a mile pulled while getting the limber loaded.	G.B.P. appendix 2
Bn. encampment MAMETZ WOOD	4th		Cold wet day. Spent cleaning guns & men.	G.B.P.
	5th		Fine cold day. 151 Inf. Brigade made attack on the BUTTE de WARLENCOURT, were held up by M.G. fire. Finally withdrew to original front line.	G.B.P.
Bn trenches as before	6th		This Company relieved 151 Coy in trenches as before. Quiet relief no casualties.	G.B.P.
	7th		Fine bright day. Great aerial activity. Casualties in the company. One wounded accidentally. A good deal of promiscuous shelling of the back area. 1 Communication down to transport lines.	G.B.P.
	8th		Another clear day. One enemy aeroplane brought down near transport lines. Heavy shelling of supports & trenches. & at night both sides put up barrage. Casualties 2 killed & 3 wounded.	G.B.P.
	9th		Duller day. Lt. COMMINS relieved Lt CARPENTER who returned Lt TYLOR who came down to transport lines 1 man wounded	G.B.P.
	10th		Various officers of 149 Inf. Coy & the O/C. 2. Coy. M.G. Corps came round to see the line & make arrangements for relief. No casualties	G.B.P. appendix 5
	11		This Coy relieved by the 149 Coy and took over their camp on relief. Two sections remained in the FLERS Line in support to the 149. One man wounded	G.B.P. Appendix 4
In Camp near BAZENTIN LE GRAND	12		Dull Day. Rev A. C. McANLEY C. F attacked this Coy left to join 60th Division. Received cuddle hints of without turnout but up by artillery.	G.B.P.
	13.		Four guns under Lt DADD went up to HEXHAM ROAD to be in support to attack tomorrow before midnight.	G.B.P.
	14.		149 Inf. Brigade attacked this morning. Result not known & prisoners taken. CAPT. BIRLIS to report 56th Coy. ordered received tonight for Duty as O/C	G.B.P.

WAR DIARY of 150 Coy MACHINE GUN CORPS 50th DIVISION

INTELLIGENCE SUMMARY

VOL. 10 NOVEMBER 1916.

Army Form C. 2118.

(Erase heading not required.)

Instructions regarding War Diaries and Intelligence Summaries are contained in F.S. Regs., Part II. and the Staff Manual respectively. Title Pages will be prepared in manuscript.

Place	Date	Hour	Summary of Events and Information	Remarks and references to Appendices
	15		Two guns sent up to bring trench from Hessian Rd to replace two of the 149 Bde guns. Two men wounded	RLhn
	16		Lt Higinson relieved Lt Badel at Hessian Rd. By Bristol trap went the four guns in & two left & removed went to & came right. One gun knocked out in duty trench. Transport lines shelled at night & one light draught horse killed. No casualties	RLhn
	17		1st Batt relieved 12 guns in line. Transport lines shelled at night and killed two mules & wounded eleven. No casualties	RLhn
Becourt Camp	18		Company moved to Becourt Wood Huts	RLhn
"	19 to 25		Major Thorpe proceeded on leave 15.4.15 - 24.11.16. Elementary machine work & general cleaning	RLhn
"	26		Elementary Training & cleaning	RAAT
"	27		Training & cleaning. Lt THOMAS from the 144 Coy, arrived to take over 2nd in command to this company	RAAT
	28 to 29		Training	RAAT
	30		Large working party: getting ready for move to CONTAY & VADENCOURT	RAAT

M Connell
for OC 150 MG Coy

War Diary. 150 M.G. Coy
appendix I

SECRET.
==========

Copy No. 7

150TH INFANTRY BRIGADE OPERATION ORDER NO.55.

Ref.Trench Map
LE SARS. Sheet
1/10,000.

1st November, 1916.

1. The following reliefs will take place to-night:-

    (a) 4th Yorks will relieve 4th East Yorks in right Sector.

    (b) 5th Yorks will relieve 5th Durham L.I.in Left Sector.

2. After relief the Brigade, with a view to the future, will be distributed as follows :-

    4th East Yorks. - 3 Coy's. STARFISH, 1 PRUE, Headquarters STARFISH.

    5th Durham L.I. - 2 Coy's PRUE, 2 FLERS LINE, Headquarters FLERS LINE.

    4th Yorks Regt. - 1 Coy.SNAG & MAXWELL. 1 Coy.FLERS LINE.
    2 Coy's FLERS SWITCH. H.Qrs.M.22.d.7.0.

    5th Yorks Regt. - 1 Coy.SNAG & MAXWELL. 1 Coy.**MILL AREA**.
    2 Coy's.FLERS SWITCH. H.Q.,M.22.d.4.1.

3. The Brigadier General Commanding hopes that every effort will be made to-morrow to lie low and avoid shewing the enemy the larger numbers in our trenches.

4. The following times are allotted in the forward area for reliefs :-

    Right Sector .... 6 p.m. to 11 p.m.

    Left Sector ....11 p.m.-to 4 a.m.

    To save congestion the 4th Yorks will relieve the three rear Companies of 4th East Yorks by daylight before 6 p.m.

5. Relieving Battalions will arrange among themselves for the handing over of Stores, e.g. - Lewis Gun drums, tools etc, as far as possible to save carriage.

6. Reliefs to be reported when complete.

7. ACKNOWLEDGE.

Captain,
Brigade Major,
150th Infantry Brigade.

```
Copy No. 1  Filed.
        2.  War Diary.
        3.  4th East Yorks.
        4.  4th Yorks Regt.
        5.  5th Yorks Regt.
        6.  5th Durham L.I.
        7.  150th M.G.Coy.
        8.  150th T.M.Bty.
        9.  44th Inf.Brigade.
       10.  149th Inf.Brigade.
       11.  7th Durham L.I.
       12.  50th Division "G".
       13.  50th Division "Q".
       14.  Staff Captain.
       15.  Brigade Transport Officer.
       16.  Brigade Signalling Officer.
       17.  Brigade Dump Officer.
       18.  Spare.
       19.   "
       20.   "
```

ADDENDUM TO OPERATION ORDER NO.55 DATED 1ST NOVEMBER, 1916.

SHEWING POSITION OF BATTALIONS AFTER RELIEF.

| 1 Coy. 5th Yorks. | 1 Coy. 4th Yorks. | .... | .... | Front System. |

| 1 Company. 5th Yorks. | .... | .... | .... | MILL AREA. |

| 2 Coy's. 5th D.L.I. | 1 Coy. 4th Yorks. | .... | .... | FLERS LINE. |

| 2 Coy's. 5th Yorks. | 2 Coy's. 4th Yorks. | .... | .... | FLERS SWITCH. |

| 2 Coy's. 5th D.L.I. | 1 Coy. 4th East Yorks. | .... | .... | PRUE. |

| 3 Companies. 4th East Yorks. | .... | .... | .... | STARFISH. |

War Diary. Appendix II Nov 2-1916.

Relief Orders for 3/4 Nov. 1916.

(1) Coy. will be relieved by 10 guns of 151st M.G. Coy. on the night of 3/4 inst.

(2) The relieving Coy. will be disposed as follows & will take over following Belts & tripods:—

Position	Guns brought in	Belts taken over	Tripods taken over	Officer	Remarks
H.Q.	NIL	NIL	NIL	O/C. Coy.	Tripods in position will be left in position.
MILL	ONE	16	ONE (spare)	NIL	
SNAG. DUG OUT	FOUR	80	FOUR	ONE	
SNAG. TRENCH	TWO	16	TWO	NIL	
Dug out on road East end of SNAG	NIL	8	NIL	NIL	
PIMPLE	TWO	20	TWO	ONE	
LEFT S.P.	ONE	8	ONE	NIL	

It will be seen that six Tripods will be brought out, 4 at Coy. H.Q. 1 from Mill and 1 from dugout at end of SNAG Tr.

(3) Officers will wire to Coy. H.Qrs. by 9 P.M. that they are able to hand over all full belt boxes as in (2) and also the numbers of the Tripods to be handed over. Empty Belt Boxes will be brought out including all German boxes in possession.

(4) Any man who should be in possession of a Rifle coming out of the trenches without will be required to pay the value of a rifle. This also applies to Steel Helmets and waterproof Sheets. Fighting stores (Bombs etc.) will be handed over. A signature will be obtained from the Off. or N.C.O. for all stores handed over.

(5) The Coy. S.M. will ensure that all gear is at Coy. H.Q. by 2 P.M. from the old H.Qrs. & that the leather cases are ready for carrying guns on the limbers. Any gun cases in trenches will be brought out. Any Team not having a gun-case will carry its gun back to Camp.

(6) Guides will be ready at Coy. H.Q. for relieving teams at 5 P.M. and relieved teams will report to Coy. H.Qrs. to the C.S.M. for orders as to loading guns, etc. on to limbers, and will then proceed under their Officers to Coy. Transport Lines and pick up guides for Camp.

(7) Paper trench maps & Tables of Indirect fire will be handed over.

(8) Officers & NCOs in charge of positions will report completion of relief to O/C. Coy. at Coy. H.Qrs.

H.M.R Sharp Major
Comdg. 150th M.G. Coy.

No. 380/1 **WAR Diary**
Appendisc 3.
2/Lt MORRISON
SNAG d.o.

1. Your 2 guns in MAXWELL
Tr. will be relieved tomorrow
a.m. by 2 guns & teams of
149 M.G. Coy.

2. The relieving teams will arrive
at SNAG d.o. about 5.0 p——
where you will have one
guide & per gun ~~~~~~~~
or take death in yourself.

3. Hand over all belts also
tripods, bring out spare
parts & guns only

4. After relief you will proceed
to 57 HQ & pack guns on
limber & return with teams
to Transport lines, reporting
to Capt PURVIS.

5. Gun boots & blankets will be
handed over & a receipt ob——

RS 360/2.

2/Lt Turvey } } may do.

Packet Orders

1. You will be relieved by 4 teams of 149 Coy about 5.0 tomorrow 11th.

2. See 3 + 5 of RS 360/1 to MORRISON.

3. On relief you will bring out teams with guns & spare parts, report to Coy HQ where a guide will take the teams under 2/Lt MOON to reserve position in FLERS line.

4. You will proceed to Transport lines.

5. Acknowledge.

HQ 6.30 p. 10/11

D Matthews
Major

tained for them.

b) Acknowledge by wire (or orderly)

DM Sharp
maj

HQ 6.30 p 10 ¼/6

R 360/3

2/Lt PADD (Ample)

1. You will be relieved by 3 teams of M.G. Bay dt about 5 pm tomorrow 11th

2. You will hand over buffoes, belts, gum boots + blankets + obtain a receipt for same from relieving officer

3. On relief teams will bring guns + spare parts to Bay HQ where they will meet a guide for reserve position nr FLERS. & will proceed there under 2/Lt COMMINS.

4. You will proceed to Transport lines

5. Acknowledge.

6. You must give relieving officer all possible information re your flank (48th Div) guns.

H 6.30 pm 10/16   D Russhay

BS 360/4

Sgt BROWN
          M.G.

1. You will be relieved about
5 pm tomorrow 11th by a
team of 149 M.G. Coy.

2. You will hand over belts &
tripod, obtain a signature
for same.

3. On relief you will bring
the team with gun &
spare parts to Bat HQ
where it will proceed to
a reserve position in FLERS
line under 21st Coy MGS.

4. You will go to Transport
lines after handing your
team over as in 3.

5. Acknowledge.

                    E Nesshorp
                         Major
HQ 6.30 pm 10/11/16

2/Lt COMMINS.

Relief Orders

1. 7 Guns will be relieved by 5 skeleton teams of 14 & 149 Coy between 7 & 10 a.m. on 11th. No jumbles required. You will on relief send 4 men to Coy HQ to carry out the 2 guns spare parts care (at Coy HQ) & then send all the men from 7 teams to Transport lines, clean up guns, put them away, reporting to Capt PURVIS

2. You will remain yourself at Coy HQ to take up to present position same night.

3. Acknowledge. — D.M.Sharp Maj

AQ 6. 10 p.
10.11
16

BS 359

2/Lt Carpenter

1. Placing guns in advanced posts — This will be done under direction from 4 Yks. Coy. Cmdr. with whom you must keep in touch.

2. Relief.

You will have 1 guide per gun at HEXHAM RD end of PIONEER ALLEY (near Batt HQ) at 1 p.m. tomorrow. You relief by 147 MG Coy.

You will bring out guns & all belts you can, except the clean ones you took up with.

You will then come to Coy HQ (leave men in CRESCENT ALLEY near HQ)

& exchange your tools for
new ones tools, & take
our spare parts to work
lines.

P. M. Sharp
Maj.
Comdg 150 M.G. By

Appendix 4.   COPY NO. 4

150TH INFANTRY BRIGADE OPERATION ORDER NO.60.

1. The 149th Infantry Brigade will relieve the 150th Infantry Brigade on night of 11/12th November 1916, with advanced Brigade Headquarters at SEVEN ELMS.

2. 150th Infantry Brigade will remain in support of 149th Infantry Brigade. 151st Infantry Brigade will be in Reserve.

3. The relief will be carried out in accordance with attached table by arrangements between C.O's concerned.

The advanced posts will be relieved by special arrangement before moonrise, incoming Battalions sending on their parties to Battalion Headquarters at 6 p.m. Greatest care to be taken in this relief.

4. Machine Gun Coy. will leave 2 sections at disposal of 149th Infantry Brigade.

5. Command of Sector will pass at 8 a.m. 12th instant to B.G.C. 149th Infantry Brigade.

6. Primus Stoves will be brought away by Units.

Gum Boots will be handed over and receipts obtained and forwarded to Brigade Headquarters.

7. Reliefs to be reported to Brigade Headquarters, SEVEN ELMS

8. Acknowledge.

Captain,
Brigade Major,
150th Infantry Brigade.

Copy No. 1. Filed.
"   "   2. War Diary.
"   "   3. 4th East Yorks.
"   "   4. 4th Yorks.
"   "   5. 5th Yorks.
"   "   6. 5th Durham L.I.
"   "   7. 150th Machine Gun Coy.
"   "   8. 150th Trench Mortar Battery.
"   "   9. 50th Division "G".
"   " 10. 50th Division "Q".
"   " 11. 149th Infantry Brigade.
"   " 12. 151st Infantry Brigade.
"   " 13. Brigade Transport Officer.
"   " 14. Brigade Signalling Officer.
"   " 15. Staff Captain.
"   " 16. Brigade Dump Officer.
"   " 17. 5th Australian Infantry Brigade.
"   " 18. 143rd Infantry Brigade.
"   " 19. Spare.
"   " 20.   "

TABLE of MOVES.

	Relieved in trenches by	Go to Camp at	And take over a camp from	Time of Relief in trenches	Remarks.
4th E.Yks.	5th N.F. Major Wright	New Huts S. 9. d.	6th N.F.	Day 11th Novbr. by 4 p.m.	No guides.
4th Yks.	4th N.F. Col. Gibson	High Wood.	5th N.F.	12 Midnight to 5 a.m. 12th Novbr.	Guides as arranged between C.Os.
5th Yks.	6th N.F. Major Temperley	Prue & Starfish	7th N.F.	8 pm to 12 midnight 11th Novbr.	Guides at Seven Elms 8 p.m. 11th inst. to meet 6th N.F. - 4 Officers and 16 other ranks.
5th D.L.I.	7th N.F. Colonel Jackson	BAZENTIN LE GRAND	4th N.F.	Day 11th Novbr. by 4 p.m.	No guides.
M.G.Coy.	M.G.Coy. 149th Bde.	BAZENTIN	M.G.Coy. 149th	11th/12th Novbr.	Leaves 2 sections in support of 149th Brigade as at present distributed.
T.M.Bty.	T.M.Bty. 149th.				
Bde.H.Q. "G"	"G" 149th	BAZENTIN	G. 149th	8 a.m. 12th Novbr.	
"Q"	Stands fast at BAZENTIN.				

Army Form C. 2118.

150 M.Gun Coy.

WAR DIARY
INTELLIGENCE SUMMARY
(Erase heading not required.)

CONFIDENTIAL
December 1916
Vol XI

Place	Date	Hour	Summary of Events and Information	Remarks and references to Appendices
VADENCOURT	1-12-16	7·0 PM	The Company left hutments at Bécourt at 9·0 am and proceeded to Vadencourt	
			Arrived noon took over billets	
	2.12.16		Arranging billets & settling down	
	3 & 5		Coy Training & Sports	
	6.12.16		Lt. C. Wood with 5 other ranks proceeded on leave to UK (10 days) Coy Training & Sports	
	7/8/9		Coy Training & Sports	
	10th		4 Transport reinforcements arrived Coy Training & Sports	
	11.4		14 M Gun Reinforcements arrived Coy Training & Sports	
	12.4		Lt Turing Proceeded on leave to UK (10 days) Coy Training & Sports	
	13.4		6 other ranks proceeded on leave to UK Coy Bathed	
	14."		Coy training and relosliver practice	
	15."		Coy Training. Anti-Aircraft gun of 92 gun Anti-Aircraft Btry arrived at Authie &c for use of this Coy	
Sports at Authie 021C4·3	16th		7 men joined this Coy from the infantry for transfer to M.G.Coys CONTAY	
	17th		Church Parade. 2nd Lt CARPENTER proceeded on leave to UK (10 days) & other ranks " "	
	18th		Major Sharp returned from leave. 6 mules arrived completing establishment	
	19		Coy Training & Sports. 6 M.G. reinforcements arrived	
	20		Coy Training & Sports	

R. Turing 2nd Lt
i/c Coy
150 M.G.C

Army Form C. 2118.

WAR DIARY
or
INTELLIGENCE SUMMARY

(Erase heading not required.)

150 M.Gun Coy.

Vol. XI

CONFIDENTIAL

Place	Date	Hour	Summary of Events and Information	Remarks and references to Appendices
VADENCOURT	21		Coy. Training & Sports	RAFT
	22		Coy. Training & Sports	RAFT
	23		Coy. Training & Sports	RAFT
	24		Church Parade	RAFT
	25		Christmas festivities: concert & dinner	RAFT
	26		Training: Lt THOMAS & 5 O.R. proceeded on leave to U.K	RAFT
	27		Coy. Training	RAFT
	28		Coy. Training Lt TURING returned from leave	RAFT
	29		Coy. Training	RAFT
	30		Coy. handed over to 144 M.G. Coy & proceeded to N°1 camp MILLENCOURT. Lt DADD & 4 O.R proceeded on leave to UK. Anti aircraft guns at CONTAY taken over by 144 M.G. Coy.	} RAFT
	31		Church Parade: Coy proceeded to MAMETZ WOOD & took over camp at X.23.D 5.8. from 3rd M.G. Coy.	RAFT

R. Turing Lt
150 M.G. Coy.

WAR DIARY OF THE 150th M.Gun. Coy.

INTELLIGENCE SUMMARY

Army Form C. 2118.

VOL. XII CONFIDENTIAL

(Erase heading not required.)

Place	Date	Hour	Summary of Events and Information	Remarks and references to Appendices
Bazencourt	1/4/17		Settling down in new camp	
"	2/4/17		R.E. Working parties on roads & infantry camp	
"	3/4/17		2 Lt. Ly Con. and 3 O.R. proceeded on leave to U.K.	
"	4/4/17		R.E. Working parties	
"	5/4/17		" "	
"	6/4/17		149 Inf. Bgd. Coy relieved in the line by 3rd Coy	
"	7/4/17		& proceeded to join the Coy	
"	8/4/17		H.Q. Coy transferred to 2nd Bn 6/L.F.	
"	9/4/17		Working parties for men out of the line	
"	10/4/17		Coy moved to High Wood camp (last) in da decent camp	
"	11/4/17		Coy in line Wickney and Bazen ? relieving 149 M.G. Coy	
High Wood	12/4/17		" "	
"	13/4/17		" "	
"	14/4/17		Coy relieved in the line by 149 Coy	
"	15/4/17		Cleaning up men and guns in huts by entire	
"	16/4/17		Repairing huts and clearing up	
"	17/4/17		Working parties for 149 M.G. Coy	
"	18/4/17		" "	
"	19/4/17		" "	
"	20/4/17		Coy relieved 149 M.G. Coy	
"	21/4/17		Coy H.Q. established in the line	
"	22/4/17		Coy transferred to boundary street M Hudson Post Division	
"	23/4/17		Relieved by 1st Australian M.G. Coy	
"	24/4/17		" "	
Bazencourt	27/4/17		Coy returned to Bazencourt camp	

Army Form C. 2118.

WAR DIARY OF THE 150th M.GUN. Coy.
or
INTELLIGENCE SUMMARY
VOL. XII   CONFIDENTIAL

(Erase heading not required.)

Instructions regarding War Diaries and Intelligence Summaries are contained in F.S. Regs., Part II. and the Staff Manual respectively. Title Pages will be prepared in manuscript.

Place	Date	Hour	Summary of Events and Information	Remarks and references to Appendices
Harcourt	28/1/17		Settling down in camp	A. 1
"	29/1/17		Church Parade	A. 2
"			Cleaning of guns and equipment	A. 3
Buire	30/1/17		Company moved to Buire	
"	31/1/17		Settling down in billets, drying guns & gear and checking deficiencies	

Lt Col
150 M Gun Coy

CONFIDENTIAL
Army Form C. 2118.

WAR DIARY of 150th M.G. Company.

INTELLIGENCE SUMMARY Vol: 13. For Month of February 1917.

(Erase heading not required.)

Instructions regarding War Diaries and Intelligence Summaries are contained in F.S. Regs., Part II. and the Staff Manual respectively. Title Pages will be prepared in manuscript.

Vol 13

Place	Date	Hour	Summary of Events and Information	Remarks and references to Appendices
Buire Sur l'Ancre	1st	PM 10:30	Very cold – Training in morning football in afternoon – Limbers cleaned and oiled	
	2nd	" "	" " Inspection by B.G.C. Route march all day	
	3 "		Training and re-equipping men overhauling guns & equipment	
	4 "		Lt Thomas left to Camiers Course with 2 O.R. Coy Batted at Buire – 2 men returned from leave. Sgt Anderson left for England to Cadet school	
	6		Played 149 M.G. Coy at football. Draft of 4 Transport men arrived from Base – 3 men returned from leave	
	7		Preparing for move to Morcourt. Major Sharp, Lt Morrison, 2 Lt Ramken, 2Lt Cormitt left Coy to recommobilise Munition	
	8		moved from Buire to Morcourt	
Morcourt to Morcourt	9		Lt Hawke arrived, left for Lira, & was proceeding in the line to take over from French	
	10		Remainder of Coy moved in to the line, Enemy quiet 2 men returned from leave	
	11		151 M.G. Coy Fish man hut at Forcourcourt	
	12		1 casualty, slightly wounded by shrapnel – 4 men returned from leave	
	13		Cold inclined to Thaw. Shelling by enemy heavier. Enemy aircraft busy during morning	
	14		Intermittent shelling and wind dangerous. Dump at Barry heavily shelled by 4 air shells. 8 men slightly gased	
	15		Fine day fairly quiet. Light rain fell during night. Hostile artillery active	
	16		Rained fairly heavily all day. Trenches taking in badly and impassable in many places.	
	17		Hostile Artillery very active. Two sections relieved by 151 M.G.Coy during night	
	18		Coy H.Q. moved back to Forcourcourt. Two sections left in line on an Anti aircraft duty	
	19		The two sections out resting and cleaning up. Weather rainy ground very muddy.	
	20			
	21		Major Sharp away reconnoitring new part of line more expected	
	22		orders for move to CAPPY received. Weather very wet. Two o Tun sections turnout of line 6 am	
	23		Move orders cancelled, 2/Lt Thomas returned from Camiers. also 3 OR	
	24		Two Sections moved up to line to relieve 149 M.G.Coy very wet – Trenches impassable	
	25		The Two other sections moved into line to relieve 149 M.G. Coy relief complete 9.0 P.M	
	26		Enemy Artillery quiet. Fine and warm weather. Received orders to dummy attack 13 guns to fire in conjunction with Artillery	
	27		Enemy Quiet – Fine and warm weather	
	28		Weather foggy. Visibility of our positions and light work carried out. Hostile Artillery very active during evening	

8-2-5 2499 Wt. W14957/M90 358823 1/16 J.B.C. & A.J Forms/C2118/12.

CONFIDENTIAL

Army Form C. 2118.

WAR DIARY of 150th MACHINE GUN COY.
INTELLIGENCE SUMMARY
For month of MARCH - 1917
VOL. IA

(Erase heading not required.)

Instructions regarding War Diaries and Intelligence Summaries are contained in F.S. Regs., Part II. and the Staff Manual respectively. Title Pages will be prepared in manuscript.

Place	Date	Hour	Summary of Events and Information	Remarks and references to Appendices
ESTRÉES Cemetery	1/3/17		Misty morning. B.G.C. visited Coy H.Q. Enemy aeroplane bombed our observation balloon and set fire to it.	No 1
"	2/3/17		Foggy morning. Enemy active on the first caved bombs trenches which inspired a Coy movement of enemy men and Troops of an enemy line	No 2
"	3/3/17		Morning clear and bright. 2nd in command and 70 missiles of 48th found a weakness in Coy Coy enemy's artillery	No 3
"	4/3/17		Morning clear. Enemy wire bombed for 5 minutes. We retaliated	No 4
"	5/3/17		Heavy snow. Orders for relief by 177 Coy arrived. Enemy very bad	No 5
"	6/3/17		Reg'd. S.O.S. was seen on our left. A heavy barrage ensued and continued for 15 minutes. Demonstration of a company barrage by our artillery. Enemy retaliated	No 6
"	7/3/17		Cold. Heavy shelling on the left caused by raid on the enemy's line made later relieved by two section of 177 Coy	No 7
"	8/3/17		Remainder of Coy relieved by 177 Coy	No 8
"	9/3/17		Coy moved to Bayonvillers	No 9
Bayonvillers	10/3/17		Coy settled in billets. General cleaning	No 10
"	11/3/17		Clothes & parades. Bow repairs fitted and tried	No 11
"	12/3/17		Inspections by G.O.S. Limbers washed by hail	No 12

CONFIDENTIAL

WAR DIARY of 150th M. Gun Coy

Army Form C. 2118.

for month of MARCH 1917.

VOL. 14.

INTELLIGENCE SUMMARY

(Erase heading not required.)

Instructions regarding War Diaries and Intelligence Summaries are contained in F.S. Regs., Part II. and the Staff Manual respectively. Title Pages will be prepared in manuscript.

Place	Date	Hour	Summary of Events and Information	Remarks and references to Appendices
Bayonvillers	13/3/17		Inspection by C.O. at 11 a.m. Inter-section football in the afternoon	No 1
"	14/3/17		Coy training. Lecture by C.O. & Officers and N.C.O.'s Football Coy v 149 Coy	No 1
"	15/3/17		150 Coy 1 149 Coy 2	No 1
"	15/3/17		Coy training. Numbers for wind	
"	16/3/17		Coy training 2 sections on range. 2 Plt sent to Villers-court at	No 1
"			Cappy. Football 150 Coy 1 151 Coy 0	
"	17/3/17		Coy training. Demonstration by Coy of an indirect barrage	No 1
"	18/3/17		Church parade. Inspection of billets by C.O. Football Coy v	No 1
"			1 last York Coy won 2.0	
"	19/3/17		Coy training. Demonstration with rifle grenades by Lt Field	No 1
"	20/3/17		Route march in full battle order	
"	21/3/17		Coy training. Lecture by 2nd in command. Football Officers	No 1
"			v Sergeants result Officers 3 Sergeants 2	
"	22/3/17		Coy training. Route march. Football Coy v B Coy 5th Fusiliers 1st round	No 1
"			Bde competition 150 Coy 16 Coy 0	
"	23/3/17		Coy training. Lecture on range Football 150 Coy v	No 1
"			5th D.L.I.	

CONFIDENTIAL.
Army Form C. 2118.

WAR DIARY of 150th MACHINE GUN COY.
or
INTELLIGENCE SUMMARY for the month of MARCH 1917

VOLUME 14.

Instructions regarding War Diaries and Intelligence Summaries are contained in F.S. Regs., Part II. and the Staff Manual respectively. Title Pages will be prepared in manuscript.

Place	Date	Hour	Summary of Events and Information	Remarks and references to Appendices
BAYONVILLERS	24/3/17		Coy training. Rifle grenade practice	No.3
"	25/3/17		Church parade. Lecturers time arc./detail	10.3
"	26/3/17		Raining. Coy lectures in billets	18.3
"	27/3/17		Field firing on range in co-operation with infantry	12.3
"	28/3/17		Inspection by III Corps Commander. Bde photographs taken	12.3
"			for 150 Russian regiment. Bde march past cinema graphed	12.3
"	29/3/17		Coy training. Orders for move in 30th received	12.3
"	30/3/17		Coy moved to BUSSY. 6 inefficient men returned to base	12.3
BUSSY	31/3/17		Coy moved to RAINEVILLE	12.

Mulherine Mcmayor
Comdg. 150th M.Gun Coy

150TH MACHINE GUN COMPANY — MACHINE GUN CORPS.

Army Form C. 2118.

WAR DIARY or INTELLIGENCE SUMMARY

Volume No: 15
APRIL 1914.

(Erase heading not required.)

Vol 15

Place	Date	Hour	Summary of Events and Information	Remarks and references to Appendices
RAINEVILLE	1/4/17		Inspections and training	
VICOGNE	2/4/17		Company moved to LAVICOGNE	
BAGNEUX	3/4/17		Company moved to BAGNEUX area DOULLENS	
LIGNY-SUR-CANCHE	4/4/17		Company moved to III army area LIGNY-SUR-CANCHE	
"	5/4/17		Company training	
"	6/4/17		Company training	
HOUVIGNEUL	7/4/17		Company moved to HOUVIN-HOUVIGNEUL	
SARS-LEZ-BOIS	8/4/17		Company moved to SARS-LEZ-BOIS	
"	9/4/17		Company training	
LATRE St QUENTIN	10/4/17		Company moved to LATRE St QUENTIN	
ARRAS	11/4/17		Company moved to ARRAS and were billeted in caves at RONVILLE	
RONVILLE	12 13 14 15 4/17		Company remained in reserve in the caves at RONVILLE	

150th MACHINE GUN COMPANY • MACHINE GUN CORPS.

Army Form C. 2118.

WAR DIARY or INTELLIGENCE SUMMARY

VOLUME No 15. April 1917. Sketch No R.

(Erase heading not required.)

Instructions regarding War Diaries and Intelligence Summaries are contained in F. S. Regs., Part II. and the Staff Manual respectively. Title Pages will be prepared in manuscript.

Place	Date	Hour	Summary of Events and Information	Remarks and references to Appendices
RONVILLE	16/4/17		Company moved from reserve to support of 1st & III section to TILLOY. III & II to WANCOURT. Coy HQ at TILLOY. Transport and Q.M. Stores remained at RONVILLE	
"	17/4/17		CO and 1 section & Transport officer went up to WANCOURT & saw the positions held by no 3 inf. Bde. + were informed at HQ no 9 Inf Bde that the guns were at their disposal from 17th for offensive purposes. Arrangements were made for 2 sections to hold high ground S.W. of WANCOURT. 2 sections to remain in the HARP in reserve. The dispositions were completed by dusk. Weather very stormy. HQ moved to dugouts in HARP (at TILLOY) occupied by 2nd & 1st + 2nd Batns. N.F.	
	18/4/17		Were informed that night 17/18 enemy had retaken WANCOURT TOWER. At 12 noon 21st Battalion N.F. & 2 retook it after a short bombmt. no. 4 & no. 12 guns fire was effective in covering fire + 2 sections the 17th & 18th were busy mopping + dugouts by working of cooling gear of 2 sections. 149 M.G. Coy guns were operated on form very appreciable damage. Were fired from P. guns in rounds. From I very heavy.	

150TH MACHINE GUN COMPANY. WAR DIARY

MACHINE GUN CORPS Army Form C. 2118.

VOLUME No 15
April 1917 Sheet 3.

INTELLIGENCE SUMMARY

Place	Date	Hour	Summary of Events and Information	Remarks and references to Appendices
	19th		Day fairly quiet. Enemy in artillery fire on our front made efforts our front. Casualty Lance Corporal i/c Cluster ranked near HANCOURT.	X7
	20th		Pos. i/c Section ordered to reline 8 Guns 149. M.G. By in positions in and about HANCOURT TOWER N5 & R. COJEUL, and 3 of 4 sections to relieve 2 Sections 149 M.G. By in about high ground S.W. of HANCOURT. HQ moved to HQ 149 M.G.B.	X
	21st		Day used in completing arrangements for attack by VIII Corps expected for 4.45am 23rd. 20 Rnds. brought up to advanced H.Q. of each unit after 8 p.m. to Entree Place N21 A-7. 80 unused stocken in hut shed near detailed to support scheme of 4 Estab. in right & Note in left of Pte. two 3 & 4 Sections in reserve in support. Regt. return ordered to stay in neut. about N21 a SE. great position was recommended by 2/Lt Packer at dusk.	X [?]
	22nd		Find assault points in assault under weather. Time of ground hard & barrel became grass & dump P293. 82 Rnds Eyots. HQ & 3 of 4 Sections of fire which the became burned dump P293. 11.30 in a bad state of very solid, also our aerial activity. Enemy front on of our captured position. 5PO BOWMAN had Harton shot-down a German airplane	G [?]
	23rd		Enemy new on HANCOURT which high tell new MONCHY. Enemy attacked TOWER HILL before drums back our Inf. Enemy Very Proprietary duty gave our troops at 1900 attack consisted at 4.45 a. as flying/ct Pros't. In Pte. Towed would hotly its dropped a Barrager. Pro. BOWMAN has 2 Pvrs. 2/Lt DOMMIN. 5/Lt HALL more 2/L. & 2/Lt TAYLOR, Lt MORRISON & 2/Lt HANSEN morning. Slightly wounded remained at duty. 35 ot. killed wounded & missing or ten being relieved by GOC 75 Inf Bde. Coy took up billets in ARRAS.	[?]
	24th			

150th MACHINE GUN COMPANY

MACHINE GUN CORPS — Army Form C. 2118.

WAR DIARY or INTELLIGENCE SUMMARY

VOLUME No 15 April 1917 Authot

(Erase heading not required.)

Army Form C. 2118.

Instructions regarding War Diaries and Intelligence Summaries are contained in F. S. Regs., Part II. and the Staff Manual respectively. Title Pages will be prepared in manuscript.

Place	Date	Hour	Summary of Events and Information	Remarks and references to Appendices
ARRAS	2 & 5	6.30 p.m	Moved by train from ARRAS to MONDICOURT. Transport by road. Reached billets at GAENAS.	D
GAENAS	26	—	Rested, cleaned guns & gun firmiture & kits.	B
"	27	—	Rested, rest gained.	
"	28 ⎫ 29 ⎬ 30 ⎭		Refitted w for in trouble. No reinforcements received * 1 officer 2/Lt RUSSELL reported having arrived at Div. Reinforcement Camp & been inoculated there by a tent accident	B
GAENAS	+		* 2/Lt JENNER arrived from DOULLENS 9ᵃ	D

WAR DIARY
INTELLIGENCE SUMMARY

150th COMPANY MACHINE GUN CORPS Army Form C. 2118.

MAY 1917. VOLUME No: 16.

Vol 16

Place	Date	Hour	Summary of Events and Information	Remarks and references to Appendices
Evennes	1-5-17		Company moved to Rosignol Farm.	R/hr
Rosignol	2-5-17		Company moved to Blainville. Weather intensely hot.	R/hr
Blainville	3-5-17		Company moved back to Rosignol Farm arriving at 8.30 hr.	R/hr
Rosignol	4-5-17		Company bathed, but no clean clothing.	R/hr
Rosignol	5-5-17		Company moved to Evennes arriving at 8 hr. 2/Lt R. Watson & three Gunners joined the Company.	R/hr
Evennes	6-5-17		Company training	R/hr
Evennes	7-5-17		Two sections on Range, remainder training. Lt T.A.S. Rader joined Company	R/hr
Evennes	8-5-17		Same as for 7-5-17.	R/hr
Evennes	9-5-17		Same as for 8-5-17.	R/hr
Evennes	10-5-17		Company bathed at Hurloy. Inter team competition on range.	R/hr
Evennes	11-5-17		Company training. 2/Lt W.S. Beddall & 2/Lt T.R. Bartlet joined the Company	R/hr
Evennes	12-5-17		Brigade Field & musq scheme.	R/hr
Evennes	13-5-17		Inspection of Company by Brigadier Shute.	R/hr
Evennes	14-5-17		Company training	R/hr
Evennes	15-5-17		Brigade Field & musq scheme. Draft of 33 O/Ranks joined Company.	R/hr
Evennes	16-5-17		Company training.	R/hr

150TH COMPANY. MACHINE GUN CORPS Army Form C. 2118.

WAR DIARY or INTELLIGENCE SUMMARY

MAY 1917.

VOLUME No 6.

Place	Date	Hour	Summary of Events and Information	Remarks and references to Appendices
Evreux	17-5-17		Company moved to Rosignol from St Maurice granted to troops train to Paris.	Rbh.
Rosignol	18-5-17		Company moved to DOUCHY LES AYETTE	Rbh.
Douchy	19-5-17		Company training. Lt Thomas admitted to Hospital. Lt Tyler + 2 ranks departed for Machine Gun School at Camiers.	Rbh.
Douchy	20-5-17		Company training	Rbh.
Douchy	21-5-17		Brigade Field Day.	Rbh.
Douchy	22-5-17		Company training	Rbh.
Douchy	23-5-17		Company moved to Rosignol farm	Rbh.
Rosignol	24-5-17		Company training. Major Sharp admitted to Bapfa Rest Station	Rbh.
Rosignol	25-5-17		Company training. 6 ranks joined Company from 2nd Sept.	Rbh.
Rosignol	26-5-17		Brigade Field Day. Sgt Hibot awarded D.C.M.	Rbh.
Rosignol	27-5-17		Company travelled.	Rbh.
Rosignol	28-5-17		Company starting up Battle	Rbh.
Rosignol	29-5-17		Brigade Field Day.	Rbh.
Rosignol	30-5-17		Company training	Rbh.
Rosignol	31-5-17		Company on Range. Inter team competition	Rbh.

Rhum W/Lt (illegible)
Comdg. 150th M. Gun Coy.

150th MACHINE GUN COY.

JUNE 1917

MACHINE GUN CORPS.
VOLUME No. 14

Army Form C. 2118.

WAR DIARY
or
INTELLIGENCE SUMMARY.
(Erase heading not required.)

Instructions regarding War Diaries and Intelligence Summaries are contained in F. S. Regs., Part II. and the Staff Manual respectively. Title pages will be prepared in manuscript.

Place	Date	Hour	Summary of Events and Information	Remarks and references to Appendices
Roclincourt Bulleroy	1/6/17		Coy training. Wet & windy day	WB
	2/6/17		Coy training. T.S.O.R. Prescot returns	WB
	3/6/17		O.R. No reports received	WB
	4/6/17		Lt Nicol returned	WB
	10/6/17			WB
	11/6/17		Coy Training. Lt Wood A returned to Coy from leave	WB
	12/6/17		Bright weather - Lt Taylor joined Coy from Base	WB
	13/6/17		Coy training. Perfect weather	WB
	14/6/17		Lt R.C Neary proceeded to U.K. 5.6.17. to attend Office	WB
	15/6/17		S.S.M & left Boulogne 11.30 pm. Took Boat from Boulogne 9 am. returned from leave 12/6/17 5 pm by relief to	WB
	16/6/17		15 Div. H.Q.	WB
Bovelles West of Tournai Boingles	17/6/17		Company Brigade joined the Coy. Hostile artillery quiet - weather very hot.	WB
	18/6/17		Hostile artillery active for short periods through the day & night	WB
	19/6/17		2/15 Rendy proceeded to U.K & left camp.	WB
	20/6/17		Enemy artillery more active during the period	WB
	21/6/17		Orders to carry out attack by 3rd Divn Trench M. with 6 M.G. Zero Midnight 22-23	WB
	22/6/17		Zero midnight 9th Inf Brig attacked trenches 5482 SW of Fontaine les Croisilles No 25577 Pte Lindly wounded	WB
	23/6/17		Left 6 MGs final 20 pm sunrise. No 8754 Pte Paige -- No 25577 Pte Lindly wounded	WB
	24/6/17		Received orders that 150 In. Bde. would attack enemy trenches 500x NW Fontaine Croisselles that the Coy would support the attack with as many guns as possible. Dawning 7am. No 8564 5.151 Madge. 1 other rank in M.S.Coy gassed, patrol sent into No Mars Land. No 8564 Pte Newlands wounded.	WB
	25/6/17		Zero 12.30 am attack was successful the Coys 4 guns fired throughout, only allowed the day & night	WB

(63703) Wt W3309/M1235 75,000 11/15 D.D. & L. Ltd. Forms/C.2118/14

160th MACHINE GUN COY.

JUNE 1917

WAR DIARY or INTELLIGENCE SUMMARY

MACHINE GUN CORPS.
VOLUME No 14.
Sheet 2

Army Form C. 2118.

Place	Date	Hour	Summary of Events and Information	Remarks and references to Appendices
In the Field Fontaine - Croiselles	27/6/17	—	Very heavy shelling all night and all morning and a concentration of all enemy Artillery from all directions, a great part of front line and support areas were blown in at 5-0 P.M. a heavy counter attack was launched but was driven back by M.G. fire and Artillery. The bombardment continued and the enemy again attacked about midnight. They were again repulsed. Pte Reeve A. 25967 wounded. Pte Jarrold 67023 wounded -Pte Walton 83287 wounded- Pte Hall 88139 - Pte Thomson 17240 - Pte Lee 90653 -Pte Newcombe 85774 - Ditto Ditto.	W.I.
"	28/6/17		Pte Mawby 88875 Missing - Pte Blackman 71366, Pte Road J 86512, Pte Bean 63133, wounded shellshock. Heavy shelling by enemy through day, although considerable lights from S.O.S. were sent. Orders to support attack by 221st Bde in Hindenburg Support line. Enemy Artillery quiet towards night.	W.I.
"	29/6/17	Zero 3.50 AM	6 M. guns laid on Fontaine Croisilles to prevent the enemy bringing up reinforcements	W.I.
"	30/6/17		Quiet along our front only intermittent shelling. Raining heavily	

WAR DIARY or INTELLIGENCE SUMMARY

150th MACHINE GUN COMPANY
MACHINE GUN CORPS
JULY 1914

Army Form C. 2118.
VOLUME No. 18
SHEET No. 1
Confidential

(Erase heading not required.)

Instructions regarding War Diaries and Intelligence Summaries are contained in F.S. Regs., Part II. and the Staff Manual respectively. Title pages will be prepared in manuscript.

Place	Date	Hour	Summary of Events and Information	Remarks and references to Appendices
Bapaume	July 1st		Company relieved by the 62nd M.G. Coy & came back to camp at Bapaume. Strength 12 O. & 191	R.M.
	2/7/17		Company cleaning up after tour in line. Lt. home & 2/Lt Rankin rejoined from leave.	R.M.
"	3/7/17		Company training	R.M.
	4/7/17		Moved into new camp at Tranville Sitinae. Major Sharp rejoined bn from leave.	R.M.
	5/7/17		Company bathed. Lt. Morrison granted 10 days leave	R.M.
	6/7/17		Company training. Transport shoeing & refitting. 2/Lt Watson admitted to hospital.	R.M.
	7/7/17		Company training	R.M.
	8/7/17		Company bathed - 1 Officer & 7 N.C.Os for action went to reconnoitre trenches.	R.M.
	9/7/17		Company training	R.M.
	10/7/17		Company taking over from 149th M.G. Coy. Lt Tyler granted 10 days leave to U.K.	R.M.
	11/7/17		Relieved 149th M.G. Coy in Chérisy Sector. Very quiet during relief. Major Sharp went to Divison.	R.M.
	12/7/17		In the line. Enemy Trench Mortars very fine. 1 Battalion N.C.	R.M.
	13/7/17		Fairly quiet during day. 1 O.R. slightly wounded.	R.M.
	14/7/17		Rather quiet till 9.P.M. but it was very heavy during the night. Enemy successful very active. 2/Lt wounded. O/C S.R. Battn pinned the company. Caught pt who usual dickering and big dummy de nuit. Enemy very quiet.	R.M.
	15/7/17		Two hrs very heavy after the rain. Enemy aircraft very active. 4 enemy planes day. Our guns carried out a gas shell bombardment killed enemy. and & great Trenches still very bad. Bombardment by guns I will entrain on enemy lines.	R.M.
	16/7/17		Very little retaliation for same.	R.M.
	17/7/17		Very quiet day in the line. Enemy transport kept hitting work. Enemy aircraft very active.	R.M.

150TH MACHINE GUN COMPANY.

WAR DIARY or INTELLIGENCE SUMMARY.
(Erase heading not required.)

MACHINE GUN CORPS
VOLUME No 18.
SHEET No 2.
JULY 1919.
Army Form C. 2118.

Place	Date	Hour	Summary of Events and Information	Remarks and references to Appendices
	18/7/19		One of the reserve guns put out of action. Casualties nil. Exceptionally quiet during the night. No ammunition returned from Leave.	Rbhm
	19/7/19		At 4.15 am enemy put a very heavy barrage on our front & support lines & attempted a raid but same was repulsed. One dead German was found in our lines. Casualties 2 O.R's & one tripod damaged by shell fire. Remainder of day very quiet. No 3 Section relieved No 2 Section in the front line.	Rbhm
	20/7/19		Fairly quiet all day & night. No 4 Section relieved No 1 Section. 10 Reserves granted 10 days leave.	Rbhm
	21/7/19		Enemy aircraft very active. Two of our reserve guns taken away by 149th M.G. Coy in accordance with Divisional scheme.	Rbhm
	22/7/19		Fairly quiet day. Two men sent to Army Rest Camp. 2nd Lt Tyler returned from leave.	Rbhm Rbhm
	23/7/19 24/7/19		2nd Lt Tyler took over command of Coy. Enemy very quiet during the day. But artillery had a frantic S.O.S. barrage lasting for one minute. Very little retaliation for same. Three guns in reserve relieved by 151st M.G. Coy.	Rbhm
	25/7/19		Very quiet both day & night	Rbhm
	26/7/19		Three Sections relieved by the 151 F.M.G. Coy.	Rbhm
	27/7/19		Remainder of Company relieved by 151 M.G. Coy. Enemy aircraft very active.	Rbhm
	28/7/19		Company having "cleaning up" after tour in line. I.O.R. & Services in reserve	Rbhm

MACHINE GUN CORPS. JULY 1917
Army Form C. 2118.

WAR DIARY
or
INTELLIGENCE SUMMARY. VOLUME No 18.
(Erase heading not required.)

150TH MACHINE GUN COY SHEET No 3.

Instructions regarding War Diaries and Intelligence Summaries are contained in F. S. Regs., Part II. and the Staff Manual respectively. Title pages will be prepared in manuscript.

Place	Date	Hour	Summary of Events and Information	Remarks and references to Appendices
	29-7-17		Company bathed. 8 guns sent to D.A.D.O.S. for examination	Nil.
	30-7-17		Company training. Inspection by E.O.	Nil.
	31-7-17		Company training. 8 guns to D.A.D.O.S. for examination	Nil.

Allison Lt.
for O/C 150th Machine Gun Coy

150TH COMPANY. MACHINE GUN CORPS.
1/8/17

150TH MACHINE GUN COY.

WAR DIARY or **INTELLIGENCE SUMMARY**

Army Form C. 2118.

MACHINE GUN CORPS VOL: 19.

SHEET No: 1

VOLUME 19. AUGUST 1914.

Vol 19

Place	Date	Hour	Summary of Events and Information	Remarks and references to Appendices
Campsat: M: Rd Cushat Sheet 51b S.W.	August 1st		Parade cancelled owing to heavy rain. Men mobilised & map reading. Right section carried out from 8-15 & 10-45 pm. an avoidance with training programme. Marched gun implements etc. in compass bearing exercise by L.O. at 8.10 pm.	Vol 5
"	2nd		Officers went up line to 149th M. Gun Corps H.Q. (No: 2 2.9 Sheet 51 b.S.W. 1/20,000) to arrange fatig. Section officers of the 3-4 Sections stayed the night to reconnoitre position during day light.	Vol 5
"	3rd		4 teams of No. 4 Section and 2 teams of the 1 Section relieved 6 teams of 149th Machine Gun Coy. field complete at 9.30 pm.	Vol 5
and Coy HQ N1a2.9 (S.W.1/20000)	4th		Remaining teams overhauled gun stores and moved up with C.O. & Coy HQ. to relieve 149th Machine Gun Coy. Trench strength on this date being P. Off: 125 O.Ranks. Coy. H.Q. taken over and established at N.1a 2.9. (S.W.51b)	Vol 5
"	5th		Relief of 149th Machine Gun Coy. reported complete to 150 Bde & 1 Bde H.Q. at 1.15 am. Enemy M.G. active against teams of No.4 Section. Enemy aircraft flew at a low altitude in rear of Coy H.Q. and sent M.G. against Battery positions. Wired P.A. GRITSHAW and from Base Depot.	Vol 5
"	6th		Our guns carried out harassing fire in conjunction with 8 pdrs on enemy trench system. Guns retaliated against position located by Maj. P. Eaton. 2nd Lieut L.E. PHILLIPS joined from Base Depot. Enemy parachute (red) floated over our lines at 9 pm and fell in rear of Coy H.Q. Who was captured by artillerymen. Enemy artillery quiet. E. aircraft active during afternoon and was successfully engaged by A.A guns. One enemy plane was forced to fall & flames behind his lines.	Vol 5
"	7th		Visibility poor and consequently artillery fairly quiet. Wind dangerous received at 5pm. 5 Enemy aeroplanes flew over our line at 9pm and were engaged and driven back by anti A.A. guns.	Vol 5
"	8th		Repaired bombardment by our artillery especially during day. Wind. Capt: Wicker at 10' Ralph. Lieut Remble from lay guns. Lieut Heavy proceeded to U.K. from G. instruction at Brillion. Lieut Paddell reported to Coy. from leave to U.K.	Vol 5
"	9th		Few Enemy aeroplanes flew at a great height over our lines at 9 am. Trench being bombarded by our artillery. Gunemptied at 6 pm. Enemy's artillery engaged a country battery with heavy artillery and during afternoon. At 9:30 6 8 2 pdr Hows + Heavy guns put 3 shells over our lines. Our James Park embarrassed by lines now formed guns eye during + brilliant enemy's good bombardment firing morning & afternoon.	Vol 5

150th MACHINE GUN COY.

WAR DIARY or **INTELLIGENCE SUMMARY**

Army Form C. 2118.

MACHINE GUN CORPS.

SHEET No: 2   VOLUME No 19.   AUGUST. 1914

Place	Date	Hour	Summary of Events and Information	Remarks and references to Appendices
Coy HQ N16a 2.9 Sheet 57 c S.W.	9th August (cont)		Silenced enemy trench mobile guns of No 1 T.M. Section fired 1,500 rounds each at suitable targets during the barrage bombardment. 1st Rank wounded by shell fire.	VAT
"	10th		Enemy fairly very active on our left sector during afternoon in retaliation for our bombardment of yesterday. Usual harassing fire was maintained throughout the night by our guns. Two mobile guns fired 2,000 rounds on ST ROHART'S FACTORY (6.6.d.05 Sheet 51 & S.W.)	VAT
"	11th		Anti aircraft position built in RAKE TRENCH (O.14.0.5.6) Spare men on teams assisted R.E.'s in construction of dug outs at Nos 5, 10 & 12 positions. Enemy shelled the vicinity of Coy HQ with 4.1 H.V. guns about 6 p.m. and 8 p.m. Usual firing on night lines was carried out.	VAT
"	12th		Anti aircraft position built in dug outs. Registration of ammunition of Aug outs at Nos 5, 10 & 12 positions carried 4,000 rounds on night lines.	VAT
"	13th		Our artillery fairly active throughout the day. Cargo-Cambrai Road receiving much attention. Visibility very good. During the night our guns at 4.30 p.m. fired to WOOD sypered on from Bks. Our guns co-operated with 18 pdrs in harassing fire.	VAT
"	14th		Hazy morning and enemy very quiet along whole Sector. Guns standing by for list of S.O.S. signal wheel placed to approach. Two mobile guns fired 1,000 rounds on during night Enemy airforce fairly active, particularly against Coy Position Heavy thunder storm at 6 p.m.	VAT
"	15th		Enemy artillery active during morning and the valley in rear of Coy HQ received attention. A few shells also dropped in the vicinity of Coy HQ. During the night, guns carried out usual night firing. Two guns in ambush fired 1,500 rounds on enemy works in TRIANGLE WOOD. Two mobile guns fired 1,050 rounds on LT ROBERTS FACTORY and LANYARD TRENCH. Sergt Batt. & BUCK RESERVE was employed. Lieut. of the 3 Section returned from short leave, which Carol to Coy HQ.	VAT

150TH MACHINE GUN COY.

Army Form C. 2118.

WAR DIARY or INTELLIGENCE SUMMARY.

MACHINE GUN CORPS.
VOLUME No. 19. AUGUST 1914.
SHEET 3.

(Erase heading not required.)

Instructions regarding War Diaries and Intelligence Summaries are contained in F. S. Regs., Part II. and the Staff Manual respectively. Title pages will be prepared in manuscript.

Place	Date	Hour	Summary of Events and Information	Remarks and references to Appendices
Coy HQ. N16 a.2.9. (51st Divl/2000)	August 16th		Enemy field guns shelled vicinity of Coy HQ. at 2pm and marched HIGGER TRENCH in rear of HQ. Two of our guns (mobile) fired 2,500 rounds on new enemy works in TRIANGLE WOOD. Guns fired 2,000 pounds on to ST ROHARTS FACTORY. Two of our emplacements were made for mobile guns in the COPSE. Enemy artillery fairly quiet. ARRAS-CAMBRAI Road slightly shelled at 9pm.	Vol
"	17th		Gas alarm given by gas guard at 10am which proved false. Two mobile guns fired 2,000 rounds in the course of the day and night. Two other guns mounted in KEY RESERVE fired 2,500 rods on targets round ST ROHARTS FACTORY. There was no retaliation from the enemy. Two lamps assisted REP in construction of deep outs. Enemy observed using signal lamp from Kite Balloon during evening. Meant L.J. HAWKER to hospital.	Vol
"	18th		Misty in morning. Enemy shelled HENINEL with 4.7 Hows during afternoon. WANCOURT was also slightly shelled. Our guns carried out harassing fire throughout the night. 2000 pounds being fired from KEY RESERVE & tracks to left by train ROBERT.	Vol
"	19th		2 teams of No.9, 2 teams of No.2 & 1 team of No.1 Ry. Section relieved by 151st Machine Gun Coy. Relief complete by 10.30 pm. These teams proceeded to BEAUFORT Lines. Enemy shelled Coy HQ. with light shrapnel. Our guns fired 2000 rounds on enemy approaches during night according to programme.	Vol
"	20th		Very quiet throughout day. Enemy aeroplane flew over our lines at 8.30am and was driven off by one of our guns at Coy HQ, Remainder of Coy relieved by 151st Machine Gun Coy. Relief complete at 10.5 pm. Trench strength of Coy on completion of tour:- 9 Offs. 125 O.Ranks.	Vol
CoyHQ. M.Aubusson	21st		Day of rest. Coy cleaning up equipment etc.	Vol
"	22nd		Coy bathed at NEUVILLE VITASSE during morning. Gun pars & spare parts overhauled.	Vol
"	23rd		The B.G.C. 150th Inf. Bde. inspected transport at 2.30pm and Coy and guns at 3pm. B.G.C. complimented Coy on smartness of turnout.	Vol

150TH MACHINE GUN COY.

WAR DIARY

MACHINE GUN CORPS.

Army Form C. 2118.

SHEET No: 4

INTELLIGENCE SUMMARY. VOLUME 19. August 1914.

(Erase heading not required.)

Instructions regarding War Diaries and Intelligence Summaries are contained in F. S. Regs., Part II. and the Staff Manual respectively. Title pages will be prepared in manuscript.

Place	Date	Hour	Summary of Events and Information	Remarks and references to Appendices
Coy.H.Q. M.4/c/at (51.b.S.W.)	24th and 25th	-	Usual training was carried out according to programme. Firing on range was carried out and digging of emplacements.	nil
"	26th		Day of rest throughout the Brigade. General cleaning up during day.	nil
"	27th		Overhauling of kit and guns preparatory to moving up line. C.O. and officers went to reconnoitre trenches. Weather very bad and an exceptionally high wind.	nil
Coy.H.Q. N30.b.6.2 (51.b.S.W.)	28th		Coy. moved up to relieve 149th Machine Gun Coy. Relief complete at 5pm and H.Q. established at N.30.b.6.2. (Sheet 51.b.S.W.) Weather very bad and an enemy quiet throughout the night.	nil
"	29th		In the early morning enemy trench mortars + Fish Tail bombs were very active against BULLFINCH TRENCH (O25d.9.6.) Our guns fired at irregular intervals throughout the night.	nil
"	30th		In the course of the night harassing fire was carried out on enemy positions round CHERISY, and particularly the cross roads at 0.32. 6.5.9. 5,000 rounds went fore. The enemy were fairly inactive during the day. Coy H.Q. was shelled with light guns, and during the night trestle M.G.s and light guns worked for the two guns firing in to CHERISY.	nil
"	31st		Two guns mounted near QUARRY fired 6,000 rounds on enemy tracks and roads north of CHERISY. Two guns in BROWN TRENCH fired 4,000 rounds on targets in FONTAINE - LEZ - CROISELLES. All gun emplacements were improved and strengthened. What appeared to be an enemy dump was blown up, South of FONTAINE at 8.15.pm. The weather was very bad, and the enemy was very quiet throughout the day.	nil

V.A.Tyler Captain.
Comdg. 150th Machine Gun Coy.

150TH COMPANY, MACHINE GUN CORPS.
No. 3714.
Date.................

CONFIDENTIAL

Army Form C. 2118.

150TH COMPANY, MACHINE GUN CORPS.

WAR DIARY or INTELLIGENCE SUMMARY.

(Erase heading not required.)

150TH MACHINE GUN COY.

VOLUME 20. SEPTEMBER 1914. MAP REF: SHEET 51b S.W.

Place	Date	Hour	Summary of Events and Information	Remarks and references to Appendices
Coy. H.Q. N.30.b.8.2. (QUARRY)	September 1st.	10.30 p.m.	Day's visibility poor. At 10.30 pm gas was projected with the aid of T.M's. A heavy bombardment by our field artillery was maintained simultaneously, with apparently good effect, but the exception of slight fire from Minenwerfer and Rifle Grenade bombs, there was hardly any retaliation. Our two guns mounted Coy. H.Q. (N.30.b.8.2.) fired 3,000 rounds on target near CHERISY. Another two guns in "BROWN TRENCH" fired 4,000 rounds on target near FONTAINE.	
"	"	8.30 p.m.	800 rounds on FONTAINE. Harassing fire was maintained by our guns during the night. Enemy artillery unusually quiet. (Assumed by Lieut. B. WOOD, deputising W.A. TAYLOR (C.O.) left to take Rest and temporary command.	
"	2nd.		Enemy generally inactive. Our two guns in "BROWN TRENCH" (N.36.d.4.3.) fired 4,000 rounds on FONTAINE, and two other guns mounted near Coy. H.Q. fired 3,000 rounds on target near CHERISY. Hostile Machine Guns were rather more active than usual, one gun pounded for two guns mounted near QUARRY.	
"	3rd.		Our guns carried out usual harassing fire during the night. Two mobile guns in BROWN TRENCH fired 3,500 rounds on tracks converging on FONTAINE. Two mobile guns near QUARRY fired 4,000 rounds on CHERISY and tracks leading there. There was slight retaliation in the way of M.G. fire on the guns firing from BROWN TRENCH. Otherwise there was no pronounced activity. Condition work greatly improved at Coy H.Q. A splinter proof Officers Mess, sand bagged and camouflaged, was erected at the entrance to the dug out. New latrines were dug and splinter proof roof house built. Weather fine.	
"	4th.		Usual night firing was carried out on pre-arranged targets in the vicinity of FONTAINE and CHERISY. Total rounds fired 6,250. At 9 am R.E.8. (two seaters) engaged one of our contact machines, which put up a good fight and succeeded in driving the enemy plane to withdraw. Hostile M.C. shewed marked activity against our aeroplanes, which was fairly active as visibility was good.	

A 5834. Wt. W14973/M687. 730,000. 8/16. D.D. & L. Ltd. Forms/C.2118/13.

150TH COMPANY.
MACHINE GUN
CORPS.

Instructions regarding War Diaries and Intelligence Summaries are contained in F.S. Regs., Part II. and the Staff Manual respectively. Title pages will be prepared in manuscript.

WAR DIARY
or
INTELLIGENCE SUMMARY.
(Erase heading not required.)

VOLUME 20. SEPT: 1917.   SHEET 2. MAP REF SHEET 51.B S.W.

Place	Date	Hour	Summary of Events and Information	Remarks and references to Appendices
Coy HQ. (N.30.6.8.2.) QUARRY.	Sept: 5th.		Two mobile guns in BROWN TRENCH fired 3,000 rounds on FONTAINE. The two guns mounted near Coy HQ fired 2,000 rounds on tracks about CHERISY. Slight retaliation by hostile M.G. at irregular intervals. A few gas shells dropped in the vicinity of Coy HQ during the night.	
"	6th:	10.30pm 10.10pm	Usual night firing was carried out according to programme. A hostile M.G. fired with great accuracy on the two positions near the QUARRY. An enemy plane was engaged by our patrol and descended out of control behind enemy lines.	
"	7th.		Enemy artillery fairly active during the morning IBIS, BROWN, and MALLARD trenches receiving great attention. Mobile guns fired according to firing programme, on enemy tracks and trenches. Total number of rounds fired during night 6,250. Lieut A.L. JENNER M.C. joined Coy from Base. New posts were commenced in CONCRETE TRENCH (N.36.c.)	
"	8th:	11am.	Our guns carried out usual harassing during the night in co-operation with 18 pdrs. Enemy aeroplane flew at a low altitude over our lines and were engaged by A.A. and M.G. Dt patrolled our front line being driven down into own lines. Work on new emplacements was carried out during darkness and eight shelters were completed in CONCRETE trench.	
"	9th.		Lieut G. HUDSON M.C. arrived and took over Command of Company. Visibility good and aerial activity increased. Our guns carried out usual fire by night time work on positions in CONCRETE TRENCH continued during darkness.	
"	10th.		5,250 rounds were fired in the course of the night by our mobile guns in co-operation with 18pdrs. The enemy dropped a few gas shells in the vicinity of Coy HQ during the night. Hostile M.G. swept our positions near the QUARRY at irregular intervals, in retaliation to the two mobile guns firing on CHERISY.	

Army Form C. 2118.

WAR DIARY or INTELLIGENCE SUMMARY.

(Erase heading not required.)

VOLUME No 20. SEPT: 1917.   SHEET 3 MAP REF. SHEET 51.6.S.W.

Instructions regarding War Diaries and Intelligence Summaries are contained in F. S. Regs., Part II. and the Staff Manual respectively. Title pages will be prepared in manuscript.

Place	Date	Hour	Summary of Events and Information	Remarks and references to Appendices
Coys H.Q. N 30.6.8.2 QUARRY.	Sept: 11th.		Harrassing night firing was carried out in accordance with programme. Two mobile guns in BRON TRENCH fired 3,500 rounds on prearranged targets. Two guns near QUARRY fired 2,000 rounds on enemy's silences in front of CHERISY. Work on new emplacements in CONCRETE TRENCH was completed. 16 emplacements are now ready for occupation.	
"	12th.		Enemy T.M.s active during the night. Minenwerfer bombarded MALLARD TRENCH (O.25.C.Central) inflicting several casualties on our T.M.Batt. Carrying Party. 20,000 of S.A.A. was drawn and carried to CONCRETE TRENCH. Our guns carried out usual night firing on night lines. 5,250 rounds being fired.	
"	13th.	5pm 4pm	Coy relieved by 151st Machine Gun Coy and proceeded to transport lines, with the exception of H.Q. personnel which proceeded to CONCRETE TRENCH (N 36 c 58) when Coy H.Q. was established. Relief was reported complete at 5pm. German dump near FONTAINE was hit and blown up, by our artillery at 4pm.	
N36.c.5.8. CONCRETE TR:	14th.	11noon 6pm	All guns in position in CONCRETE TRENCH. Emplacements deepened and improved during the day. At 6pm a few shells were dropped in the vicinity of Coy H.Q. but generally quiet with intermittent shelling. Registration with observation was carried out which resulted in some minor corrections in the firing table as regards elevation.	
"	15th.	2.9pm 1.40pm	A raid was carried out during the day, and the 16 guns of this unit co-operated with artillery in barrage fire. The raid was carried out in three places. During the 1st phase 46,000 rounds were fired, and during the second phase 40,500 rounds. Our guns did not support the 3rd phase which was prepared by gas projectors and T.M.s. An allowance of 30 yards was allowed during firing for atmospherical conditions. All phases were entirely successful and infantry succeeded in destroying dugouts and securing confirmation of enemy orders of battle. The enemy was completely taken by surprise and in response to the S.O.S. signal which was placed on our front works by the operator their was no retaliation to our fire.	

(8834 Wt W4973/1687. 750,000 8/16 D.D.&L. Ltd. Forms/C.2118/13.)

150TH COMPANY. MACHINE GUN CORPS.
Army Form C. 2118.
No. ....
Date ....

WAR DIARY
or
INTELLIGENCE SUMMARY.
(Erase heading not required.)

VOLUME 20. SEPT: 1914.

Instructions regarding War Diaries and Intelligence Summaries are contained in F.S. Regs., Part II. and the Staff Manual respectively. Title pages will be prepared in manuscript.

150TH COMPANY. MACHINE GUN CORPS.

SHEET 4. MAP REF: SHEET 51a S.W.

Place	Date	Hour	Summary of Events and Information	Remarks and references to Appendices
Coy: H.Q. CARLISLE LINES M.14.a.8.6	Sept 17th	5.30am	Coy: went out of line in the early morning and proceeded to Winter Camp (M.14.a.8.6). The day was spent in cleaning up, and resting.	
"	17th		3 Officers proceeded on 3 days Course of instruction with artillery. 1 Officer + 1 M/Rank proceeded to 50th Divisional Gas Course. During the day gun Pit was overhauled and spare parts checked.	
"	18th	8.30am	Coy: paraded for baths at NEUVILLE VITASSE. Resting for the remainder of the day.	
"	19th	9.0am	8 guns were sent to Ordnance to be overhauled and inspected. E.O. inspected Coy: during morning and transport during the afternoon. Nos: 1 + 2 Sections carried out fire practice during the afternoon on range at M.24.c.0.6. Q.M. Stores were moved from M.14.a.8.6 to tail head at M.23.d. E.A. flew over camp at 11.20 am at a high altitude and were fired upon by AA. A concert party in the mens' hut, at 7.0pm.	
		9.30pm		
		4.0pm		
"	20th	11.0am	B.Q.C. inspected Coy: at 11-0am. 3 Off: returned from Artillery Course and 1 Off + 1 O.R. from Course at Div: Gas school.	
"	21st	4.30pm	Coy: moved up to relieve 149th Machine Gun Coy. L.O. established at N.16.a.2.9. Relief reported Complete at 12.30am (22nd).	
N.16.a.2.9	22nd	4am	Enemy put down T.M. Barrage on our trenches in front of BOISVERT (O.9.a.9.) S.O.S. was observed from the troops on our immediate left, and steady fire was maintained for half an hour. At 4.30am E.A. flew low over own front system and was effectively engaged by our gun at Coy HQ (N.16.a.2.9) which fired 500 rounds. 12 P.O. fired on our immediate left caused enemy's trenches at 2.30pm this action was preceded by a heavy bombardment by guns of all calibres. The enemy, in response to Golden Rain rockets, put down a heavy T.M. barrage on our front line and close support. Mobile guns fired 3,000 rounds during the night.	
		4.30am		
		2.30pm		

150th COMPANY, MACHINE GUN CORPS.
Army Form C. 2118.

No. ....
Date ....

WAR DIARY
or
INTELLIGENCE SUMMARY.

(Erase heading not required.)

VOLUME 20. SEPT. 1914.

SHEET 5. MAP REF: SHEET 51 B.S.W.

Place	Date	Hour	Summary of Events and Information	Remarks and references to Appendices
Coy. H.Q. N.16.a.2.9.	23rd	9 am.	Aircraft was very active over our lines. Our guns successfully engaged two E.A. forcing them back over their own lines. Two roving guns engaged target from 0.20.6.9.4 to 0.20 d 9.6. 3,000 rounds being fired.	
"		11.30am	Enemy put down Barrage on M.G. Divisional front which was replied to by our artillery and no action developed.	
"	24th		Mobile guns fired 3,000 rounds at targets at 0.20. b.9.1 and 0.20.d.98. Our artillery carried out a chemical bombardment just after midnight. Enemy bombarded our front system and our M.G. replied. Visibility very poor owing to heavy mist. New Limber proof dug out was built to form Section H.Q.	
"		12.30am 4.30am		
"	25th	12.10 to 1.5 am 3am 2.30pm 3pm	4,000 rounds were fired by two mobile guns on prearranged targets in conjunction with 18 pdr. Artl. M.G. replied and appeared to be searching for our two guns. Our gun mounted at Coy H.Q. fired on E.A. which flew over our lines and forced him to retire. Enemy working party observed at 0.15a central and fired on by our mobile guns. Second burst that was seen to drop into trench. Later a horsed ambulance appeared about 0.15.a.4.1 and our gun was laid to take away stretcher case.	
"	26th	9b 11am	Enemy artillery shelled WIANCOURT and attempted counter battery work. Weather fine and visibility good. Usual night firing was carried out by our mobile guns according to programme. 5,000 rounds being fired.	
"	27th	5am 1.15pm	Our artillery carried out chemical bombardment, during which our guns carried out harassing fire. Our guns firing from N.18. 6.9.4. fired 5,000 rounds. Enemy retaliated from gas bombardment with T.M. and M.G. fire on our front works and this Coy port. Hostile artillery shewed increased activity during the day. Enemy plane under cover of low clouds crossed our lines and fired on one four late following which succeeded in flames. Our gun at Coy H.Q. and L.P. signals at E.A. as he returned, with no apparent effect.	

150TH COMPANY, MACHINE GUN CORPS.
Army Form C. 2118.

No. ....
Date ....

Instructions regarding War Diaries and Intelligence Summaries are contained in F. S. Regs., Part II. and the Staff Manual respectively. Title pages will be prepared in manuscript.

WAR DIARY or INTELLIGENCE SUMMARY.

(Erase heading not required.)

VOLUME 20 Sept. 1914. SHEET 6. MAP REF. SHEET 51 c. S.W.

Place	Date	Hour	Summary of Events and Information	Remarks and references to Appendices
Coy HQ N.16.a.2.9.	28d	12.6 1am 3.45am	Our two mobile guns fired 3000 rounds on night firing targets. Enemy M.G. marched to our bivouac in retaliation to our fire. At 3 p.m. an enemy party was observed about 0.15.a. central, and fire was opened on them. They dispersed and dropped into a trench. Enemy artillery fairly active during the day. Observation being very good, counter battery work was attempted by the enemy.	[initials]
		3 pm.		
		11.30 pm.	Our aeroplanes were very active flying from 10 p.m. They showed navigation lights and sounded klaxon horns when passing over our lines.	
"	29d	1-11 am	Usual harassing fire was maintained during darkness. Two guns at 0.19.d.5.1. and 0.19.a.4.4. fired 4,000 rounds. One night firing targets as per programme. The enemy did not retaliate. Hostile M.G. reached EDJEUL VALLEY and road leading to CHERISY and LION DUMP during darkness. Hostile (post?)	[initials]
		9.45 am.	New low car our lines and 250 rounds was fired at it from gun at Corp. HQ. Enemy has to retire. 1 officer (Lieut. BRACTON) and 29 ranks left for Course at G.H.Q. Small Arms School (M.G. Branch) ETAPLES	
"	30"	12-15 am.	Our artillery bombarded new enemy works and guns of our guns co-operated. 4000 rounds were fired during artillery barrage from positions about 0.13.d.55.95. and 0.14.a.3.4. There was no reply in retaliation to our fire from the enemy. Hostile artillery fairly inactive during the day being round mist in morning but visibility good about 12 noon. Enemy's altitude fairly passive. Casualties during period in line from Viet. cont. Nil. Strength of Coy at month end 11 officers 183 (? ranks). Trench strength available 8 offs. 125 O. ranks.	[initials]

R. L. Venner Lt. for Capt.
Comdg. 150th Machine Gun Coy.

150TH COMPANY, MACHINE GUN CORPS.

No. ....
Date 30.9.14

CONFIDENTIAL

150TH COMPANY, MACHINE GUN CORPS.

Army Form C. 2118.

No. ....
Date ....

150th MACHINE GUN COMPANY WAR DIARY
or INTELLIGENCE SUMMARY

OCTOBER 1917. VOLUME No 21.

SHEET No 1.

Instructions regarding War Diaries and Intelligence Summaries are contained in F.S. Regs., Part II. and the Staff Manual respectively. Title pages will be prepared in manuscript.

(Erase heading not required.)

Place	Date	Hour	Summary of Events and Information	Remarks and references to Appendices
Coy: H.Q. N.16.a.2.9 (51.B.S.W.)	Oct: 1st.		2,000 rounds were fired on night firing lines, in conjunction with artillery. The enemy retaliated with M.G. fire. Hostile activity was normal. IBIS TRENCH and BISON TRENCH received attention during afternoon. Enemy bombarded 152nd Divisional front with gas shells and T.M.s	RWh
		3.30pm 8.0.	Enemy transport distinctly heard at night behind NUT TRENCH (O.21.C.1.4.5) by String 4.(104/153R.)	RWh
"	2nd.		Roving guns fired 1,000 rounds on targets according to programme. Four gun positions were prepared in trench joining PANTHER and LION TRENCHES. HENINEL received attention from enemy 15cm during the day and T.M.s were dropped in the vicinity of 151st and BROWN TRENCHES. Operation Order 96 issued in anticipation of raid by 12th Division on the Boisleux. (O.O. 96 attached)	RWh
"	3rd.		Operation cancelled owing to unsuitability of atmospheric conditions. Rain during morning and visibility poor. Mobile guns fired 2,000 rounds on targets N.W. of VIS-EN-ARTOIS.	RWh
		3 /pm.	R.F.C. reported enemy moving on 12th Divl front. Our own shell with the retaliation, and the intended action did not materialise. Until M.G.s were fairly active during darkness.	RWh
"	4th.		Mobile guns carried out usual harassing fire during darkness. A 19.4 pattern 94 mm. heavy Gun (German) was discovered in a camouflaged shell hole about O.13.0 5/4.(51.B.S.W) The gun had apparently not been previously reported, 90 rounds, portable spare parts lay around it. The matter was reported to 150th Inf Bde HQ. and the gun clearly marked. Weather bad and visibility poor. The enemy was generally inactive, his M.G. as usual, swept the COJEUL VALLEY, during darkness.	RWh
"	5th.	3pm.	Enemy aircraft fairly active during afternoon and evening. Coy was relieved by 154th Machine Gun Coy and proceeded to CARLISLE LINES.	RWh

150TH COMPANY, MACHINE GUN CORPS.

WAR DIARY OCTOBER 1914 VOL 2.

INTELLIGENCE SUMMARY. SHEET 2.

Place	Date	Hour	Summary of Events and Information	Remarks and references to Appendices
ACHIET-LE-PETIT G.P.O. 52 (57c N.W.)	Oct: 6d.	12.30	Coy moved from CARLISLE LINES to new training area at ACHIET-LE-PETIT. Order of march; full marching order. Weather very bad, and saw most of the day. Accommodation at new camp; tents and bivouacs.	RChm
"	7d.		Parade served at 11 am.	RChm
"	8d.	4.30am	Training commenced. Physical drill from 9.30 to 8 am. During the morning spare parts were checked and deficiencies made good. Lieut W.T. CLYDE, 154th Machine Gun Coy attached to this unit to assist Coy in training.	RChm
"	9d.	9am	Lecture by O.C. to all Officers. Squad drill and handling of arms during morning. Additional tools drawn from camp, and sent new accommodation under canvas & gun huts to B.A.D.O.S. for overhauling and repair.	RChm
"	10d.		Physical training as usual from 4.30am to 8am. All men in possession of revolvers fired on range at G.S.A.S.S. (sy. 2 N.W.) during the morning. Remainder of Coy. doing squad drill and handling of arms. Deficiencies in spare parts and small kit issued.	RChm
"	11d.	8.30pm	Coy on range with limber on Lala Being private fourteen team. Saw most of the day battle at Batho in ACHIET-LE-PETIT.	RChm
"	12d.		Brigade Scheme postponed owing to weather. Training on mechanism and stoppages carried out in tents. Learning order received for move on 16th inst.	RChm
"	13d.		Usual training carried out.	RChm
"	14th.		Coy bathed at 10.30 am. Parade for divisional series at 1.30 am. Coy footed team played both Yorkshire Regt and won 3 goals to one.	RChm

150TH COMPANY, MACHINE GUN CORPS.

No. ....
Date ....

WAR DIARY
or
INTELLIGENCE SUMMARY.

(Erase heading not required.)

150TH MACHINE GUN COY.   OCTOBER 1917 VOL: 21.

SHEET 3.

Place	Date	Hour	Summary of Events and Information	Remarks and references to Appendices
ACHIET-LE PETIT.	15th		Usual training carried out. All gun gear overhauled and checked. Camp cleared in anticipation of move. All maps of this area returned to Brigade HQ. Nucleus P.H. & R.M. GRIMSHAW proceeded on ten days leave to U.K.	R.P.M
"	16th	4.30 p.m. 8-0 p.m.	Coy moved with transport to entrain at MIRAUMONT station. Coy went left by first train which departed at 8 p.m.	R.P.M
CASSEL & RUBROUCK.	17th	5 am. 11 am.	Arrived at CASSEL where Coy detrained. Marched to RUBROUCK, a distance of about 12 km arriving there at 11am, where accommodation was found in billets. Bn. transferred from VI Corps III Army to II Corps V Army.	R.P.M
"	18th	3pm	Remainder of 150th Inf Bde arrived here. Bombing drill and handling of arms during morning. Lecture by Comdg. Officer at 2pm. Lieut. R.C. MOON rejoined Coy from extended Course in U.K. and assumed duties of 2nd in Command. Coy paid during afternoon.	R.P.M
"	19th		Training during the morning. Gun drill and handling of arms. Lecture by Comdg. Officer in afternoon. Warning order received for move on Sunday. Weather fine.	R.P.M
"	20th		Usual training carried out. Lecture to Officers and Sergeants by Comdg. Officer.	R.P.M
RUBROUCK and LEDRINGHEM.	21st	10am	Coy moved with transport to billets on the outskirts of LEDRINGHEM, arriving there at 11.30am. German aeroplane flew over ARNEKE at night and dropped bombs. He was engaged by A.A. Rmts. No. of victims at football, and admitted into hospital.	R.P.M
LEDRINGHEM and PROVEN.	22nd	8.30am 5pm	Coy left billets at LEDRINGHEM and marched to the station at WORMHOUT where the unit - less transport - entrained for PROVEN. Transport proceeded by road and arrived at PROVEN (Rot Ovre) at 7pm. Accommodation billets and huts.	R.P.M

WAR DIARY or INTELLIGENCE SUMMARY

150th COMPANY, MACHINE GUN CORPS.

150th Machine Gun Coy. OCTOBER 1917 Vol: 21. SHEET 4.

Place	Date	Hour	Summary of Events and Information	Remarks and references to Appendices
PROVEN.	23rd		Coy; resting during the day. Warning order received for move on 24th.	R.Ch.
PROVEN and ELVERDINGHE	24th	10.30am	Unit entrained at PROVEN for ELVERDINGHE, Transport proceeded by road. Arrival at ELVERDINGHE at 2pm. Into billets allotted to this Coy occupied by 9th (Service) Batt: Durham Light Infantry and Coy had to pitch tents at night. Transport lines and war H.Q. established at B.20.c.8.8. (Sheet 28) Commanding Officer reconnoitred line opposite SCHAAP-BAILIE.	R.Ch.
"	25th	11.0am	Coy moved into the line to prepare positions. Barrage emplacements dug and bivouacs made. 19 Ranks of 4th Batt: Yorkshire Regt.(T.F.) and 19 Ranks of 5th Batt: Yorkshire Regt.(T.F.) attached to this unit as carrying party.	R.Ch.
		9.30pm	Enemy aircraft flew over and dropped a number of bombs on POPERINGHE and ELVERDINGHE. They were engaged by A.A and M.Gs. Returns for two days sent up the line. Throughout the night enemy harassing fire was maintained by our artillery.	R.Ch.
Coy HQ. Junc. V.28.a.9.4. (Sheet 20.S.W.4).	26th	4.40am	Our artillery developed into an intense barrage which fort to them fire at 5.40am when the 149th Infantry Brigade attacked towards SCHAAP-BAILIE. 150th Machine Gun Coy; provided a 16 gun barrage for 1 hour and then stood to on S.O.S. line all day. The attack was unsuccessful owing to hostile machine guns in nebus which had not been knocked out mowing down infantry advancing through the mud. 149th M.G. Coy; lost a number of guns. 150th M.G. Coy; advanced 4 guns on night and on 4th railway to defend the line. Guns were dug in consolidated shell holes. The weather very much hampered operations as it rained nearly all day without ceasing. During the day LANGEMARK was heavily shelled. Casualties NIL carrying party 19 Ranks 4th Yorkshires and 4 Ranks 5th Yorkshires wounded.	R.Ch.
"	27th		4 guns were mounted for A.A. work at Coy HQ. (see marginal reference.) 9 guns on S.O.S. barrage between TURENNE CROSSING and SCHAAP-BAILIE. 4 guns in line in defensive positions established on consolidated shell holes. Continuous heavy hostile shelling with gas shells throughout the day. Lofft; and 20 O/Ranks of this unit entrained at PROVEN STATION and proceeded to Elverdinghe Details Camp O. 1500. Lyffd. Relieved 149th M.G. Coy; in the line.	R.Ch.

Army Form C. 2118.

WAR DIARY
or
INTELLIGENCE SUMMARY

Army Form C. 2118.

50th MACHINE GUN COY.   OCTOBER 1917 Vol. 21.

SHEET No. 5.

(Erase heading not required)

Place	Date	Hour	Summary of Events and Information	Remarks and references to Appendices
Coy. HQ. (in) U.18.a.9.4. Sheet 20 SW4	28th		Hostile artillery rather quiet during the day, but increased at night. A number of g.s. shells being used, several went thought to contain mustard gas. Enemy shelling of our front reached its greatest intensity at 3:45 a.m. Enemy aircraft showed great activity during the day. During the morning bombs were dropped about U.18.b.55. (BIXSCHOOTE 4000) and in the evening on the vicinity of U.18.A.O.R. Our M.G. did not know our targets except low flying E.A. which were manoeuvring by engaged during the morning. Our aircraft were very active throughout the day. Transport was heavily shelled whilst conveying rations to the line and one of our horses was destroyed. Hostile aircraft flew over and dropped a number of bombs on ELVERDINGHE. Casualties Nil. The weather showed a marked improvement and visibility about was very good.	Nil.
"	29th	6:30 p.m.		
		11:30 a.m.	Squadron of hostile aeroplanes flew over in close formation, and dropped bombs on ELVERDINGHE ROAD. E.A were rather less active than usual on our front system. Our guns fired on barrage line in conjunction with artillery. The enemy fired a number of g.s. shells which fell in the vicinity of U.18.a.9.4. (BIXSCHOOTE 4000) The nature of these gas shells was doubtful.	Nil.
		3:30 p.m.	Our artillery put down a heavy barrage on the edge of HOUTHULST FOREST, which lasted from 3:30 p.m. until about 4:45 p.m. Casualties: 197 Rank R. wounded by shell fire.	
"	30th		Very hot was overhauled and barrage positions prepared. Weather very hot and visibility poor. Enemy fired about a dozen rounds into ELVERDINGHE with a high velocity gun but one of that shells exploded. During the night the enemy dropped a number of bombs in roads in the rear area, from Woesten. E.A. were engaged by A.A and M.G. fire without success. Casualties. Officers (2/Lieut G.R. ACTON) and 10th Rank wounded by shell fire.	Nil.

	150th COMPANY, MACHINE GUN CORPS.	WAR DIARY or INTELLIGENCE SUMMARY.	October 1914 Vol: 21. Sheet 6.	
Place	Date	Hour	Summary of Events and Information	Remarks and references to Appendices
Coy Hq: Lint. U.18.a.9.4. Sheet 20 sw.4	3/9.		Enemy artillery active from dawn to dusk in response to our heavy barrage. Enemy M.G. active especially from huts V.1.d (WESTROOSEBEKE) which caused some casualties during an operation by 150th Inf: Bde. The barrage guns of this unit did not fire, as no S.O.S. Signal was observed during the operation. Two M.Gs, under 2/Lieut: W.J.S.RANKEN, M.G.C. went forward to consolidate the ground taken by no. 1 Coy. Owing to only slight gains being made, the guns eventually dug in at shell holes about U.6.d.5.6 (Sheet 20 S.W.4.) Own aircraft showed great activity during the day. The weather showed a slight improvement, and visibility was good about mid day. No further news of the operation is yet available.	

R W [signature] Lieut for Captain
Cmdg. 150th M. Gun Coy. M.G.C.

150th Machine Gun Coy.
Operation Order No: 96

SECRET
Copy No: 8
October 2nd 1917.

Map ref: VIS-EN-ARTOIS. Edition 6a. Scale 1/10000.

(1.) At 12·50 p.m. on the 3rd inst: a raid will be carried out by the 36th Infantry Brigade assisted by Artillery, Trench Mortars, and M.G. barrages.

(2.) The area raided will be SPOON TRENCH from O.9.d.4.8 to O.8.b.8.6.

(3.) (a) The 150th Machine Gun Coy will co-operate with six machine guns as follows. Two left roving guns under 2/Lieut: W.J.S. RANKEN in DURHAM ALLEY, O.13.d.40.95. Battalion Commander should be warned. These two guns will barrage HILL SIDE WORK including the area formed by joining following four points O.21.a.45.75, O.21.b.20.65, O.21.b.10.35, O.21.a.4.5.

(b) Four guns under 2/Lieut: P.H. GRIMSHAW. These will be situated in the trench joining PANTHER TRENCH and LION TRENCH. They will search the area formed by joining the following four points O.9.a.30.15, O.9.a.80.00, O.9.c.65.80, O.9.c.10.50. Again Battn. Commander should be informed.

(4.) The Artillery will fire from Zero i.e. 12·50 p.m. till Zero + 15.

(5.) Machine Guns will open fire at Zero and will fire at the rate of 1 belt per 4 minutes until Zero + 20 minutes.

(6.) The two gun teams in NIGER TRENCH will report with guns and kit to 2/Lieut: P.H. GRIMSHAW at 8 a.m. 3rd inst. After firing and clearing up firing points they will proceed to EGRET TRENCH under further orders.

(7.) An orderly will be sent round with 12th Division time.

(8.) Acknowledge.

Copies:- 1. C.O.
2. File.
3. 150th Inf Bde.
4. 50th D.M.G.O.
5. 36th Machine Gun Coy.
6. 2/Lieut: P.H. GRIMSHAW.
7. 2/Lieut: W.J.S. RANKEN.
8. War Diary.

Issued at 6·15 p.m.

Captain.
Comdg: 150th M. Gun Coy.

CONFIDENTIAL.
Army Form C. 2118.

VOLUME No. 22

WAR DIARY
or
INTELLIGENCE SUMMARY

150th COMPANY, MACHINE GUN CORPS.

160th Machine Gun Coy. Machine Gun Corps.

November 1914

(Erase heading not required.)

Instructions regarding War Diaries and Intelligence Summaries are contained in F. S. Regs., Part II. and the Staff Manual respectively. Title pages will be prepared in manuscript.

Place	Date	Hour	Summary of Events and Information	Remarks and references to Appendices
Coy.H.Q. U.19.a.9.4. Sheet 20 S.W.L.	1st	12.10am	From 12 midnight, enemy maintained a heavy bombardment with gas shells, reported to be Phosgene. One of these shells fell immediately behind Coy. H.Q. causing casualties. 1/Pavt. Bellet and C.S.Major were severely wounded and died later. The Commanding Officer (Captain G. Hudson M.C.) was also wounded and sent to hospital. 2/Lieut W.J.S. Ranken was also gassed & having L. McDonald, and to hospital. 2/Officers and 6 O. Ranks gassed but remained at duty. Sergt. Telward by 151 & Macleod Gunley. Transport was heavily shelled in front of LANGEMARCK. The near half of one limber was destroyed, the Transport Sergeant's horse badly wounded by shell fire. After relief Coy. was transport proceeded to DUBLIN CAMP (P.M.C.M. Sheet 28) where they were billeted in huts.	Nil
DUBLIN CAMP A.H.0.14.	2nd		Men very fatigued after having endured 4 days under the most trying and severe conditions, and Coy resting during the day. 2/Lieut P.H.Grimshaw admitted to hospital suffering from flu-poisoning.	Nil
"	3rd	9.30am	Guns cleaned and Spare parts checked during the morning. 1 enemy aeroplane came up from transport lines. Enemy aeroplane flew over camp but did not drop bombs.	Nil
"	4th	10am	Inspection of guns at 10am. Route march at 11am, followed by Lecture of Coy. Commander. 1 Corporal transferred from this unit to 149th Machine Gun Coy.	Nil
"	5th	11.30am	Physical training under Sergeant Trayall. Guns were cleaned and all billets. Company still during morning.	Nil
"	6th		Captain G.R. McPhail joined this Coy. from 149th M. Gun Coy., and assumed command. 30 O.Ranks arrived from base as reinforcements. Physical training under Instructor, Gun drill and Coy. drill during morning. Recreational training in the afternoon.	Nil

(A7094.) Wt. W12890/M1293. 75,000. 11/17. D. D. & L., Ltd. Forms/C.2118/14.

150TH COMPANY, MACHINE GUN CORPS.

WAR DIARY
or
INTELLIGENCE SUMMARY.

(Erase heading not required.)

Army Form C. 2118.

Instructions regarding War Diaries and Intelligence Summaries are contained in F.S. Regs., Part II. and the Staff Manual respectively. Title pages will be prepared in manuscript.

150th Machine Gun Coy.   November 1917 Vol. ?
SHEET 2.

Place	Date	Hour	Summary of Events and Information	Remarks and references to Appendices
DUBLIN CAMP. R.H.C.I.4.	Nov: 7th.	Noon	Belt filling completed during morning, also rehearsed and stoppage practical. Inspection of Coy. by Commanding Officer at noon. No movement to and inspected brigade Hq and in Waterloo Camp at Carriere. Enemy aircraft over at night, but did not drop any bombs.	
"	8th.		Usual training carried out during the day. Enemy aircraft brought down by one of our airmen, which crashed on ELVERDINGHE. Duds cast bombs and endeavoured to advance.	
"	9th.		Warning order received to move on 11th inst. at 8.30 p.m. and went packed.	
"	10th.		Transport moved off for new area and Officer (Lieutenant) and Perpanks proceeded in advance party. Weather very bad and the transport had some trouble, with two limbered wagon wheels which broke. Camp and surrounding areas thoroughly cleaned and huts scrubbed out.	
"	11th.		Coy. moved from DUBLIN CAMP at 11.45 am and entrained two transports at International Corner Station. Arrived at WATTEN at 6.30pm. Thence by march route to MENTIQUE, arriving there at 8.45 pm. Kits were conveyed by motor lorry from WATTEN to new area. Accommodation huts.	
MENTIQUE R.16.a.R.1 (Sheet 8/4 S.E.)	12th.		Physical training during the morning. Guns cleaned. Intend to complete in clothing submitted. Weather good.	

WAR DIARY
INTELLIGENCE SUMMARY

150TH COMPANY, MACHINE GUN CORPS.
Army Form C. 2118.

150TH COMPANY MACHINE GUN CORPS
150TH MACHINE GUN COY.
NOVEMBER 1914. Vol. 22.
SHEET 3.

Place	Date	Hour	Summary of Events and Information	Remarks and references to Appendices
MENTQUE P.16.a.2.1. (Sheet 27a S.E.)	13th.		Physical Training immediately after breakfast. Stoppages and mechanism during morning. Indents to complete clothing submitted.	R.W.
"	14th.		Indicator and Recognition target from about P.22 central during morning. Coy paraded for baths at TOURNEHEM at 3pm. 5 officers and 20 O/Ranks proceeded on joint went from Bath as reinforcements and Roll and 20 O/Ranks reported Coy. from Divisional Details Camp. Coy Para at 5pm. Weather fine. Coy strength now 18 officers and 144 O/Ranks.	R.W.
"	15th.		Parade 5.45am. Coy firing on rifle range at P.12.6.(27yS.E.) Targets allotted 1 to 8. Men without rifle threw them from transport section. Shooting at both 200 and 500yds very good, considering the bad visibility during the shoot. Number of men practised 83. Number of men who obtained 162% of total marks 50. Number of men who obtained 50% of total marks 44. Coy played 5th Bat. Durham Light Inf. at football and won. Rgoals to 1.	R.W.
"	16th.		Tactical Scheme with limbers under section order arrangements. Action, Stability and changing of targets against time. Mechanism. Stoppages and gun drill. Recruitment Training during afternoon. No.26346 Pte. BOWLAND W.H. awarded R1 days F.P. No.1. Coy old Straw cleared from billets and replaced by new.	R.W.
"	17th.		March with limbers terminated by tactical scheme. Indicator and recognition of targets practiced by 3rd. 4th Sections. Had to move their billet to make room for a Coy of 4th East Yorks. Regt.	R.W.

150TH COMPANY, MACHINE GUN CORPS.

WAR DIARY or INTELLIGENCE SUMMARY

Army Form C. 2118.

150th Machine Gun Coy.   November 1914 Vol 22.   Sheet 4.

(Erase heading not required.)

Place	Date	Hour	Summary of Events and Information	Remarks and references to Appendices
MENTQUE P.16.a.2.1. (Sheet 246 S.E)	18th	9am	Church Parade at 9am. Billets inspected by Commanding Officer during the morning. Capt. P.H. Schmidt and Small Box Respirators handed in to Q.M. Store slightly marked with varnish and name. Small kit issued in the afternoon. Additional blanket issued to each man.	RHM
"	19th		Usual training carried out during the day. Recruits and Range Parties detailed for Picton, for special training under 2/Lieut T.R.BAXTER. Recreational training in afternoon.	RHM
"	20th	9am	Coy: on range firing 30 yards practice. Brig: General demo's; inspected Coy: transport at Picton. Football team played 1st round in Divisional competition and lost to R.S.C. 1 goal to Nil.	RHM
"	21st		Tactical scheme carried out under section arrangements, in the vicinity of P.30 central. Inter section football during afternoon.	RHM
"	22nd	2.30pm	Officer (Lieut P.H.MORRISON.) proceeded on 4 days leave to PARIS. Squad drill and Coy: drill carried out under supervision of Coy: Officer. Issue of clothing to S.Majr BROWN.J.C. joined this unit from 143rd Machine Gun Coy. Concert held in canteen tent at 9pm. All officers + N.C.O's and section corpls. reconnoitred ground for Bdei futsal day tomorrow.	RHM
"	23rd	9.30am	Brigade scheme carried out during the morning, Commencing 9.30am. 2 Limbers per section communication kept up with H.Q. by visual signalling, which was very successful. All blankets sent for fumigation.	RHM
"	24th	1.45pm	Morning spent in cleaning up billets preparatory to move to TOURNEHEM. Coy: paraded with transport ready to move off at 1.45pm, and proceeded by march route to TOURNEHEM, arriving there at 2.30pm. R.N.C.O's of this unit awarded Military Medal for gallant work in the YPRES area. Coy's present strength 11 off. 144 O/ranks.	RHM

WAR DIARY or INTELLIGENCE SUMMARY

150th COMPANY, MACHINE GUN CORPS Army Form C. 2118.

NOVEMBER 1917 Vol. 22. Sheet 5.

Place	Date	Hour	Summary of Events and Information	Remarks and references to Appendices
TOURNEHEM J.31.a.5.9. 2/A.S.E.	NOVEMBER 25th	8.45am	Coy: paraded for baths at 8.45am. Divine service during morning.	RLM
"	26th	8.30am	Physical training under Senior Officer on parade. Squad drill – mechanism – stoppages – toy drill during the morning. Recreational training in afternoon. Cross country run of 3 miles. All small box respirators examined by Bde. Gas N.C.O. and found up to order. All black cartridges being exchanged for new issue into 5 newest A. JENNER proceeded on one months special leave to U.K.	RLM
"	27th		Physical training cancelled owing to rain. Handling of arms, gun drill and cleaning of gun pit during morning. Recreational training in afternoon.	RLM
"	28th		Physical training as usual. Indicator & recognition of targets – ranging and fire control – Panaphone and visual gun signal practised. Cross country run in afternoon. Pte. C. WOOD proceeded on one months special leave to U.K.	RLM
"	29th		No.4 Section Co operating with 5th Batt: Durham Light Inf: in Battn: Scheme. Physical training as usual. Handling of arms, gun drill and mechanism practised during the morning. Weather very fine.	RLM
"	30th		Usual training carried out. Coy strength 11 Officers 146 O. Rank & Co.	RLM

Winn H. W. Captain
Comdg. 150th Machine Gun Coy.

Volume XXIII   Confidential

Vol 23

War Diary

of

150th Machine Gun Coy.

From Decr 1st 1917

To Decr 31st 1917.

150th COMPANY, MACHINE GUN CORPS.

WAR DIARY
or
INTELLIGENCE SUMMARY.
(Erase heading not required.)

Army Form C. 2118.

SHEET No: 1.

DECEMBER 1917 Vol: 23.

Place	Date	Hour	Summary of Events and Information	Remarks and references to Appendices
TOURNEHEM J.31.a.5.9. (Sheet 24a NE)	1st.		Physical training – gun drill – handling of arms during morning. Officer inspected Coy at 12.30 p.m. in the following order. Nos 1 and 2 sections in full Marching Order. No. 3 section in fighting Order, No. 4 section in great coats. Weather dull, but fine. 3 O.R.'s proceeded on 14 days leave to U.K. All old steel helmets separated and colours painted on.	nil.
OUEST-MONT K.24.a.I.B. (Sheet 24a NE)	2nd.		Morning spent in cleaning up billets and packing "limbers" boy. Paraded with transport at 12.45 p.m. and moved off at 1.0 p.m. Arrived at OUEST MONT at 2.45 p.m. where Coy was accommodated in billets. Weather fine.	nil.
"	3rd.		Physical training – squad drill – advanced gun drill – Coy drill. New M.G. anti aircraft mounting tested and reported on. This mounting was found satisfactory, but could be improved if made of heavier material. Coy. Strength 144 officers 144 O.Ranks. Weather fine, frosty.	nil.
"	4th.		Usual training carried out during the day. Issue of clothing and spare parts in afternoon.	nil.
"	5th.		All Small Box Respirators and P.H. helmets certified serviceable. Old containers replaced by new ones. S.B.R's and P.H. helmets re-issued at Q.M. Stores. Examination of gas helmets – Gas Drill – handling of arms. Coy. paraded for baths at EPERLECQUES but pipes were frozen at baths. Weather dull. Rain fell during night.	nil.
"	6th.		Coy on "B" range for rifle practice. Firing commenced at 9 a.m. Coy's practice and field shooting, as a whole was good. Number of men practised:- 45. Commanding Officer Lieut Beddall reconnoitred forward area, under Brigade arrangements.	nil.

150th COMPANY, MACHINE GUN CORPS

WAR DIARY
or
INTELLIGENCE SUMMARY.

(Erase heading not required.)

SHEET No. 2.

Army Form C.2118

150th COMPANY MACHINE GUN CORPS. DECEMBER 1914. Vol 23.

Place	Date	Hour	Summary of Events and Information	Remarks and references to Appendices
OUEST MONT K24.a.1.B. Sheet 24a.N.E.	7d.		Usual training carried out during day. Lieut R.O. MOON and 2/Park proceeded to CAMIERS, for Vickers course. Divisional Sports jumping finals in afternoon. Weather fine. Coy. Recd. out at 3pm.	MW
"	8d.		Warning Order received for move into forward area. Usual training carried out.	MW
"	9d.		Transport less one G.S. limbered wagon, wcc. cart & water cart, moved off at 8.30 am under D/Lieut Bethell and proceeded by road to new area. Remainder of Coy. paraded for Baths at 2pm. Weather mild.	MW
RIDGE CAMP G.11. A 8.2. (Sheet 28 N.W.)	10d.		Reveille 3.30am. Coy paraded ready to move off at 6.30am. One blanket per man carried, remainder conveyed by motor lorry. Remainder of Transport proceeded by road to ST OMER STATION, where it entrained. Coy. entrained at WATTEN STATION at 8.30am and detrained at BRANDOEK STATION at 1.0 pm. Coy. proceeded by march route to RIDGE CAMP (via marginal scheme). Transport arrived at 3.0 pm. Q.E.A. flew over VLAMERTINGHE at 3.15pm and bore unsuccessfully engaged by A.A. guns.	MW
"	11d.		Nos 2,3,& 4 Sections and 8 fighting limbers moved to POTIJZE CAMP (I.3.6. Central) at 5.30am. Rations for two days carried on the man. Transport Lines and war est. established at POTIJZE CAMP. A Battalion Scheme is being tried by the four M.G. Coys. of the Division under the direct command of the D.M.G.O. The staff being usual tactical efficiency. The H.Q. personnel being selected from the four Coys. This unit has sent 2/Lieut R.H.MORRISON, who is temporarily appointed Head Quartermaster. Advanced Coy. HQ established at TYNE COTT D.17.a.2 Right flank Guide. The enemy engaged in counter battery work, and using many gas shells. Fethur and staff slightly gassed but remaining at duty.	MW

A5834 Wt.W4973/M687 750,000 8/16 D.D.& L. Ltd. Forms/C.2118/13.

Army Form C. 2118.

SHEET No 3 VOL. 23

160th COMPANY, MACHINE GUN CORPS **WAR DIARY**

or

INTELLIGENCE SUMMARY.

DECEMBER 1917.

(Erase heading not required.)

Place	Date	Hour	Summary of Events and Information	Remarks and references to Appendices
SHEET 28.N.E.1.	12th		The relief of the 100th M.G. Coy by this unit was reported complete at 6.0 a.m. Two gas barrages were passed through during the relief of No.s 10, 11, 13 and 13 positions, at 1.0 a.m. and 3.0 a.m. on travelling along No 5 and SOUTHERN extension track, most of the men felt the effects of the gas but the relief was carried out satisfactorily. The GRAF and surrounding areas were heavily shelled between 6.0 and 7.0 a.m. S4 position (D.16.c.2.9) was heavily shelled by H.E. and shrapnel, one tripod was smashed and one gun slightly damaged. One E.A. was brought down by our A.A. BATTERIES on the eastern lip and another was forced to descend at 9.0 a.m. At 5.30 pm our guns fired 250 rds at two enemy aeroplanes, no effect was observed. Hostile Artillery was very active from 11.0 a.m. onwards ABRAHAM HEIGHTS, BEECHAM, SEINE and HILLSIDE FARM being heavily shelled – Casualties Nil.	Nil
	13th		Hostile Artillery fairly inactive at 7.0 a.m few light shells were dropped in the vicinity of HAMBURG and CREST FARM. In the course of the night our machine guns maintained a harassing fire on the railway cutting S.E of PASSCHENDAELE STATION and traffic on the Neighbourhood of ASSYRIA (D.18.c), 2,500 rounds were fired.	Nil
	14th		Heavy hostile shelling of forward gun positions at D.12.a. towards 5p.m, shortly by shrapnel. Enemy aircraft fairly active towards dusk (4p.m) they were heavily engaged by our A.A guns at BEECHAM and were forced to retire after having expended 500 rounds. During the night of the 13th/14th unusual harassing fire was maintained on suspicious enemy positions near PASSCHENDAELE ROAD (E.7.a) and EDDY TRENCH (E.13.c central) – Casualties Nil.	Nil

150th COMPANY, MACHINE GUN CORPS   SHEET NO. 4. VOL. 23

WAR DIARY or INTELLIGENCE SUMMARY

(Erase heading not required.)   Army Form C. 2118.

DECEMBER 1917

Place	Date	Hour	Summary of Events and Information	Remarks and references to Appendices
SHEET 28.N.E.1	15th		Enemy Machine Guns fairly active during the early part of the morning along road leading S.E. from PASSCHENDALE through D.12. One Enemy M.G. presumed to be firing from ECHO COPSE (E, Y, q, S, 1) traversed the railway in the region of DEEP CROSSING (D.17.B). Our guns replied to the enemy's M.G. fire which resulted in stopping his fire. Positions in D.11.C were slightly shelled by shrapnel towards 8 and 9 pm – with no effect. Cattle movement (3 men) were observed near ERRATIC FARM (E.Y.O) towards dawn and were promptly fired on. Casualties - Nil.	Arif
	16th		All gun teams in the line were relieved from 4 to 6 a.m. by the 245 M.G. Coy. All tripods, ammunition and trench stores were handed over to the incoming teams. Guns only were taken out. Relief was carried out satisfactorily and was reported complete at 6 a.m. All mustering gathered at TYNECOT (COY HQ) D.19.a.2.1 and formed to TRANSPORT LINES at POTIJZE Camp (F.9.a.8.2.) arriving at 9.0 a.m. The remainder of the day was allowed as a rest.	Arif
POTIJZE CAMP 17th (F.9.a.8.2)			Stores – namely, duck boards, corrugated iron, sandbags, boards, etc were drawn from the D.M.G.E. with a view to the general improvement of the camp. Transport less fighting limbers moved to BUSSEBOOM (G.16.c.) by marched route in charge of 2nd Lieut F. BETHELL.	Arif
SHEET 28.N.W.	18th		The morning was employed in the cleaning of kit and harness. During the afternoon erections and improvements were made with camp. Officers Mess Dristores and 50 of Ranks bathed. During chunks were merged and 60 yards of trench boards laid.	Arif

150th COMPANY. MACHINE GUN CORPS. Army Form C. 2118.
No. ....
Date 1/1/18

WAR DIARY
or
INTELLIGENCE SUMMARY.
(Erase heading not required.)

150th COMPANY MACHINE GUN CORPS.   SHEET N°5 VOL. 23.

DECEMBER 1917.

Instructions regarding War Diaries and Intelligence Summaries are contained in F.S. Regs., Part II. and the Staff Manual respectively. Title pages will be prepared in manuscript.

Place	Date	Hour	Summary of Events and Information	Remarks and references to Appendices
POTIJZE CAMP I.9.a.8.2 (SHEET 28 NW)	19th		During the morning, sections were employed in cleaning of guns, gun gear, ammunition and belt filling. Limbers were packed ready for action. Transport under 2/Lt F. BETHEL moved from BUSSEBOOM to Coy. H.Q. at POTIJZE Camp.	Nil
SHEET 28 N.E. (PASSCHENDAELE)	20th.		Nos 1, 3, and 4 Sections paraded for the trenches at 4.0am, to relieve 149 M.G. Coy. relief was completed satisfactorily and reports complete at 4 am. Coy. H.Q. was established at TYNE COTT. (D.14.a.4.2). Casualties Nil.	Nil
		Nil.	Enemy Artillery fairly active in the vicinity of Nos 1,2,73 position (D.14.a) Light shells and shrapnel was used against these positions at various times of the day. One salvo of 9in shells was dropped slightly to the rear of No 4 position (D.12.C.1.2). "B" Battery (D.11.b.) carried out night firing programme on the enemy's line from E.Y.a.54 to E.1.C.5.2 Firing 1000 rounds per gun, total number of rounds fired (right of 30/31st) 4000 rounds. Enemy average fairly active towards 10.0 A.M. one plane was engaged by our AA Machine Gun with good results. 410 rounds fired – Casualties Nil.	Nil
	22nd		Enemy activity diminished during the last 24 hours. "B" & "C" Batteries received attention and 4.2 HE shells at intervals throughout the night and day. Hostile Aircraft was active over the sector practically the whole of the afternoon. Most of the enemy planes were out of M.G. range, but a few her engaged by our AA M. Guns. Over 3000 rounds were fired. About 3pm, one of our planes flying very low was engaged by hostile M.G. fire and was seen to collapse. A scheme up harassing fire was carried out in the region around the junction of the PASSCHENDAELE-MOORSLEDE ROAD, and a railway between the towns of (Continued)	Nil

A5834 Wt.W4973/M687 750,000 8/16 D.D. & L. Ltd. Form/C.2118/13.

150th COMPANY MACHINE GUN CORPS. No. CM2118 Date 1.1.18

150th COMPANY MACHINE GUN CORPS

WAR DIARY or INTELLIGENCE SUMMARY

SHEET N°6 VOL.23.
DECEMBER 1917

(Erase heading not required.)

Places	Date	Hour	Summary of Events and Information	Remarks and references to Appendices
PASSCHENDAELE SHEET 28 NE	22nd		(Continued) 12 midnight and 2am. 3000 rounds were fired.	M/W
	23.		Hostile machine gun acting towards 6.7 am. Traversing over forward positions of D.12.a and D.12.c. Often firing with considerable accuracy. "B" Battery D.11.C.31 fired 2,500 rounds on targets Echo Corpse (E.Y.A.), Erratic Farm and Passchendaele Station.	M/W
	24.		At 4.0 am. Nos 1, 3, and 4 sections in the line were relieved by the 245 M.G. Coy. All guns were taken out and tripods, belt boxes and S.A.A. Iwas, and Lewis ammo handed over to the incoming teams. Relief was reported complete at 4.15 am. Sections marched to transport lines at POTIJZE CAMP, arriving 9.15 am. The remainder of the day was allowed as a rest.	M/W
POTIJZE CAMP (J.9.a.8.2.) SHEET 28 NW	25.		Sections paraded for baths, 200 o/Banks baths. The remainder of the day was spent in cleaning equipment and guns.	M/W
	26.		Cleaning of guns, gun kit and ammunition, belt filling during the morning. Material taken from the D.M.G.O. for the erection of a Nissen Hut.	M/W
	27.		Coy paraded for packing of fighting limbers preparatory for going into the line.	M/W
PASSCHENDAELE SHEET 28 NE	28th		Nos 1.2. and 4 sections paraded at 12 midnight (27/28th) and proceeded to the line to relieve the 245 Coy in the PASSCHENDAELE Sector. Coy H.Q. was established at TYNE COTT (D.H.a.u.2.). Hostile artillery (6.8 and shrapnel) were active on the region of D.13.a. & D.12.c. from 4.30 pm to 6.6 pm. 16 hostile aeroplanes were active during the morning. Between 4.30 am and 9.0 am. 5 aeroplanes more observed flying at an altitude of 5000 ft. 45000 rounds were fired by our A.A. Machine Guns. (over)	M/W

A 5534/Wt.W 4973/M 687 750,000 8/16 D.D. & L. Ltd. Forms/C 2115/13.

WAR DIARY

150 COMPANY MACHINE GUN CORPS

SHEET No. 7   VOL. 23

INTELLIGENCE SUMMARY

DECEMBER 1917

(Erase heading not required.)

Place	Date	Hour	Summary of Events and Information	Remarks and references to Appendices
PASSCHENDAELE SHEET 28.NE	28 (cont)		without effect. At 12 noon 5 Aeroplanes were observed. 1500 rounds were fired at them without effect. Casualties Nil.	Nil
	29		There was great artillery activity throughout the day. D.12.C. was shelled from 10 to 12 midnight on the night of 28/29. Active throughout the day and night on PASSCHENDAELE RIDGE from 3 p.m. to 4 p.m. AUGUSTUS WOOD on D.11.C and D.14.A. also N.E. Corner of D.16.C. from 8.30 p.m. to 9.30 p.m. (night of 28/29). Area on D.10.A and D.11.C were shelled from 2.30 p.m. to 4 p.m. Area on D.12.C. was shelled intermittently throughout the day, especially on PASSCHENDAELE ROAD. Several E.A. were observed together at 8.0 a.m. and 10.0 a.m. One Aeroplane at 1 a.m. flew low and openly at about D.S.A.H.8 with machine guns. Two Aeroplanes were observed about N.8 a.m. but were beyond machine gun range. Two of our own guns were used throughout the night at 28/29 on target E,7,d,5,3. 1750 rounds were fired. - Casualties Nil -	Nil
	30		Hostile artillery fairly active. D.12.C was shelled with H.E. and gas shells between 4.0 & 9.6 p.m. on night of 29/30. D.11.A. from 5.0 to 6 p.m. by H.E. shells. D.12.A and D.12.C were shelled occasionally throughout the day. Lewis & 2" 5.9" shells "Woolly bears" through to GRAF WOOD came much heavy Machine Gun fire about 7.0 am. Looking for about 4 mins. These guns are thought to be in number appeared to be firing from EXERT COPSE. Intermittent shelling throughout the day on D.16.d. Also on PASSCHENDAELE ROAD about D.15.c. D.10.d. + D.10.c. D.11.A. + D.11.c also active that evening. (Continued.)	Nil

50TH COMPANY MACHINE GUN CORPS.

150TH COMPANY MACHINE GUN CORPS.

Army Form C. 2118.

150th COMPANY MACHINE GUN CORPS WAR DIARY

SHEET NOS. 101.23

INTELLIGENCE SUMMARY

DECEMBER 1917

(Erase heading not required)

Instructions regarding War Diaries and Intelligence Summaries are contained in F.S. Regs., Part II. and the Staff Manual respectively. Title pages will be prepared in manuscript.

Place	Date	Hour	Summary of Events and Information	Remarks and references to Appendices
PASSCHENDAELE SHEET 28.N.E.	30 (cont)		Hostile Machine Guns were very active during night of 29/30th on D.12.a, V.18.1.c firing from the direction of GENEOZE WOOD (E.1.D). Four guns maintained a harassing fire throughout the night from 4.0pm to 6.0am. 2 guns at D.16.b.65.72 fired three belts her gun on Railway in D.12.a and at E.Y.C. Total number of gunmmdo fired 1800. 1000 rounds were also fired on 2.4 central (two guns firing) Casualties — Nil	
	31st		Intermittent shelling throughout the 24 hours in D.16.L.2 & L.9.a. At 6.0am the enemy shelled the forward area heavily with about 15 8 and shrapnel burets, in the vicinity of HAMBURG (D.16.L) and AUGUSTUS WOOD (D.11.C.) Manual shelling in area D.11.d from 10.0am D.12. noon, D.13. & 9.11 very active. S.O.S. was put up in the aft. of 3rd, lasting at 6.5am. Our guns fired a total of 8,250 rounds. There was shelling in the Lands of Mules & gun-fire at intervals throughout the day. The M.G. fire returning from WRATH WOOD Z.7.D.11 (w.25 & L.64) and where landed on the intercot of PILLBOX (77.m.m.) 70.y.1340 (C.Morser. H.50 & 116.4.64 Chenille, to pere burning off the Pill-Box. He inflicted a second lift & same a third but some distance away. The shell fortunately was a dud, but remained of great threat and Courage until the man that came and set on he dug and over 30 Boers. Like Shell had not hit him a dud. Harassing fire was maintained as on D.16.o.6.2 from 940 pm to 10pm and 10.15pm to 11.15pm. 1000 rounds were fired by 2 M.G. on Roma Junction in E.1 central and 6.0am 1000 rounds fired by 2 M.G. on the Same target. Between 6.0pm throughout from D.16.b.75.72 — Casualties — Nil	Nil

(A7092) Wt. W12830/M1293. 75,000. 1/17. D.& L., Ltd. Forms/C2118/14

150 M S Av
Vol 24

150th COMPANY, MACHINE GUN CORPS WAR DIARY

CONFIDENTIAL. Army Form C. 2118.

VOL. 24 SHEET

INTELLIGENCE SUMMARY.

OR

(Erase heading not required.)

JANUARY 1918

Place	Date JAN.	Hour	Summary of Events and Information	Remarks and references to Appendices
POTIJZE. I,30.c.3 Sheet 28 NW.	1st		150th Machine Gun Coy relieved by 245th Coy. Sections arrived at POTIJZE CAMP at 9am. Horses but drawn from A.M.G.O. and erected by men of this unit. Day spent in cleaning of equipment and personnel.	Clo.
"	2nd		Tools in sections of Horses but continued. Camp, which was in a very dirty condition cleaned up and rubbish burned. Warning Order received for move into / reserve area. Weather keen frost.	Clo.
WINNIZEELE. J.35.d.4.9. Sheet 24.	3rd		Transport moved off at 8.45am. for WINNIZEELE AREA via YPRES - POPERINGHE ROAD. Weather frosty and ground very bad for transport. Animals harboured well. Frost very. Remainder of Coy moved from YPRES SQUARE at 11 am, arrived in WINNIZEELE AREA, J.35.d.4.9. at 3p.m. Accommodation billets.	Clo.
"	4th		Physical Training 9 to 10am. Cleaning and checking gun kit. Kit inspection by Section Officers at 2pm. Training during day.	Clo.
"	5th		Physical Training Carried out. Squad and Coy Foot Drill mechanism and Staff/S.A.A. Recreational training during afternoon. Indents to complete in short parts etc. submitted.	Clo.
"	6th		Physical training 9-10am. Loading limbers during morning. Rifles and ammunition was cleaned. No Divine Bread in billets.	Clo.
"	7th		Normal training carried out. Weather cold, frosty at night.	Clo.
"	Sat.		Mechanism and Stoppages during morning, in billets owing to heavy fall of snow. Lei guns sent to Div Ordnance Workshop to overhaul. Repair Field Gun & impossible owing to weather.	Clo.

150th COMPANY, MACHINE GUN CORPS.
Army Form C. 2118.

WAR DIARY

INTELLIGENCE SUMMARY

150th Machine Gun Coy. M.G.C.   January 1918. Sheet 2. Volume 24.

Place	Date Jan.	Hour	Summary of Events and Information	Remarks and references to Appendices
WINNIZEELE. J.35.d.4.9 Sheet 27	9th		Coy. paraded for Baths at STEENVOORDE at 8.45 a.m. 6 guns sent to Rein. Ordnance for overhaul and repair. VICKARIS (Bandstand) Anti aircraft mountings tested and found satisfactory. The mounting would be greatly improved by means of heavier material. Snow fell during the day and was particularly heavy in afternoon.	Clr.
"	10th		Physical training - gun drill - indication and recognition of targets. Two guns sent to Ordnance for overhaul and repair. Weather thawing, high wind.	Clr.
"	11th		Visual training - test of elementary training - Company drill under C.S.M.	Clr.
"	12th		Physical training, squad drill, gun drill, mechanism and stoppages. Recreational training during afternoon. Inter section football match, feathers milder.	Clr.
"	13th		This division held the annual day of Prayer. Parade service at 10 a.m. followed by Holy Communion. Volunteers. Voluntary service at 5.30 p.m. further service party.	Clr.
"	14th		Slight fall of snow during night. Usual training carried out during day. Central and store packed and preparations made for transport for move tomorrow.	Clr.
"	15th		Transport moved to new area at 8 a.m. two limber waggons and contents. Weather very bad. Continual rain and wind. Packing up ready for move. Advance party of 1 Off. and 20 Ranks moved to sign on at 9.50 a.m. 50 Rank preceded on two day Pigeon Course. Transport halted for night at RENESQUE.	Clr.

150th COMPANY, MACHINE GUN CORPS

150th COMPANY, Army Machine Gun Corps.

WAR DIARY or INTELLIGENCE SUMMARY

(Erase heading not required.)

150th Machine Gun Coy: M.G.C.

JANUARY, 1918. SHEET 2.

VOLUME 214

Place	Date	Hour	Summary of Events and Information	Remarks and references to Appendices
SETQUES E.8.a.95.00	16th	11.45am	Out billets and surroundings were thoroughly cleaned during morning. Coy moved to TILQUES AREA and entrained at GODWAERSVELDT at 4.15pm, arriving at WIZERNES (S.O.N.E) at 9.45pm. Thence by march route to SETQUES arriving at 7.30pm. Blankets and stores conveyed to and from entraining and detraining stations by motor lorry. There did not arrive at SETQUES until 2.30am (17th). 1 limber, 1 G.S. wagon and 2 carts were left on transport train arriving at SETQUES at 8am (17th). Weather fair but no rain in bad condition. Usual precautions being observed.	Clo
"	17th		Training in billets owing to bad weather. Machineguns and Staff Tapes.	Clo
"	18th		Repairing limbers during morning. Ammunition to complete to establishment received. Recreational training during afternoon. Weather fine.	Clo
"	19th		Work on cleaning transport, guns and limbers continued. Recognition of targets. N.S. Officers attended lecture on Gas Censorship at 2.15pm. Coy paid out at 8.30pm.	Clo
"	20th		Baths at SETQUES at 8am. Divine Service at 11.30am and voluntary Service at 5.30pm. Weather fine.	Clo
"	21st	11.30am	Gas drill, gun drill, musketry and gun signals, physical training. Commanding Officer inspected Signallers' Equipment at 11.30am. Brigade Signal Officer was also present. G.O.C. inspected Transport at 2.30pm and every officer present with the turnout. Weather bad, rain during the morning.	Clo

150th COMPANY, MACHINE GUN CORPS.

Instructions regarding War Diaries and Intelligence Summaries are contained in F. S. Regs., Part II. and the Staff Manual respectively. Title pages will be prepared in manuscript.

150th COMPANY, MACHINE GUN CORPS.

Army Form C. 2118.

WAR DIARY or INTELLIGENCE SUMMARY.

60th Machine Gun Coy. M.G.C. JANUARY 1918. SHEET 4. VOLUME 24.

(Erase heading not required.)

Place	Date JAN.	Hour	Summary of Events and Information	Remarks and references to Appendices
SETQUES W. E.8.a.9500	22nd		Usual training carried out. Cmd. Drill, combined oral and Company drill. Weather very fine.	Ch.
"	23rd		Mechanism & stoppages, range finding and semaphore. Coy had photographs taken by letters in afternoon. Coy dinner followed by Concert in schoolroom. SETQUES at 5 p.m. 5 reinforcements received from Base Depot.	Ch.
"	24th		Exchanged Vickers guns with 245th Machine Gun Coy, 16 guns of our original guns which had been handed over on relief when lost in the line. Lecture by Lieut. NICOL,C, on Barrage light followed by Barrage drill under action arrangements. Mechanism and stoppages. Working orders received for move to forward area on 29th inst. Weather fine. Recreational training during afternoon.	Ch.
"	25th		Preparations made for transport to move into forward area. Line of march Rd at 2.30 p.m. Weather fine. and limbers packed. Line of march Rd at 2.30 p.m. Weather fine.	Ch.
"	26th		Transport moved off at 6.30 a.m. and proceeded by march route to forward area. Cleaning of kits during morning and Company drill under C.S.M. Transport billeted at OUDERZEELE for the night.	Ch.
No.2 CAMP POTIJZE.	27th		Coy moved off at 8.30 a.m. and marched to WIZERNES where they entrained at 11 a.m. for ST.JEAN arriving there at 8.30 p.m. Kits, limbers and tools cart proceeded by own line. From at 6 a.m. and arrived at POTIJZE at 2 p.m. Remainder of Company arrived at 3.45 p.m. Coy marched from ST.JEAN to No.2 CAMP POTIJZE. Rations moved up with 33rd Machine Gun Coy to relieve 33rd Division. Weather fine. Enemy quiet.	Ch.

150th COMPANY, MACHINE GUN CORPS.

Army Form C. 2118.

WAR DIARY or INTELLIGENCE SUMMARY.
(Erase heading not required.)

150th Machine Gun Coy. M.G.C.

JANUARY 1918   SHEET 5

VOLUME No. 24.

Instructions regarding War Diaries and Intelligence Summaries are contained in F. S. Regs., Part II. and the Staff Manual respectively. Title pages will be prepared in manuscript.

Place	Date	Hour	Summary of Events and Information	Remarks and references to Appendices
POTIJZE No. 2 CAMP	28th		Guns of this unit relieved 248th M. Gun Coy in Barrage Positions and established at DAH HOUSE (D.21.6.8.9.) and (D.22.b.8.N.E.) at 4.30am. M.Gs fired shots throughout the night. Weather very good.	O.W.
DAH HOUSE D.21.6.8.9.	29th		Enemy dropped gas shells round EGGIST FARM during the morning and a few 77mm shells in the afternoon. The attitude of the enemy seemed peaceful. 1300 rounds were fired in harassing fire during darkness into EVERY FARM and BACORE WOOD (D.21.6.9.C.) Enemy replied with M.G. fire.	O.W.
"	30th		Enemy artillery was rather more active during the day Visibility good and T.M. were fairly active over our front system during the afternoon. Harassing fire was carried out by our guns at enemy tracks at irregular intervals during the hours of darkness. Enemy M.G.s were fairly active at night.	O.W.
"	31st		Very few shells dropped around Coy H.Q. at 10am without causing any damage. Weather good. Enemy very quiet during the day. Guns fired down to gas SOS Alarms Coy in.	O.W.

Oliver P.B. / Captain
Comdg. 150th Machine Gun Cor.

CONFIDENTIAL

150th COMPANY MACHINE GUN CORPS.

WAR DIARY or **INTELLIGENCE SUMMARY**

GUN CORPS. Vol. 25.
FEBRUARY, 1918.

(Erase heading not required.)

Instructions regarding War Diaries and Intelligence Summaries are contained in F.S. Regs., Part II. and the Staff Manual respectively. Title pages will be prepared in manuscript.

Place	Date FEB.	Hour	Summary of Events and Information	Remarks and references to Appendices
POTIJZE. NOR CAMP. I.u.d.o.8 (Sheet 28 N.W.)	1st.		Coy relieved by 245th Machine Gun Coy at 2.30am and returned to rear H.Q. No 2 Camp POTIJZE. Enemy very quiet. Weather cold. Coy resting & remainder of day.	DMM
"	2nd		Baths at YPRES 9.30am to 12 noon. Cleaning guns, gun kit and packing limber during afternoon. Weather fine.	DMM
"	3rd		Divine service in morning. Inspection and kit cleaning up of camp.	DMM
"	4th		Preparations made for relieving 149th Machine Gun Coy in the line. Coy moved up at 11.30am. Our artillery active in support of a raid made by the Leicesters on our right. 5 hostile balloons descended opposite our front during the confused event due to the raid. Coy lay table 9pm. Casualties NIL.	DMM
Adv. HQ. HEINE HOUSE. D.11.C.4.3.	5th.		Coy took over 149th Coy in front posters and H.Q. were established at HEINE HOUSE at 3am. Our artillery was active at morning and stand-to. Hostile artillery fairly quiet. Enemy dropped barrage on PASSCHENDAELE RIDGE & CREST FARM. (P.6.d.10) like received attention at our band 4pm PASSCHENDAELE ROAD about D.11.d.9.2 was shelled with H.E. Enemy aircraft was active all day at excellent work. Good. An E.A. flew high our POTIJZE 2pm and was engaged by A.A and M.G. fire. 10-10am the loud firing E.A. over M.G. at working bars of CREST FARM. Seattle LERRATIC FARM. Our gun carried out harassing fire on commission with S ordis Lewis light. Lise large 7 flows were brought to Cuis by Casualties NIL	DMM

150TH COMPANY. MACHINE GUN CORPS.			Army Form C. 2118.

WAR DIARY
or
INTELLIGENCE SUMMARY
(Erase heading not required.)

150th COMPANY MACHINE GUN CORPS. SHEET 2. Vol. 25
FEBRUARY 1918.

Place	Date FEB:	Hour	Summary of Events and Information	Remarks and references to Appendices
Adv H.Q. HEINE HOUSE. D.11.c.4.8.	6th.		Hostile artillery rather more active than usual. PASSCHENDAELE RIDGE was shelled with 5.9's in the early morning. D.I.R. Camp received attention from 4.20 a.m. and 7am field guns at 12.57 pm. Our artillery quiet. Harassing fire was maintained by our guns every darkness. Enemy M.G. situated on ENTREE COTT. Aircraft on both sides active throughout the day. Casualties nil. Weather good.	Nil
"	7th.		Enemy quiet throughout the rest. Our guns carried out usual harassing fire during darkness on enemy tracks and roads. At 10.30 pm a discovery of two green lights went up 4' by the enemy attend any attempt. Result inconclusive luckily. Usual enemy lines from 9.30 to 11.30 pm. Enemy signalling with lamps about 10.30 pm. Weather changeable. Visibility poor. Casualties nil.	Nil
½ camp POELZE I.4.d.2.8. (Hut 29 NW)	8th.		Three sections relieved by 245 Coy at dawn and returned to M.D. Camp POELZE. Bur. Took over a portion of front previously held by 66th Div: Day spent in cleaning up and resting. Weather dull. Both sides inactive.	Nil
"	9th.		Cleaning guns and gear. Pt. Parker Limbers Transport bringing up No. 14 hot. out of live was heavily shelled two mules wounded and Limber had to be abandoned. Limber was filled up at night, but to part upon. One gun in Limber blown up. No. 14 Section relieved by Coy machine gun. Casualties nil.	Nil
"	10th		Baths 8.10.8am at YPRES. Drew fuses at 3.15 pm. Weather cold and uncertain.	Nil

150th COMPANY MACHINE GUN CORPS

Army Form C. 2118.

WAR DIARY
or
INTELLIGENCE SUMMARY

FEBRUARY 1918. SHEET 3
150TH COY. MACHINE GUN CORPS
VOLUME 25.

(Erase heading not required.)

Place	Date FEB	Hour	Summary of Events and Information	Remarks and references to Appendices
Nr.Champ Bruze 14.a.0.2.R. (Sht 28 N.E.)	11th		Cleaning and checking gun kit in preparation for line. Lieut. MOON went up line to reconnoitre positions. Weather fine but dull.	Nil
Coy. Hqd. No 6 G4.9 19 Rd. (ZONNEBEKE)			Coy relieved No. 245 M.Gun Coy in night posn. Austn gun F.1, P.2 and 3 and relieved 149 M.Gun Coy in left sector between 6 p.m. relief reported complete at 4.50 p.m. G.S. established at DENN'S CROSSING (D 26.6.9.4.) Artillery activity high on our immediate right. Weather good. Weather dull.	Nil
"	13th		Intermittent shelling round ZONNEBEKE during the night with 4.2" from N.E. direction. Majority of these shells went blind and appeared to come from a long distance. A few 9.00 shells fell round SEINE DUMP. At 11 a.m. enemy dropped 900 shells in the vicinity of GRAVENSTAFEL. Our guns carried out harassing fire on enemy tracks from dusk until dawn. Hostile M.G. replied at irregular intervals. Enemy M.G. directed in rear of our forward guns on PASSCHENDAELE ROAD. Aircraft NIL. Visibility poor. Raining most of the day.	Nil
"	14th		Enemy activity normal. SEINE DUMP received attention during the early hours of the morning from enemy artillery. Between 10 and 11 am enemy field guns searched the mule track from about Log. 6a. to "D" Battery but shells fell about 50x on either side. 4 details M.G. going up in the direction of MOORSLEDE received tracer leading to on PASSCHENDAELE ROAD. Coy M.G. carried out on training and strengthening of gun positions. Numerous articles were collected and dumps formed at DON HOUSE and by "D" Battery. Several men of other units who had been by 7 out unburied were buried by our men. The routes were informed as to grave locations. The transport who assisted whilst conveying rations up the line. Coy much scan wounded. Weather dull. Enemy activity Nil.	Nil

150TH COMPANY,
MACHINE GUN
CORPS.

Army Form C. 2118.

WAR DIARY
or
INTELLIGENCE SUMMARY.

150th Coy. Machine Gun Corps.   FEBRUARY, 1918.   Sheet 1. Vol. 23.

(Erase heading not required.)

Place	Date FEB	Hour	Summary of Events and Information	Remarks and references to Appendices
Coy.HQ.D.26.6.9.4. (ZONNEBEKE)	15th		Usual harassing fire was carried out during darkness on enemy tracks and approaches. Enemy retaliated with M.G. fire from the direction of MOORSLEDE. Artillery activity normal during the day. SEINE DUMP and ZONNEBEKE received attention from gas shell and H.E. At 3.45 p.m. S.E.5. flew over our lines at a very high altitude. A.A. position by Bn. batteries was completed. Casualties Nil. Weather wet.	[sig]
"	16th		Enemy more active than usual. Between 9 am and 12 pm SEINE DUMP and ZONNEBEKE light railway running through BEECHAMS was shelled with 5.9". It was quieter than usual. Eight balloons were up opposite our front from 9am to 2.30 pm. Enemy aircraft going over carried out gun of this sort. Several E.A. flew low over our lines during that day. Enemy dropped a few M.G. shells and YPRES end at about 11.30 am. Weather good party. Visibility good.	[sig]
No.8 Camp POTIJZE I.14.d.2.8. (about 1⅛ N.E.)	17th		Coy relieved in line by H/215 Coy. Relief complete at 6 am. Coy proceeded to No.8 Camp, POTIJZE. Baths at YPRES at 2.30 pm. Weather frosty.	[sig]
"	18th		Day spent in cleaning guns, kit and transport. Artillery active over whole sector particularly on the right sector. Weather fine.	[sig]
"	19th		Cleaning guns and working limbers. Camp cleared and rubbish burned. Preparations for move tomorrow.	[sig]
WESTBECOURT. V.14.d.5.8. (24a.S.E.)	20th.		Coy moved to TILQUES area. Stores etc proceeded in motor lorry by road. Coy left POTIJZE at 10.30 am and arrived at WESTBECOURT at 9 p.m. Coy entrained at YPRES at 2 p.m. and detrained at WIZERNES, thence by march route to WESTBECOURT, a distance of 15 Km. N.W. transport details i.e. Qr. Limbers, Mess cart and water cart, proceeded by rail from NAMERTINGHE to WIZERNES. Remainder of transport proceeded by road and moved from POTIJZE to BRANDHOEK.	[sig]

150TH COMPANY.
MACHINE GUN CORPS.

WAR DIARY or INTELLIGENCE SUMMARY.

150th Coy Machine Gun Corps FEBRUARY 1918. Vol. 25. Sheet 5.

Place	Date FEB.	Hour	Summary of Events and Information	Remarks and references to Appendices
WESTBECOURT. V.14.a.5.8. (24i S.E.)	21st.		Transport moved from BRANDHOEK to STEENVOORDE. Coy spent day in cleaning up and resting. Weather fine.	
"	22nd.		Practical training during morning and recreational training during afternoon. Transport return moved from STEENVOORDE to RENESCURE.	
"	23rd.		Transport joined unit at 3 a.m. Coy's work during morning and Physical training. Recreational training during afternoon. Weather fine.	
"	24th.		Commanding Officer attended Sunday service. Coy attended Church service (voluntary) during morning. Divine service at 10.30 a.m.	
"	25th.		Weather bad and snowing to rain, freezing hard. Coy confined to billets.	
"	26th.		16 men from 165th Inf Bde joined Coy to be trained on machine guns. Army gave orders that the Coy was to commence an elementary course which on Coy of Phys Training, saluting, and Company drill carried out during the morning. One afternoon was devoted to recreational training as will be the afternoon during the training period. 30 Ranks wild Coy for Bath Coy.	
"	27th.		Rapid digging of emplacements during morning. Afternoon gun drill, Physical training. Weather fine and sunshine.	
"	28th.		Coy paraded to baths at PEQUIN at 9 a.m. and training for rest of day including Squad and gun drill, education and reception of Orders and gas drill.	

[Signature] W H [?] Captain

Volume ~~XXV~~   Confidential

Vol 2b

War Diary

of

150th MACHINE GUN COY

From Feby 1st 1918

To Feby 28th 1918.

Appendix B

SECRET   2nd Bn Northumberland Fusiliers.   Copy No. 9

OPERATION Order No. 48   17/12/1918

Ref. VALENCIENNES, Sheet 12
1/100000.

1. Battalion will proceed to WARGNIES LE GRAND by route as circulated with O.O. No. 47 dated 16th inst. Head of column passing Town gate at 0900 hours to morrow.
Order of march. "H.Q." "D" "A" "B" and "C", Transport.
Headquarters will move off at 0850 hours followed by Companies in the above order at 100 yds interval.

2. Dress as laid down in O.O. No. 47 dated 16th inst.

3. Blanket limbers will be in the square close to Battalion H.Q. and will be loaded by 0830 hours.
Officers Kits will be loaded on baggage wagons by 0830 hours.

4. O.C. "C" Coy. will detail 1 officer and 6 other ranks as slow moving party. This party will move in rear of transport and will collect all stragglers.

5. C.Q.M.Sgts will parade outside Orderly Room at 0830 hours and will proceed to new area on bicycles.
On arrival they will report to Lieut. H. ST. C.L. 'Amie. O.C. "B" Coy will detail an Officer to proceed with this party.

6. All billets will be left clean prior to marching off.

7. Revielle and breakfast will be under Company arrangements.

8. All transport will be loaded by 0845 hours.

                   Captain & Adjt.,
      2nd Bn Northumberland Fusiliers.

Copies to:- No. 1. O.C. "A" Coy.
              2. O.C. "B" Coy.
              3. O.C. "C" Coy.
              4. O.C. "D" Coy.
              5. O.C. "H.Q." Coy.
              6. Transport Officer.
              7. Quartermaster.
              8. File.
             No. 9 War Diary.
             No. 10 "
             No. 11 R.S.M.
             No. 12 Medical Officer.

50th Division.

Became "B" Company 50th MACHINE GUN BATTALION

150th MACHINE GUN COMPANY

MARCH 1918

CONFIDENTIAL

150th COMPANY, MACHINE GUN CORPS.

WAR DIARY or INTELLIGENCE SUMMARY

(Erase heading not required.)

Army Form C. 2118.

150th COMPANY MACHINE GUN CORPS. VOLUME No 26.

MARCH 1918

Instructions regarding War Diaries and Intelligence Summaries are contained in F.S. Regs., Part II. and the Staff Manual respectively. Title pages will be prepared in manuscript.

Place	Date March	Hour	Summary of Events and Information	Remarks and references to Appendices
WESTBECOURT (PAS-DE-CALAIS)	1st		Physical training, Musketry and Stoppages. Company out during morning and recreational training during afternoon.	
"	2nd		Visual training carried out during day. Weather bad. Division of work for elementary class for infantry men being transferred. Lecture given by Lieut at night.	
"	3rd		Divine Service 9/0am. Weather bad. Football match with do. 149 Coy cancelled.	
"	4th		Coy paraded for Baths 8, & 9.30 am (at AQUIN). Training Taken over when commenced. Coy divided into 2 – Group (A) "Infantry men being transferred (B) "Refresher course (C) Remainder of Coy on advanced gun drill, barrage and Compass work. Training programme issued to Officers i/c Groups and to NCOs acting as instructors on A and B Groups. Weather dull.	
"	5th		Training carried out as per programme. Visit Coy cancelled in afternoon. Coy team won Tugs of War. football match 1.149 Coy.	
"	6th		Weather good. Route march. Inspectable Coy from 9 am to 1pm. Recon. Kit inspection order. Good pull-ups. Out at 4pm.	
"	7th		Visual training carried out during day. Lecture by Lieut Sexton officer i/c gun numbers this date and the last through Baths & training. Officers i/c Sections, holding conferences with gun numbers after training until time for afternoon training.	

150th COMPANY. MACHINE GUN CORPS.
Army Form C.2118.

WAR DIARY
OR INTELLIGENCE SUMMARY.
(Erase heading not required.)

150th COMPANY   MACHINE GUN CORPS   MARCH 1918   SHEET 2
VOLUME No. 26

Place	Date MARCH	Hour	Summary of Events and Information	Remarks and references to Appendices
WESTRECOURT (PAS-DE-CALAIS)	8th.		Operation Order for move received at 5.30am. Coy. and transport marched to WIZERNES at 3pm. and entrained with 150th Inf. Bde. Group at 8.14pm. Weather good. Travelling all night.	RWm
GUSY SUR SOMME	9th.		Arrived and detrained at BOVES at 9am. thence by march route and transport to GUSY, arriving there at 11.30am. Coy. accommodated in billets at GUSY.	RWm
"	10th.		Day spent in cleaning up Kit and Personnel. Rations received and warning order received for move tomorrow.	RWm
HARBONNIERS	11th.		Coy. moved off at 9.30am. with transport and proceeded by march route to HARBONNIERS arriving there at 3pm. Weather good.	RWm
"	12th.		Cleaning of Gun Kit and Personnel. Recreational training during afternoon. Training programme commenced during week.	RWm
"	13th.		Coy. on range during morning firing guns, tripods and gun bags. Ammunition taken. Ranges 100, 500 & 1000 yds. and 1 off proceeded up the line to reconnoitre ground.	RWm
"	14th.		Orders re. Coy. GS. recon. Operation Orders for emergency entraining received. Usual training carried out during morning and Recreational training during afternoon. Coy. firing during afternoon.	RWm

WAR DIARY or INTELLIGENCE SUMMARY

150th Company Machine Gun Corps
Volume 26
March 1918. Sheet 3.

Army Form C.2118.

Place	Date March	Hour	Summary of Events and Information	Remarks and references to Appendices
HARBONNIERS	15th		Party of 1 NCO and 18 men detailed to work with Div: Branch Officer on improving the sanitary conditions of the area. Physical training, mechanism, stoppages, squad and company drill carried out.	Nil
"	16th		Training as per programme carried out. Lieut Sargeant took 4 first Gallery Rifle and musketry course at the Rest Camp Range Harvaux through Div: Gas Chamber to test the Box Respirators at Guerhevellar. Good signal slow carried out, all umpires for the scheme by Div: Hamel. Offr to Luck not arrive at the appointed time, boy went the wrong direction. Conjuria Battalion football final rep. team 3 goals, Linh	Nil
"	17th	11-15am	Church Service at Harry Coy Parade for both MORCOURT and HAMEVCOURT at Recreational Ground. Inter Section football during afternoon.	Nil
"	18th		Brigade scheme carried out, coy paraded with 16 guns and tripods and 6 belts (empty) per gun. Four guns only were used for counter attacking. G.O. at Dej: Yr. at 5pm & carried model of forward mode.	Nil
"	19th		Compy Off. and three off. proceeded with 150 inf. Bde Group to reconnoitre forward position. Sword Training carried out. Weather fine.	Nil
"	20th		Gas Drill under Div: Gas N.C.O. 2nd in comm Remainder of Coy took French Gas Chamber at 2.30pm. Naval training carried out including Compass Work Makeover, Immediate Action and signed Drill took the good.	Nil

		150th COMPANY. MACHINE GUN CORPS.
		No. .... Date ....

150TH MACHINE GUN COY.   MACHINE GUN CORPS

WAR DIARY
or
INTELLIGENCE SUMMARY.
(Erase heading not required.)

VOLUME 26   SHEET 4.   MARCH, 1918

Place	Date MARCH	Hour	Summary of Events and Information	Remarks and references to Appendices
HARBONNIERS SUR-SOMME	21st		Standing to all day. Orders received at 4pm to entrain at GUILLAUCOURT at 9pm and entrained at BRIE. Transport travelled by road. Weather fine.	RNm
HANCOURT and BOUVINCOURT	22nd		Coy arrived at HANCOURT at 5am. Called in three hours rest time and no sleep. Limbers moved up to clear enemy advance and occupied a portion of the GREEN LINE. Coy 9b. (advanced) established at BERNE'S Transport. Natives went up but at 4pm Enemy artillery and aeroplanes active. BOUVINCOURT shelled 3.9 shell shrapnel and mustard gas. Withdrawn to about R.19.c.3.2. (Sheet 62c S.E.) Enemy shelling increased and transport moved to ST CREN (R.21.a.5.7) at 11.30 p.m. In the meantime the enemy made repeated and determined attacks against our unit and entire cover of barrage our unit was ordered to new defensive line BRUNETZ – VRAIGNES. Casualties – Pte Ranko killed 10h. and 1 OR wounded.	RNm
ST CREN and BELLOY-EN-SANTERRE	R.23rd	5.30am	Orders received for unit to return to BELLOY-EN-SANTERRE. Rear guard action fought to the river SOMME. Transport moved from ST CREN to BELLOY-EN-SANTERRE. The guns of this Coy. did exceptionally fine work in covering the retirement of the infantry and all ranks showed great devotion to duty. All enemy advancing in mass were severely punished by our guns. Owing the cool of the difficult operation only one gun was lost. This had to be abandoned owing to the enemy crossing from the right. Before being abandoned it was rendered useless. The SOMME was crossed at 8.15 p.m and bridge over up at 9pm. Guns were established in the W bank of the river and during the night the coy moved to VILLERS CARBONNEL where they spent the night. Weather fine. Casualties – Pte ..... wounded A. 8 Ranko wounded.	RNm

A7092   Wt. W.125-9/M7393. 750,000. 7/17. D. D. & L-Ltd.   Forms/C218/4.

150TH COMPANY, MACHINE GUN CORPS.

WAR DIARY
or
INTELLIGENCE SUMMARY.
(Erase heading not required.)

VOLUME 26
MARCH 1918 SHEET 5

Place	Date MARCH	Hour	Summary of Events and Information	Remarks and references to Appendices
BELLOY-EN-SANTERRE	22nd		Coy joined Transport at 11am while Coy moved from BELLOY to FOUCAUCOURT at 3pm. What they were in reserve to 8th Division.	RCM
FOUCAUCOURT and PROYART	23rd		2 Sections & one Pattern moved up to ESTREES where a support line was established. Enemy pushing across the SOMME to the South and transport moved from FOUCAUCOURT to PROYART where a halt was made for the night.	RCM
PROYART and HANGARD	26th		Enemy launched a heavy and determined attack against our line to the right. ESTREES and left of ASSEVILLERS and Division had to retreat to LA CHAVATTE-ROSIERES. Again 2 of the guns of this unit played a great part in single gun on some parts today. The enemy line in check. On completion of retirement our guns rejoined in transport staff at the N extremity of the line. Casualties 1 officer wounded. Transport moved from PROYART at 8.30 am to CHYEHUX and from thence to HANGARD arriving at 4pm. Weather good.	RCM
HANGARD	24th		Guns moved along CAIX road to Cayeux infantry at 12 noon. Attack by enemy was successfully repulsed and guns returned to their support late day. Retired to the E side of HARBONNIERS. 18 hours rations sent up here and all available men sent up the line under an Officer to relieve gun teams. Transport bivouacked at HANGARD for the night. Casualties 2 O/R's No reported weather good. We were displayed great daring with no aeroplanes and no contact was apparently good.	RCM
	28th		2 Sections retired yet the last 2 am transport wounded and 150 office Group and this incident to ROUVEL stating at 2pm and arriving at 6.30pm. Enemy combat quite during the last Casualties NIL weather good	RCM

150th COMPANY MACHINE GUN CORPS

WAR DIARY
or
INTELLIGENCE SUMMARY
(Erase heading not required.)

Army Form C. 2118.

150th Company Machine Gun Corps. VOLUME 8. MARCH 1918. SHEET 6.

Place	Date MARCH	Hour	Summary of Events and Information	Remarks and references to Appendices
ROUVEL and BOVES	29th		Unit retired from HARBONNIERS at dawn and took up positions on the outskirts of CAIX. Details moved from ROUVEL at 10am and marched to BOVES. Division reported in line by French troops, but 8 guns of this unit attached to 20th Division were withdrawn again at 2pm owing to enemy pressure from S. and new line established at DEMUIN. Transport arrived at BOVES at 11.30pm. Casualties NIL.	RW
GAINS EN AMIENOIS	30th		Transport and details moved from BOVES to GAINS EN AMIENOIS at 10.30am. Guns withdrew to DOMART and their guns took up position on country N. DOMART. ROYE road. Enemy still attacking in force, and at night guns were withdrawn to travel running through E in HOURGES (Sheet 14/100,000) where lost and some transport was lost. Casualties during the day. Casualties NIL.	RW
SALEUX and ARGOULES	31st		Personnel moved by march route to SALEUX and entrained. Transport moved by road and billeted for the night at BOURDON. Day detrained at RUE and march to ARGOULES, a distance of 16 km. Weather good. Enemy delivered a determined attack all over British sector during the afternoon, assisted by much artillery and our line was again withdrawn. Casualties. 1 Rank Killed, 1 Rank missing, 3 Ranks wounded.	RW

_____ Captain
O.C. 150th Machine Gun Coy.

www.ingramcontent.com/pod-product-compliance
Lightning Source LLC
Chambersburg PA
CBHW080901230426
43663CB00013B/2597